A NIGHT AT THE SWEET GUM HEAD

A NIGHT AT THE SWEET GUM HEAD

*Drag, Drugs, Disco,
and Atlanta's Gay Revolution*

MARTIN PADGETT

W. W. NORTON & COMPANY
Independent Publishers Since 1923

For information about permission to reproduce selections from this book, write to
Permissions, W. W. Norton & Company, Inc., 500 Fifth Avenue, New York, NY 10110

For information about special discounts for bulk purchases, please contact
W. W. Norton Special Sales at specialsales@wwnorton.com or 800-233-4830

Manufacturing by LSC Harrisonburg
Book design by Chris Welch Design
Production manager: Julia Druskin

Library of Congress Cataloging-in-Publication Data

Names: Padgett, Marty, 1969– author.
Title: A night at the Sweet Gum Head : drag, drugs, disco, and Atlanta's gay revolution /
    Martin Padgett.
Description: First edition. | New York, NY : W. W. Norton & Company, [2021] | Includes
    bibliographical references and index.
Identifiers: LCCN 2020054625 | ISBN 9781324007128 (paperback) |
    ISBN 9781324007135 (epub)
Subjects: LCSH: Greenwell, J. R. | Smith, William E., Jr. | Gays—Georgia—Biography. |
    Female impersonators—Georgia—Biography. | Gay activists—Georgia—Biography. |
    Gay culture—Georgia—Atlanta—History—20th century. | Gay liberation movement—
    Georgia—Atlanta—History—20th century. | Gays—Georgia—Atlanta—Social conditions—
    20th century. | LCGFT: Biographies.
Classification: LCC HQ76.2.U52 G86 2021 | DDC 306.76/60922758 [B]—dc23
LC record available at https://lccn.loc.gov/2020054625

W. W. Norton & Company, Inc., 500 Fifth Avenue, New York, N.Y. 10110
www.wwnorton.com

W. W. Norton & Company Ltd., 15 Carlisle Street, London W1D 3BS

1 2 3 4 5 6 7 8 9 0

For Don, if he could see me now

Contents

Preface

In 1996, I lived in Birmingham, Alabama, where I led a double life. I believed coming out there would come with unbearable consequences, so I kept to myself. Each weekend I arrowed east, sometimes at a hundred miles an hour, to Atlanta.

I screwed up the courage to go to my first gay bar in Atlanta. I drove down Cheshire Bridge Road, pulled into the parking lot, and took a deep breath, not knowing what to expect. When I opened the door to Hoedowns, a country-and-western joint, the catchy refrain of familiar twangy music invited me in— Wynonna Judd's "Heaven Help My Heart." On the dance floor, a carousel of men in white cowboy hats whirled in line-dance formation. Some glanced at me. I smiled back at them. I breathed a sigh of relief.

I belonged.

Two decades before, on the same stretch of road, the godfather of Atlanta gay nightlife had opened another country-and-western bar and made himself its sheriff. At the County Seat, Frank Powell built a replica of a small town inside an old warehouse, complete with wagon wheels, a country store, and a wishing well.

Powell owned more than a dozen gay bars in Atlanta from the late 1960s until he died in 1996. He built an underground universe that came to life at night, after respectable Atlanta had long gone to bed. He opened quiet drinking bars, fancy fern bars, glamorous lesbian bars, hot disco bars, and seedy hustler bars.

He named his most famous nightclub after his hometown in Florida. It was the "Showplace of the South," the Sweet Gum Head.

///

Today, American lesbians, gays, bisexuals, transgender people, and queers can get married. We can find short-term special friends or life partners on our smartphones. We can venture proudly and safely into the straight world outside the confines of bars and clubs once designated specifically as "gay" spaces.

Fifty years ago, none of those things was true. Queer people were shamed and muted, jailed, exiled, and put in danger. Often they were left no choice but to leave home, and to run away to cities where they might be accepted, or at least tolerated.

Even in those cities, gay bars were dangerous and illicit places— but they were also the birthplace of the emerging gay rights movement. Queer communities formed, and they demanded equality. It was a time of heady optimism. Many believed anything was possible, even progress. The movement had its most visible roots in New York and San Francisco, but after it flared in the riots at the seedy Stonewall Inn tavern in 1969, it spread quickly to cities such as Atlanta, a relatively progressive oasis surrounded by ultraconservative mores.

In the 1970s, Atlanta's cruisy, electric core was the Sweet Gum Head nightclub, where an intoxicating blend of drag, drugs, disco, and revolution had a pivotal role in uniting Atlanta's gay civil-rights movement—and in turning Stonewall's rebellion into art. The Sweet Gum Head is where Atlanta earned its reputation for top-flight female impersonation. It's where Atlanta drag came out of the closet.

Before RuPaul Charles, there was John Greenwell, who ran away from Alabama to Atlanta and found a new home at the Sweet Gum Head. John became Rachel Wells—and Rachel became a drag superstar. Along the way, John put the two halves of his life back together.

John left the marches and protests to activists like Bill Smith.

A son of devout Baptists, Bill took a seat as a city commissioner, then took over the most influential gay newspaper in the South, *The Barb*. When his addictions and predilections were revealed, he lost everything.

Then it all died. In the same summer of 1981 when the Sweet Gum Head closed, the *New York Times* reported on a "rare cancer seen in 41 homosexuals."

///

I met my future husband just a few months after I moved to Atlanta. I hadn't come out. We dated quietly, in moments stolen and moments made, in a gray space between old friends and new.

We visited a friend in the hospital one evening in the months before protease inhibitors became widely available. Our friend had contracted pneumonia. His spirits were fine, but his prognosis was mixed. When he was admitted, his T-cell count had fallen to 2. He dubbed those two T-cells "Itsy" and "Bitsy." They were survivors. As for him, no one could be sure.

This is what being gay will be like, I warned myself, as if it were something I could change.

I spent countless panicked, sleepless nights negotiating a new existence, one that let me be true to myself while I faced the fear that my truth could drive my life away from me, one family member at a time, one T-cell at a time.

I had run away before, and running away had exhausted me, and resolved nothing. I stood fast and brave. I survived.

Soon after I came out, a few months after that hospital visit, I bought an old Art Deco–style apartment on Cheshire Bridge Road, next door to a strip club housed in a building that had once been home to the Sweet Gum Head.

///

History has given us sagas of world war, the Wild West, the suffragist movement, and the civil-rights movement. Relatively few stories of the queer revolution have been recorded. Many memories of the battle for equality that followed Stonewall were deemed unimportant, or they were forgotten, or they simply faded as the community fought for its very survival as the AIDS era dawned. History is a bridge made of sand.

I hope this story reclaims some of the joy and optimism of that brief time, and that it charts new constellations for future generations to study. As for me, it's something of a memoir. In many ways, John and Bill and I have lived the same life, in our search for the place we call home, in search of our true selves.

That search always is urgent, but it's particularly urgent now. While same-sex marriage has normalized aspects of our queer lives to a degree, assimilation is one of many things that have eroded our sense of community. We're losing a distinct dimension of the queer experience. We're being straightwashed, even as an unashamed army of bigots wants to turn back the clock.

This story marks our progress, but should also remind us that progress is fragile and requires regular upkeep and maintenance and, occasionally, righteous anger. We must pass on these lessons and legends before they are lost. Before *we* are lost.

This isn't my story of Atlanta. It's mine too. It belongs to us. This is our story of freedom.

Atlanta, Georgia
June 28, 2020

A NIGHT AT THE SWEET GUM HEAD

Introduction

Atlanta

August 1969—December 1970

They each paid a dollar to the cashier at the office desk in the narrow lobby, and made their way toward a theater cloaked in fireproof turquoise curtains—among them, a woman in tight brown curls and wide, hopeful eyes; a man eager to see breasts onscreen; a woman eager to see them too.

A red carpet laid out in Oscars style led them down the aisle toward Andy Warhol's *Lonesome Cowboys*, in its third week at the theater despite terrible reviews. They whispered and giggled and chatted; the girl with wide eyes ate a submarine sandwich, while others munched on popcorn. They had filled about half the sea-green, rocking-chair seats when the Simplex projector woke up and lit the screen with images of naked bodies, quick-cut visuals, and non-sequitur plot points.[1]

Cowboys had cost Warhol's Factory just $3,000 to produce, and none of the money seemed to have been spent on the script. Men thrusted their pelvises in each other's faces, the camera stared blankly at naked torsos and buttocks and breasts, and actors indulged in some lightly comic cross-dressing. The nonsensical parody of western films grated on the sensibilities of high-minded cinema.

It also grated on the high-minded people who lived in the expensive houses near the Ansley Mall MiniCinema. They complained to the local police about its more lurid, even pornographic, moments.

The movie flickered in the dark, across gay and straight and lesbian faces, but in the lobby the scene exploded into action. Unknown men in suits swarmed in without a word. One stood guard in the lobby and set up a movie camera. Two marched into the theater, while a few stomped upstairs to the projection booth. Three more hovered in the lobby and locked the front doors from the inside.[2] They said nothing to the cashier. They showed no identification. They had no warrant.

"It's over!" an officer bellowed as the movie stopped and the lights in the theater startled the patrons. Police circled them like roaches they expected to scatter. They sneered at them, and asked one lesbian, "Where is your husband?"[3]

"We're being raided!" someone wailed, and it sounded like defeat.

The police demanded identification while a photographer took pictures to shame each one of them, as the flash on his camera scorched the air with a puff of chemical judgment. The theater's twenty-eight-year-old manager, Joe Russ, sat in handcuffs, while the police movie camera kept its wide eye open as the dazed moviegoers filed out, confused and furious.

Hinson McAuliffe, the bald-pated Fulton County Criminal Court solicitor, had ordered the raid. He had gone to see the movie once he heard about the risqué content. He had found it obscene, of course—and boring. He said he fell sleep several times, and complained about the movie's low caliber of photography and acting.

McAuliffe thought the movie and its viewers were deviant. He ordered photos and film of the audience so that he could recognize any "known homosexuals."[4] He wanted to check their police records for previous sex offenses.[5] He vowed to raid more theaters and bookstores in Atlanta.

City leaders had painted the city as the picture of progress—but Atlanta in 1969 was a city with just a single skyscraper. It had anointed itself a New South before the old one was dead. Draconian obscenity and sodomy laws drew long prison sentences, and while heterosexuals regularly "watched the submarine races" at

Piedmont Park after dark, gays and lesbians were harassed for walking there in daylight.

McAuliffe swore he had the community's interests at heart, but some had already taken him to court, and lodged protests in letters to the editor and in calls to local radio stations. If police had the right to take a picture of them, one caller warned the prosecutor, they had the right to break the camera.[6]

///

The world these gays and lesbians had inherited from their fathers and mothers was different from the one they dreamed of for themselves. War had ripped up the social compact and left no draft for the future. Some took that as a cue to huddle in fear.

Others took it as a cue to free themselves. They went on a pilgrimage to cities, where they could live more openly, though they still faced grave danger. Even in San Francisco and in New York, which seemed to have more homosexuals than any place on Earth, the police still raided gay bars and revoked their liquor licenses while they professed ignorance about organized crime that ran the bars and held sway over gay and lesbian lives.

In Atlanta, members of the gay community faced open hostility from all fronts: the Church, the newspaper, the police. They were confined to a few dark, depressing places where they nudged one another on the knee to gauge mutual interest. When the police raided even those places, they were forced to the sidewalks of Peachtree Road again, or to Piedmont Park.[7] They contorted their faces to avoid any expression of desire, had to feign interest in the opposite sex, had to laugh when someone threw the word *fag* in their face, had to watch the people that passed for a hint of mutual recognition.

They claimed Piedmont Park as their front yard, the Strip as their home. Atlanta's version of Greenwich Village or Haight-Ashbury, the Strip neighborhood on Peachtree Street was the center of hippie decadence and to some a symbol of Atlanta's decay, with its grand old houses that emptied out in hysteric fits of white flight. Those who abandoned the area likened the city to ruins, but gays and lesbians streamed in from places like Sumter, South Carolina, and Opp, Alabama, and Soddy-Daisy, Tennessee, and fashioned an oasis. All the animals emerged from the woods to drink from the same pool: glittery drag queens and unapologetically effeminate men, butch women in leather jackets, beautiful athletic gay men with flowing beards and beautiful gay women with flowing hair and painted faces. The Strip pulsed with the energy of a budding gay community, and Atlanta's nearby gay nightclubs grew bold and dense with newly minted queers who matured in ways forbidden at home, as they experimented with their very identity. They stumbled through the usual mating rituals like kissing, dancing, and dating. They expanded their minds with LSD, speed, marijuana, or plain old alcohol. They learned about themselves and skewered the hostile outside world through the humor and satire of Atlanta's sub-rosa drag scene.

Police still raided the gay clubs. They cruised Piedmont Park to clear it of "sex perverts."[8] They would drive by, then circle back with a camera to intimidate people from standing on public sidewalks.[9]

When the Stonewall Inn in New York City erupted in a riot in June 1969, the police probably had no idea that it could spread to Atlanta—but a year after the Christopher Street rebellion, when some 20,000 marched in New York and another 5,000 marched in San Francisco, a handful of Atlanta's gays and lesbians gathered in Piedmont Park. They banded together as the Gay Liberation Front, and handed out leaflets from a table during the spring arts festival. They couldn't march, they decided; there just weren't enough of them to avoid looking like a punch line. People were still afraid they would lose their jobs, their families, and their lives if they came out in public. Some didn't care anymore, and came out anyway. They handed out flyers, talked to straight passersby, and drew pained glances and awkward stares.

///

Mayor Sam Massell had let his jet-black hair grow long, and he told the police to leave the hippies and drag queens alone.[10] But he saw himself as a crime-fighter, and with the blessing of Georgia's governor-elect, Jimmy Carter, Massell authorized a sixty-four-man police station on the Strip.[11] He had it painted pink and dubbed it the Pig Pen.[12] A thousand people were arrested within the first few months the Pig Pen was open, and the hippies and queers and bikers who lived on the Strip fought back in a hail of bottles and fire bombs.

Massell disbanded the station, but Atlanta police wouldn't leave the Strip alone. They took aim at Club Centaur, a club that featured go-go dancing in the afternoon and nightly drag shows by Phyllis Killer and Diamond Lil, who jammed with her live band. Phyllis performed in long blond curls and swung an eighteen-foot feather boa as a jump rope while she threw lollipops from the stage. The rowdy crowd called the Centaur home; the police called it a front for the mob. They arrested a woman near the club and raided nearby apartments looking for guns and drugs and prostitutes.[13] The neighborhood rioted, and in a cloud of tear gas the cops arrested twenty-six people.[14] In November of 1970, Sam Massell ordered the Centaur shut down.[15]

Old Atlanta cheered him on. It believed that the Strip crowd had changed from flower children to sidewalk commandos and punks and freaks. Few of them understood that their old Atlanta was gone forever.[16]

The Strip descended into chaos, and its people moved on—north into Midtown and Buckhead, east to Little Five Points, and northeast along Cheshire Bridge Road. They took their fight with them. The unpredictable and unknowable borders of a police state had kept them pinned under glass, but they began to rap against it. They knew how far they had been pushed and they began to push back. They organized. They prepared for war.

The police stayed at their heels. They knew why gays and lesbians came to the city and flocked to Piedmont Park, especially in spring, when the dogwoods painted the green with white and pink petals, when the sweetgum trees began to build their prickly seed pods. They kept arresting gays and lesbians—for loitering, for jaywalking, for disturbing the peace. They hunted them. They were easy prey.

1971

///

BRING THE BOYS HOME

John Greenwell

Huntsville, Alabama

January 1971

John Greenwell could stay in Huntsville and be the town queer, or he could run away and be free, so he ran.

He threw a couple of days' worth of clothes in a cheap gray briefcase he'd had since high school, counted $11 in his wallet, each bill worn down like him, and flew out of the house that he had never called home.

He had been born in Kentucky, the son of a mother he loved and an abusive, alcoholic father he grew to hate. The family moved whenever the military shipped them to another place: Tennessee, Texas, California, Germany, Alabama. By the time he finished high school in Huntsville, John Greenwell had already lived many lives.

He had been a good student, a Boy Scout, a member of the French club, an actor in a school film about poverty. A graduate. A heterosexual. When he braved the cold and walked to the bus station on the edge of Huntsville and put his dollar on the counter and found a seat on a bus headed east, he put that John Greenwell to death.

He dreamed of becoming a hippie, of growing out his short brown hair, of life with people like him. He wanted to see the world through psychedelic eyes. He wanted to touch the bodies of gods.

The bus rumbled to life. Its air brake hissed as it pulled away. Huntsville dimmed behind it as John's eyelids flickered. He fell asleep to the urban lullaby he'd learned in eighth grade, Petula Clark's escape fantasy, "Downtown."

The bus crossed an imaginary line in the dark and Alabama

faded into Georgia. John woke for a moment, decided he would never go back, then drifted off into the comfort of his dreams.

///

Wet bus doors slapped open and woke John up in Atlanta as midnight grew near. He walked from the smartly styled Art Deco bus station toward a hotel down the street, paid $4 for the night, tossed his briefcase on the dirty mattress of his small, cold room, and charged downstairs, not knowing what he would find. John had only cruised a few city blocks toward the Strip when a one-armed man called out from his car. He didn't say much. He didn't need to. John ran back to his small, cold room, grabbed the cheap gray briefcase too small to hold any fear, raced back down the stairs, and jumped in for the ride. The newly minted couple drove south, to a house in a bad neighborhood where the stranger slept with a gun under his pillow.

///

The stranger waved goodbye to John in front of Rich's Department Store the next morning. The ornate temple to commerce towered over an entire city block, so imposing Atlantans used it to locate themselves physically as well as socially. Margaret Mitchell had bought her dress for the *Gone with the Wind* premiere in 1939 there. Martin Luther King Jr. had integrated the store's lunch counter. Coretta Scott King wore a conservative cloth coat from Rich's when the Reverend accepted his Nobel Peace Prize.[1]

Rich's had an auditorium, a china store, its own post office. Shoppers could wander past the Store for Fashion with its hat bar and wig salon, or the Parfumerie, where cloying spritzes of Chanel No. 5 clung to the air. They could smell the heady scent of yeasty breads and Lady Baltimore cakes and pecan pies that wafted from the bakery, watch children cheer as they rode the curly tailed Pink Pig monorail overhead through the toy department, or taste the tangy dressing of the Magnolia Room cafeteria's chicken salad. Shoppers from around the South made special trips to Atlanta to buy from Rich's. It was Oz compared to the Sears catalog store where John's mother had bought the scruffy overalls that followed him to Atlanta.

John pushed his way through ornate brass-and-glass doors, found a friendly face at a counter, and asked if Robert worked there. A counter clerk pointed him to the shoe department, where Robert looked up in mild shock. He never expected his young acquaintance to make the trip to the city.

They had met only briefly, in a clandestine place months before, but Robert had made a promise, and he kept his word. He brought his stray home to his lover and they made John a bed on the couch.

John exhaled, then slept deeply. He had been in Atlanta just one day. He had a place to sleep, and a few dollars in his wallet. It was nearly all he had, now that life had started all over again, after it had barely begun.

Bill Smith

The Morningstar Inn

February 4, 1971

It was wet and frigid outside, but the Morningstar Inn warmed with talk of revolution.

The Morningstar fed hippies on the fringe of Emory University from a menu full of earnestly healthy food that paired with naturally and chemically induced good vibes. Downstairs, a head shop sold "supplies for the body and mind." Upstairs, groovy people found sustenance in its macrobiotic and vegetarian fare while they sampled comics and crafts and free entertainment and sometimes rapped at meetings of radical groups like the one Bill Smith stood before that night.

Bill Smith was the town queer in high school, and queer was a problem for his devoted Baptist parents. His mother had begged him, and his military father had ordered him, to change. Neither worked.

Rather than change, Bill lurched into politics. He led the Young Democrats of DeKalb County at a time when the party threatened to tear apart Georgia's social fabric with notions of equality and justice. He campaigned for Bobby Kennedy while avoiding Vietnam with a student deferment.

Bill left home for Georgia State University in downtown Atlanta with the weight of family never far removed. He bloomed into the image of rebellion: He traded the rounded horn-rimmed glasses and weary gaze of his freshman high school photo for square-rimmed shades and a curling smile. His parted and combed hair sprang into a frizzy cloud—his "Anglo," he called it—that turned him into an upside-down exclamation mark. He ditched the button-down shirts of his restrictive youth for the down-to-earth T-shirts and jeans of a rebel.

When a fire is lit and consumes its first breath of oxygen it creates free radicals. Bill would invite over some of the local Students for a Democratic Society to his apartment. He set himself apart from the garden-variety revolutionaries with the suit and tie he wore to meetings. He wondered why on earth they would agitate about armed revolution when it would be so much easier to change the world from the inside out.

He had already come out to his friend Diane before June 1969, when the Stonewall riots filled others with the spirit of rebellion. At school he began to lay plans for a gay liberation movement in Atlanta. By early 1971, Bill and the other GGLF organizers grew confident enough to call a first public meeting. When the Morningstar Inn opened its doors to them that February evening, it grew humid with the breath of a hundred people who wanted nothing more, nothing less, than dignity.

The clatter from the open mic lifted voices in alternating

fits of unity and disharmony. Everyone could blame the usual patriarchy for gays' second-class status, they squabbled, but women in other GLF chapters had broken off into radical lesbian groups because the GLF itself was dominated by men. Others argued that more Black people were needed to combat the inherent racism evident in the GLF. Some were tired of talking and wanted action: "We should storm city hall and put an end to the shit we face for being gay," yelled Klaus Smith, a friend of Bill's who lived with a Black drag queen named British Sterling.

As the crowd nibbled on vegetarian foods and passed joints in fellowship, they gradually took a more coherent form and elected leaders. By a show of hands, they picked Berl Boykin to work on legal issues, including an end to sodomy laws, and chose writer Steve Abbott to handle publicity.

The Georgia Gay Liberation Front still needed a front man, patriarchy be damned. Bill had organized protests. He had opened his home to the movement. When the meeting ended, Bill and A. McClane had been elected GGLF co-chairmen.

A fantastic high drew the crowd together that evening. Tired of hiding, they also were tired of being left behind in the whirlwind of civil-rights progress. The GGLF gave them hope that they could one day take pride in being gay. The mission had grown clear: "Out of the closets and into the streets!"

Bill had big plans. He wanted to incorporate, to make the GGLF a legal entity. He was adamant the group had to spread beyond Atlanta, to include all of Georgia. He saw the need to elect gay and lesbian officials, to attack prejudice in the system from inside the system itself.

He had left home for school years before, but that night, wrapped in the warm embrace of the Morningstar Inn, Bill left behind his home and its consequences one more time. He never would get far enough away.

John Greenwell

Atlanta

Summer 1971

John rang up customers and stocked shelves at the SupeRx Drug Store while he waited for night to come.

He had pined for the great unknown of big-city life, just like the heroes and heroines he read about in books and saw on television. *The Wizard of Oz* went Technicolor when Dorothy hallucinated her way out of Kansas; John's life flipped into brilliant relief when he left black-and-white Alabama for urban Atlanta. The allure was absent in the SupeRx's fluorescent lighting or its dingy carpet or its mind-numbing work, stocking shelves and counting receipts and checking out customers. It all came to life at night.

The drugstore lacked a certain glamour, but it was better than his first unsteady months in Atlanta when he had waited tables, took on odd jobs, and slept with men who let him stay overnight. SupeRx paid $1.60 an hour, enough to get him a room in a house nearby. It gave him something to do until he could head out after dark, to places like the Cove, where freedom coursed along invisible conduits.

Since he was six months under the age of twenty-one, John still was too young to get into any bar, gay or straight. His salary gave him the $10 he needed for a fake ID. When the Cove's bouncers took his fake ID and pulled him out by his ear, John had to join the clique of underage revelers who waited in the lobby of bars, in the hope of finding a source for a new license, or at least a lift back home.

He had better luck at Chuck's Rathskeller. A friendly bouncer drove him home one night, then gave him a place to sleep. One night turned into three. Soon the bouncer became his roommate and friend, one who would look the other way when John slipped in the bar through a back door.

Chuck's had taken over an old juke joint and dancehall on the corner of Tenth and Monroe, near a high school on the corner of Piedmont Park. During the day the park teemed with the gay life John had dreamt about, shirtless men walking together hand in hand, women spread out sunning on picnic blankets. At night, the crowd reemerged at Chuck's, where a DJ spun dance records for hundreds of clubgoers. Atlanta drew gays and lesbians from all over the South, and on any given weekend the club put them all on display like the packaged goods once sold inside its walls.

Chuck's held drag shows late at night, taking over the mantle from shuttered clubs like the old Joy Lounge and the infamous Club Centaur. John had heard about drag before he came to Atlanta but had never seen it. He watched, rapt in curiosity at drag shows whenever he could. He saw an acquaintance, Alan Orton, perform as Barbra Streisand, his profile a mirror image of the Broadway queen. He witnessed a man named Alan Allison blossom into womanhood as Allison. He thought he saw Pearl Bailey perform "Hello, Dolly" but realized it must have been a convincing illusion.

He clapped along as the crowd gave the drag queens applause and money. They were quasi-celebrities, queens of a demimonde that existed only at night, hidden under the mantle of dark.

John had long held fantasies of fame. But drag? It just wasn't what men did in Alabama. He found it odd and disturbing, but it drew him in, nonetheless.

///

What is drag, anyway?

Drag intersects with impersonation but goes beyond it. Impersonation is nonthreatening mimicry: Jonathan Winters as Maude Frickert, Flip Wilson as Geraldine. They're men in dresses, no more. Their brilliant comedy derives not from the assumption of gender but from the assumption that the only punch line is in the contrast between their feminine look and their masculine selves.

But a gay man in a dress, or a lesbian in short hair and men's clothes, is an altogether different being. Their images course with the electric knowledge that the performers have voluntarily given up citizenship in their presumed gender. Drag decimates presumptions of sexual identity—male, female, and all the points on the spectrum between those emphatic labels.

Drag gives many people the tools to decipher the complex meaning of their sexuality, a way to choose the place where they can exist peacefully inside themselves. Some see drag as an ultimate expression of self. Some see it as a threat.

When it matters most, drag asks universal questions. If you could wipe the slate and create a new identity, what would it be? What would you keep, and what would you set aside? Would you still be yourself?

Drag teaches an important lesson: Sometimes, to find out who we really are, we have to become someone else.

Bill Smith

Peachtree Street

Spring 1971

One day in 1971 Bill wriggled into a long green dress and fastened the buttons that went from the neckline to the waist. The outfit didn't do much for his rail-thin body. He hadn't shaved his beard or his legs. They poked out like pipe cleaners below the full skirt, a shock to the senses once the eye drifted below the demure hemline. He went to hang out with the drag queens he lived with, for no reason other than to provoke authority. Police cuffed him and hauled him into court.

His friend Diane couldn't help but wonder: Whose dress was it?

Bill had come out to her at his apartment near the Cheshire Bridge strip while she sat on his velour couch, next to a miniature replica of Michelangelo's David.

He said he was a homosexual, but didn't want to be a homosexual. He told Diane he wanted to date girls, but not her. He claimed to have a girlfriend who lived out of town, which they both knew to be a lie. He fought to get her to fall out of love with him, but he lost.

The conversation didn't change their relationship. They still spent time together alone. They were introverts who danced together in his apartment, where no one watched. They dropped acid and went to the local twenty-four-hour laundromat, where the names on the washers and dryers sent Bill into fits of giggles. "I'm a Speed Queen!" He laughed. "I'm constantly agitating!" They drove around town in his old Dodge Dart, and Bill would speed up when he neared railroad tracks. They would fly over them, then fall back to Earth.

Some nights they went downtown to the Fairfield Inn, where the always-open restaurant swarmed with drag queens in the early-morning hours. They would surround the young couple and teasingly pull at Bill's girlfriend's hair.

"Ew, it's a real girl!"

"What are you doing with a real girl?"

"You're not fucking her, are you?"

He had. Bill admired the gender bending and experimentation of the Atlanta scene, and he believed in that experimentation with every nerve in his body. Sometimes he and Diane ventured out to bars, where Bill would point out a man he thought to be closeted.

She would pick up the man, and all three would wander back to Bill's apartment, where she and the stranger would begin to have sex. Bill would join in. Then Diane would slip out of the room and sleep on the couch.

Bill's roommate Charles taught Diane how to put on makeup and put together outfits. Drag queens did it reflexively, out of a sense of mission, and Charles wanted to make the world as fabulous as he had become. He dressed with a blond wig stacked on another blond wig, shaved his body hair, and wore panty hose and miniskirts. He had great legs and was proud to show them off. "Honey, who does your hair? I mean, really," he asked as he approached his next canvas. Diane was happy to have his expertise where her mother offered none.

Bill chose her clothes. He knew her sizes, and picked conservative but tasteful pieces for her, including a plaid jumper they both agreed flattered her. He had absorbed every lesson the drag queens could teach him, from his crackling sense of humor to his agnostic idea of a good time. It didn't matter whether he wore his faded jeans and hole-soled boots or a prim-looking green dress that looked familiar to Diane. What mattered to him was to challenge authority any way he could.

He put on the green dress—so proper it could have passed for one of his mother's. *Was it?* she thought—and it was the first truly radical thing he had done. It would not be the last.

Bill had learned how to pervert the system as it had perverted justice for so many. When he was marched into court, he asked the judge the obvious: "Your Honor, do I look like I'm trying to impersonate a woman?"

He was freed. He had put on drag just to pick a fight, and he had won.

John Greenwell

Atlanta

Summer 1971

When the Cadillac pulled up to his antique-strewn apartment, John knew a star had arrived. John's roommates had offered to put up some visiting performers from Louisville, including the leggy woman who strode up the driveway. She wore huge Jackie Onassis glasses, red hot pants, and a white tank top that exaggerated her height, her dark skin, her strong resemblance to Leslie Uggams.

"Hello, I'm Crystal Blue," she said softly, in a high-pitched drawl, and extended a hand to John. She mesmerized him. Her voice perfumed the air with ambiguous allure.

She took his hand and inspected his clean-shaven face, smooth skin, high cheekbones, and lean one-hundred-fifty-pound figure. He would make a beautiful woman.

"You do drag, don't you?" Crystal asked him.

He wanted to meet men. He hadn't moved to Atlanta to do drag.

"You will, honey. You will."

Over the next few days, John grew to admire Crystal. Drawing from a suitcase, she had the magic to transform herself into a new person, one without a past. John realized he could do the same, become someone else, perhaps a beautiful woman with raven hair and long eyelashes. He tended to give in to his impulses, so when Crystal offered to teach him her art, he said yes.

Crystal groomed John. With the entourage she'd brought along, she helped him pull on and pin her wig, a black helmet updo sprayed heavily with Aqua Net. It fit. John didn't have a clue how to glue on the big, thick eyelashes Crystal wore. She helped. He knew nothing about makeup. Crystal knew how to soften his male features. With her hired hands she reinvented him in a matter of minutes, and when she was done, the mirror reflected someone he did not recognize.

Wearing one of Crystal's costumes, he toted her makeup and gowns and slipped into Chuck's Rathskeller with her. He sat backstage while Crystal prepared, then watched as she transfixed the crowd with a song from the Broadway musical *Purlie,* the story of preacher Purlie Victorious Judson, who battles Jim Crow laws in his Georgia hometown, finds allies within a family held nearly in slavery, and frees them from bondage.

Melba Moore's "I Got Love" wafted from a turntable in the dim cavern of a club as Crystal wrapped her arms around herself. She walked with a confident strut and worked the crowd. *I know I'm a lucky girl, for the first time in my life I'm someone in this world!* In turn, the crowd pulled out dollar bills, first a few, then many. By the time Crystal took her third callback, the money had grown into a pile. She lifted it, and let it rain down on her.

John watched in awe at Crystal's command of the crowd. For the first time, he thought he might want to do the same.

Bill Smith

Georgia State Capitol

Summer 1971

The television camera stared at Bill as he strode down the sidewalk. He wore his usual explosion of red-brown hair and goatee, squared-off spectacles, and a white button-down shirt. He clutched protest signs and slung a white purse over his left shoulder as he led more than a hundred protesters from downtown Atlanta to Piedmont Park on June 27, 1971.

He fronted an army of lovers in warpaint and war robes, a Seussian spectacle with signs and bongos and buttons. One marcher hummed through a blue-and-orange kazoo, tootling it beneath a shock of golden hair and gold-rimmed glasses. Another wore a bowl cut, black-rimmed frames, and a mock turtleneck. He sniffed a red carnation and licked his lips luridly.

They marched two by two, animals on an ark, forced by the police onto the sidewalk and to stop for traffic lights and pedestrians. They had asked the ACLU for help with a permit to march, but were told they were not a minority.

People in cars took leaflets and stared as the group tambourined their way to the park and called to motel balconies: "Join us!"

"This is just like the early anti-war marches," one straight-identified protester marveled, "the way passers-by stare at us."[2]

Bill's eyes angled down, dark and serious, as he spoke into the television camera.

"As people find out that you are a homosexual, there's a good chance that you may lose your job," he said with a bit of a lilt in his voice. His bony shoulders shifted while he proceeded with his lecture, part plea, part civic lesson. He told dinner-hour Atlanta how being gay affected every aspect of life, even outside the bedroom.

"The state will not hire homosexuals," he said. "The schools will not hire homosexuals. The federal government will not hire homosexuals. They consider us a security risk."[3]

He parsed his words carefully. Atlanta was not San Francisco. He warned Northern friends, half in jest, not to mention General Sherman's name unless they were prepared to be bashed. He worried the Klan would shoot at protesters from the rooftops of nearby buildings. He spoke past that fear, directly to the more than 100,000 gay men and women who lived in Atlanta but had not come to demonstrate, who could lose everything—jobs, churches, family—if they joined the first Gay Pride march in Atlanta history.

Bill had worried that Atlanta still was not ready to mount a successful protest. He knew he could count on seven friends to show up, but on the day of the march more than a hundred had shown up, and some of Bill's closeted friends told him that they had driven around where the marchers had gathered, in silent support.

"Five or 10 years ago nobody would have suspected this," Bill said.[4] "It is a new beginning for the gay community."

At Piedmont Park, the march re-formed as a rally replete with guerrilla theatre. In the first skit, soldiers shot at Vietnamese peasants under orders, and had their medals ripped off when they questioned why. Next, police threw people to the ground and hurled epithets—"Queer!" "Lezzy!" "Fag!" In the final act, a panel of experts interrogated a straight couple on the *Slick Cavett Show*: "How long have you been this way?" Atlanta's first Pride ended with promises for bigger, better, and more.[5]

Bill went home to see himself on the evening news. He reported for work the next day as usual at the Board of Education's accounting room. His colleagues stared straight ahead and would not speak to him. Bill laughed and got down to work.[6]

///

"Anybody want to go down there on Bastille Day?"

It started as a trademark blend of a laugh and a dare, but Bill was serious. He wanted to take on Gov. James Earl Carter Jr., for his odious stance on gay civil rights, and the best place to do that was on the governor's turf.

Bill polled his fellow rebels, and a few joined him as he made his way up the white marble steps and under the glittering gold dome of Georgia's Capitol Building. It was July 14, the anniversary of the day when a mob stormed the Paris prison in the name of human rights.

Governor Carter had laid his hand on his family Bible when he was inaugurated on January 12, 1971. The forty-six-year-old peanut farmer from Plains had lost a difficult race to segregationist Lester Maddox in 1966, and vowed not to lose on his second attempt. Lauded and catcalled as a progressive, Carter broke bread with Maddox's faithful and ran again in 1970, feigning agreement with some of George Wallace's positions on segregation. Some state politicians had said it would be the only way he could win, but pointed out he could change those positions once in office—which he did.[7]

"The time for racial discrimination is over," Carter told a standing crowd on Washington Street in the weak sun of Atlanta winter on Inauguration Day. Some in the crowd applauded, and some groaned. "No poor, rural, weak, or black person should ever have to bear the additional burden of being deprived of the opportunity of an education, a job, or simple justice."

Carter's positions on justice flexed easily, but that flexibility did not extend to the young men who descended on his office; the governor had crowed recently about prison reforms that outlawed lesbianism for the first time in Georgia, and attached a twenty-year sentence to it. The GLF trio who would challenge the governor—Bill, Berl Boykin, and Klaus Smith—waited for a slot during Carter's open office hours, sat down with the devout Baptist, and immediately demanded equal rights for gays and lesbians as well as the abolition of sodomy laws.

Carter's temper rose as the activists made their demands. *No,* he fumed, and repeated his rejection twice, turning all the colors of the rainbow. *No. NO.*

Aides hastened the trio out of the governor's office. The stunt had failed. The streets didn't swell in protest. The laws remained intact. Georgia would continue to imprison gays and lesbians for consensual sex. Most gay men and women would continue to live in the shadows, afraid to come out.[8]

///

On August 7, 1971, a column of soldiers moved silently down the sidewalk, then stormed in a surprise attack on a crowd of innocent civilians sitting on a lush green carpet of grass. They swarmed them and took some at gunpoint, dragging others away a while people screamed *Leave us alone!* A child began to cry, hands over ears.

Then the soldiers released them. It was all an act during an antiwar protest held to commemorate the U.S. bombings of Hiroshima and Nagasaki. The Vietnam Veterans Against the War had put on the "search-and-destroy" mission the day after the anniversary (a more convenient Saturday) to make their point.

Protesters used Hiroshima Day as a proxy for the Vietnam War, which was in its second decade of direct U.S. involvement. They pamphleted and chanted: "No more Nagasakis, no more Hiroshimas, no more Vietnams!" They demanded the United States immediately withdraw all its troops from Southeast Asia.

The rally followed the general path of most marches through town, from the park across from Georgia State, up Peachtree Street to Piedmont Park. There, Bill spoke on behalf of the Gay Liberation Front, while others, including civil-rights activist Fannie Lou Hamer, spoke on behalf of women, Blacks, veterans, and those with intersecting identities.[9]

"I've been beaten in jail until my body was hard as metal," Hamer told the crowd. "My house was bombed January 28, 1971, but I'm not stopping."[10] Bill looked to Hamer for inspiration. He wanted to align the GLF protests with the civil-rights protests of Hamer and others as he wrote a new story about the person he was, what he believed in. He honed the new version of himself he had created: Bill Smith, gay civil-rights champion. He showed the world the man he had become.

Rachel Wells

Cruise Quarters, Atlanta

Fall 1971

*F*ive *minutes, everyone! Five minutes!* the stage mother yelled
in no particular direction.

Crystal and her entourage had broken down John's precon-
ceived notions about what drag was, and what it meant about the
people who did it. He had passed so easily as a woman, a friend
convinced him he should try to get onstage as he caroused one
night at the Cruise Quarters, a dank basement bar lined with a
stage and a dance floor that hosted late-night drag shows. Auditions were during the day, and John couldn't leave his drab drugstore job to try out, but a showgirl took him aside and promised
him a slot in that weekend's performance anyway.

And then it was upon him. Already nervous in a heavily draped
dress with chiffon sleeves, he hadn't settled on a drag name. Who
was he? Who could he be? He sifted through memories of childhood movies, some of them biblical, though he had drifted toward
agnostic. He remembered the story of Rachel at the well, a parable
about the everyday presence of the divine. Rachel Armstrong? It'd
be a timely homage to the first man on the moon, but it might
remind crowds of his muscular upper body.

Gowns and wigs and makeup crowded around him in the dress-
ing room as he sat in anticipation. The club's show director—an
A-list queen in pink chiffon and pink lipstick named Dee Dee
Daniels—pressed John for music first, and then for a last name.
Someone had told John once that he looked like Raquel Welch in
drag; he regularly did his hair and makeup like the Hollywood

actress, and the compliment rang true. He took it, and corrupted it, like all good drag queens corrupt their celebrity influences. Wells. Rachel Wells.

"Please put your hands together for Rachel Wells!"

The DJ cued up John's 45rpm copy of Freda Payne's anti–Vietnam War plea, "Bring the Boys Home." John hated the war, the military, and everything it stood for. He had drawn a low draft-lottery number in December 1969, but he had no intention of serving. He had seen what the army had done to his father, and what it had done to his family. He couldn't recall getting a draft notice or a letter to report for his physical, and he didn't care. Only when a friend told him that he might be arrested for failure to report did he look up the nearest draft-board office, down on Ponce de Leon Boulevard, near the old Sears Building. He had donned his most patriotic drag—red, white, and blue shirt and shorts, and a floppy hat, face fully made up—and strode into the office only to find that he needed to go to a different location downtown. He never did.

Payne's plaintive anthem proved easy to choreograph. Rachel marched on the dingy stage, raised her hand in defiance, fingers in a V, and launched into her first number and its antiwar message, which urged America to bring its soldiers home:

Fathers are pleading, lovers are all alone,
Mothers are praying—send our sons back home.

No more than twenty people sat in the Cruise Quarters, but when Rachel finished, the applause came, and then grew. Rachel got an encore, and even made a few tips. On her way off the stage, she dropped one bill on the floor. A fan snatched it up, and handed it back to her. She'd arrived.

For the next few months John worked for $15 a night plus tips. He had always wanted to be onstage, but he couldn't sing or dance. Drag depended on a good song, a good lip-sync, and a good costume. Rachel slowly subsumed John. She wore drag outside the club, outside the mint-green basement apartment she rented with friends for $35 a week. Drag had become her armor, and hidden inside that armor, Rachel began to tuck a real weapon, a paring knife for the just-in-case hours between late-night and early-morning. The danger worried her less than it thrilled her.

John Greenwell had a past: a mother he loved, a string of middle and high school friends he'd know for a year then forget, a few seconds of fame in a school-produced film. Rachel Wells had no past. Hustlers and prostitutes were her neighbors. Needles and condoms stuck to the carpet outside her apartment's metal door. She ripped up a dress, teased her hair into an explosive shock, and painted her face into an Amazonian mask. She wanted the audience to know who she was when she left the stage; she knew she needed to shock them to make them remember her. She stalked the stage and channeled her animal instinct as she careened through a violent, physical version of Janis Joplin's "Piece of My Heart," to wild applause and the nodding approval of the club's drag mother.

Old boundaries disappeared. Rachel took to the streets. She tempted fate. She showed the world the woman she had become.

Vice Mayor Maynard Jackson

Atlanta City Hall

Winter 1971

Maynard Jackson shuffled the mounting stack of papers on his desk in his office at city hall as he began to administer the daily rites of politics. The Gothic-inspired building had become his church, and he approached his mission with zeal. Behind the heavily carved arches that framed its heavy bronze doors, citizens sought indulgences for overlooked ordinances, begged for absolution from petty grievances. Jackson could grant it all, though even he answered to a higher power.

Maynard would lead one day, his family knew. When he was born in Dallas in 1938, his mother and father wrapped the baby and put him in the car for the day-long drive to Atlanta. Aunties and uncles and grandparents cooed over the baby and showered him with gifts, including a twenty-one-jewel Hamilton pocket watch.

"What on Earth would a baby need with a watch?" his parents wondered.

"Because time is important," they were told, "and he must know that."[11]

Steeped in the church and in higher learning at Morehouse College, Jackson bristled with the political ambition that would be his destiny. At thirty years old, he already fit the part of a statesman: regal, perfectly coiffed and groomed, physically imposing. When Bobby Kennedy died in L.A., Jackson resigned abruptly from his law firm, emptied his bank accounts to run for U.S. Senate against incumbent Herman Talmadge, and lost.

In 1969 he ran for vice mayor of Atlanta. Jackson campaigned tirelessly in churches every Sunday. He electrified ordinary speeches with his eloquence and a voice that smoothed over fault lines like plaster of Paris. He had the rare power to impose his beliefs on a room. Jackson won nearly every Black voter's vote, and a third of the white vote too. Jackson became Atlanta's first Black vice mayor. Only Sam Massell, the city's first Jewish mayor, sat above him in the city hall hierarchy.

Peace and love had dissolved in assassination and recession, war had divided homes by generation, but under Massell and Jackson, Atlanta had reason to hope. The pessimists pointed to epidemic crime and white flight, but optimists saw that white voters voted for Black candidates, and that preachers came out of the pulpit to protest war and chronic poverty.[12] They saw the massive highway that now circled the city, the skyscrapers that rose inside it, the digital billboard in Buckhead that had ticked over 1 million citizens in 1970. They took pride when the first Boeing 727 Whisperjet departed from Atlanta's burgeoning airport for Mexico City, its first regularly scheduled international destination.

Atlanta had set out to fulfill Dr. King's dream, and though crime ran rampant, Atlanta was a mecca, a nirvana, an Oz. It was ripe for change. It was propelled by a collective desire for the city to be something.

By 1971 the flight of white Atlanta had shifted political weight into the hands of up-and-coming Black politicians like Jackson. Massell knew his popular vice mayor was a political threat. On October 6, 1971, Massell addressed the Hungry Club, a weekly forum held at the predominantly Black YMCA on Butler Street. Massell touched on the subject of white flight and economic impact in Atlanta, then stumbled badly. He urged Black leaders to "think white" in order to "make the city more attractive as an inducement for them to stay." He went on to suggest that Blacks should "challenge the militant minority" and "rise above the inferiority complex that only blacks will politically support blacks."[13]

The aldermen who served the city were incensed. Alderman Henry Dodson said he was glad Massell had made the speech, as it had revealed his true self.

"I can think black and get along in this society," Dodson said. "I'm not going to 'think white.'"[14]

Jackson had a keen political sense of smell and he detected blood. He sensed an opportunity, but knew he would have to be patient. In the meantime, he went about his daily rituals. He approved zoning variances, refunded overcollected taxes, okayed water-main repairs, and granted liquor licenses.

On November 1, 1971, the police board passed its usual clutch of documents to the Vice Mayor's Office for his approval. Among them was the October 18 application for a liquor license for one Frank Powell, a barman who had operated the Joy Lounge and now ran the Cove, a gay bar hidden in a pocket street off Ansley Park. Powell wanted to open a new club on Cheshire Bridge Road. All it needed was Jackson's signature. Jackson rubber-stamped the license for the Sweet Gum Head nightclub and sent it up to Mayor Massell's office for his approval.

Time was important, Jackson knew. One day soon, he would show the world the leader he had become.

Frank Powell

The Sweet Gum Head

November 1971

Frank Powell wheeled his big Cadillac downtown through a sea of white Ford Custom 500s with big official shields on the front doors, while someone he trusted watched over his bars. His hearing would start at 7:30 p.m. downtown. He couldn't miss it; Atlanta's vice mayor presided over the aldermanic board, and a late arrival could sway the vote against the new club.

When he aimed his showy land yacht back out of the police station, he had much more to do. The aldermen had approved his new club's liquor license. He had to train staff, set up the room, hire more talent. It would be a long evening, and a long few weeks ahead, before opening night.

He'd already picked out a name for the place. It sounded odd, and some people thought it sounded lewd, but it wasn't. It was touching and a little bittersweet. Frank named his new bar the

Sweet Gum Head for the place he was born, the place he knew he would one day rest.

///

Louie Frank Powell was born on November 23, 1931, to James and Vallie Powell on Vallie's mother's family farm in the Florida Panhandle. The town of Sweet Gum Head had been named for the trees that carry a poetic scientific name: *Liquidambar* hints at the golden essence hidden in their tall trunks. Hardy and strong, sweetgums set autumn fire to the South, torch it with fiery orange and red and golden leaves, then shower the ground with spiky fruit. The heavily armored sweetgum balls protect seeds through winter, then break open to let their offspring take wing and drift toward new lives.

At the turn of the last century, Sweet Gum Head formed a small, tightly knit community from just a few dozen homes, one where preachers would whip up crowds into a penitent frenzy during all-day Sunday singing festivals. Frank was taught through Sunday singing that the Bible's exact words were truth, that dancing and drinking were sins, that homosexuality was perversion, that evolution lied about the origins of man, and that segregation honored Christ. He took those lessons with him when he left home to attend Bob Jones University, where homosexuality did not exist in 1951, at least not officially. When he went home after his freshman year, he refused to go back and enlisted in the U.S. Air Force.

He left Sweet Gum Head for good and surfaced in Kansas City, where he discovered the Red Head Lounge, a place where men could slow-dance in each other's arms. Kansas City had a couple of gay bars that the police left alone, as long as the homosexuality stayed confined inside. He made his way to Atlanta, where he built a small bar empire of his own, first as a bartender at Piccolo's at 1139 Peachtree, then as manager at the Joy Lounge at 563 Ponce de Leon Avenue, where drag queen Phyllis Killer polished her drag act with flashy costumes, clever stage patter, and quick feet. The police stopped by the Lounge often, so a lookout kept watch; when the police drove by, Phyllis would run and hide in a restroom or in a beer freezer until she got the all-clear.

In 1968, Frank opened the Cove with a business partner, then took control a year later. The Cove became one of the most popular bars in Atlanta when Frank hired a disc jockey and allowed men to touch each other while dancing. That touch of radicalism did more than line his pockets. It brought the gay world out of back alleys, and gave it a home on Atlanta's main drags.

///

On November 13, 1971, Frank christened the Sweet Gum Head in a space that had been initiated in rebellion decades earlier. In 1954, when the building was part of Franklin's Supermarket, labor men picketed the store, threw stink bombs, and nearly set it on fire.

By the '60s, live music wafted out of the building, then occupied by a club called the Hound's Tooth. When it failed, the club became the Prince of Darkness, then the Cheshire Cat, the "Biggest Topless A Go-Go show in town," featuring Sonny & Cher.[15] Their months-long gig at the Cheshire Cat ended with Cher pregnant with their first child, Chastity.

By January 1970 the club reincarnated itself as Soul City, and promised James Brown as an opening-week draw. Underage drinking led to dozens of arrests and one gunfight that left three wounded before Soul City went quiet. After a stint as a short-lived outpost of the Golden Horn, the room went dark.

Frank had found it, empty and unloved, behind a tire shop and a hardware store. He took drag queen Lavita Allen and DJ Tony Romano to the place from his other bar, the Cove, to get their blessing. It needed a big sound system to bathe the space in glorious music and enough tenders to man the long bar, but everyone agreed it would be perfect. Then they got down to work.[16]

On opening night, three local drag queens each performed the "Hello, Dolly" of a distinct generation: Wendy Grape mimed as Carol Channing, Lavita Allen donned a bob wig and dark eyebrows as Streisand, and Allison played it as Pearl Bailey. All three joined for a finale—and a standing ovation. Soon the reviews were in: "The Sweet Gum Head is such a cheerful, colorful bar, it is bound to stay high on the list of the most popular bars in the south."[17]

Frank called an old friend, show director Danny Windsor, to fill the stage for the weeks to come. Windsor, a former stock player and dancer at MGM, swore he'd made his debut in *The Wizard of Oz* when an actor playing one of the Wicked Witch's flying monkeys showed up drunk to work. Windsor fit into the actor's harness, and soon was shrieking at Dorothy and her friends as they wandered toward Oz. After a stint in the air force, he directed and starred in female impersonator shows at Detroit's Diplomat Club. His characters ranged from a dancer swaying to Irving Berlin to an old woman nattering about nonagenarian sex.

Windsor relied on old-fashioned talent, not four-letter words. He aimed at straight crowds, who enjoyed the strangeness and the exuberance of his shows. He worked his troupe hard: He rehearsed his show girls three hours a day, three times a week.

"I have no use for lazy people," he said, "the ones who just want to get in a dress and say 'Look at me.' That bores me."[18]

He held the "drags"—girls who simply mouthed the words and ran back and forth onstage—with special disdain. "There are those rare few who do have talent and a little imagination to come up with clever gimmicks or routines, that are good enough to make the audience forget they're listening to recordings," he admitted. "That's the name of the game."

"The true female impersonator in show business," he thought, "is the guy who can walk into a dressing room as a guy, walk out as a beautiful woman, and when the show is over, leave all that glamour hanging back in the closet and on the wig block."[19]

Windsor kept his career a secret from his family. "My mother would kill me if she knew what I was doing," he said. "She thinks I'm a pimp in Decatur."

Windsor's revue filled the space with polished drag shows. Gays and lesbians soon discovered a community of night people and a place where they would be left alone until the light of day. Open only for a few weeks, the Sweet Gum Head already become known as the "Showplace of the South." It had already welcomed the kind of rebels that Frank Powell hated.

1972

///

WHAT MAKES A MAN A MAN?

Rachel Wells

The Lighthouse on Peachtree Road

January 1972

The phone at the Lighthouse on Peachtree Road rang, cutting through the midday gloom at the family-style seafood restaurant.

John had been in Atlanta only about a year, and had been waiting tables there only for a few months. Hardly anyone knew he worked there, and most who did knew him by another name.

The phone jangled to life again, and his coworker Marlo called to him, "It's for you." Who in the world could be calling him here, or anywhere? He didn't even have a phone at his apartment. He used a pay phone outside on the street when he had to call.

It couldn't be his mother. John's parents had just moved back from Germany a few months ago. The operator had to find their number for him the day he'd mustered the courage to call home and come out. Short of time, so strapped for money he called collect, he dissolved from fear to relief when his mother asked him, "Are you happy?"

But his mother didn't know he worked at the Lighthouse. It was one of a number of secrets he still kept from her.

It couldn't be the Cruise Quarters, the dingy basement bar where John and his two roommates had worked for a few months at the end of 1971. Those jobs ended when the nightclub closed abruptly, just before Christmas.

Early in the New Year all three found jobs at the Lighthouse, which sat near the Strip. An eastern European couple ran the place, and they were fascinated by the drag queens who cruised the Strip. These same queens flocked to the Lighthouse for its cheap food—and for work.

No one knew John at the Lighthouse because he waited tables in full drag. He shaved his legs, slathered his eyelids with blue eye shadow, slipped into miniskirts and polyester floral-printed blouses, and went by his newly adopted drag name of Rachel. Occasionally, some of the fathers of the unsuspecting families who dined there gave Rachel long, quizzical looks. They sensed something was amiss but they overlooked it, and tucked into their dinners of fresh fish.

Rachel was stunning. She passed as a woman easily. At times John had to remind himself that he was still a man. His customers rarely gave it a second thought. If they knew Rachel was a man, the men who paid her for sex pretended otherwise. The audiences at her drag shows didn't care who she was offstage. They only knew that when she was *onstage*, Rachel mesmerized them with a beauty that all but erased the anxious young man beneath the gowns and makeup.

Marlo stretched out the curly phone cord as far as it would go. "Somebody named Wendy."

Rachel didn't know a single Wendy, but she took the call anyway. Wendy Grape from the Sweet Gum Head told Rachel about plans for a new show that she would produce. She wanted fresh talent to fill its big stage. She asked Rachel to join the already famous Sweet Gum Head family of performers.

John hung up the phone in disbelief. The club could have had any performer the show director liked—and they wanted him.

Still shocked and flattered a few days later, and a little bit scared, John put his nerves aside and headed over to Cheshire Bridge Road in a taxi he couldn't afford, dressed in his "boy drag" of low-rise slacks on slim hips. His unruly hair leapt in curls off his head, springing to restless life like his heroes in the musical *Hair*.

The cab slowed along the Cheshire Bridge Strip in front of a tire shop and a drugstore, across the street from a family-style restaurant, all echoes of the formerly upstanding street, now gentle reminders of its decline. To John it looked like paradise.

Ready for love, for acceptance, for applause, John hesitated for a moment. Then he took a deep breath and stepped through the Sweet Gum Head's church-style doors. He didn't care if he ever went back to Alabama. Xanadu waited inside.

///

John's new drag sisters called out to Rachel from the middle of the room. Wendy wore Steve Vismor's clothes, his friendly face, his large nose, his wide grin. Tiny, handsome Rhonda Blake wore a few days' worth of beard.

Rachel already knew Lavita. Out of drag, oval-faced Lavita had flirted with John, who looked at him in his male guise and only saw . . . Barbra.

"Come on, let me show you the dressing room," Lavita said as she led Rachel upstairs.

Lavita Allen had been born Alan Orton in New York. Stagestruck, Alan wanted to act, but obeyed his parents' wishes and studied geology at Emory University instead, then taught at Georgia State University. He was twenty, and many of his students were older than him. He made just $90 a week before taxes. He depended on generous parents to thrive, and they indulged him. Alan had the first of everything—the first new Lincoln, the first microwave oven, the first Betamax. Friends teased that his parents paid him to stay away. "You know that's not true!" he protested.

A roommate had told a bar owner that Alan did drag. In reality, he'd never put on a wig, and his wide brown eyes and curly dark hair were more like Woody Allen than Barbra. He dressed up on a dare and did it anyway, borrowing Streisand's gestures from her *Funny Girl* run on Broadway. His drag name came from a neighbor, Lavita Allen.

Lavita wrote her own funny-girl backstory: Lavita the Quaalude freak, burned out on acid, not so feminine. A comedy queen, Lavita would join the cast in a can-can and play it for laughs. It became her passive-aggressive way of fighting choices made by other, more famous, more glamorous cast mates, and it worked.

Lavita showed Rachel the cramped dressing area upstairs— workstations, makeup tables and mirrors, racks for hanging hot pants and polyester blouses—while Wendy cast the roles in the newly minted *Red, White & Blue Revue*. She would host, and perform Liza Minnelli and Carol Channing; Rhonda would deliver glamour, while Rachel played the new girl, whatever that meant. Lavita, of course, would perform as Streisand. The revue would rehearse three days a week, and perform two shows five nights a week, for $25 a night each, plus tips.

Over the next six days the *Red, White & Blue Revue* honed its first show numbers, "Aquarius" from *Hair* by the Fifth Dimension, and "Thoroughly Modern Millie / Second Hand Rose/ Mame," a Supremes Broadway medley. Rachel didn't even know what a production number was, and thought the second song was about one person, not three, but when the DJ dropped the needle, she stepped in, and stepped up. The girls knit well together; they traded the high sheen of Danny Windsor's shows for spontaneity, and it paid off handsomely. Crowds quickly learned they'd always see something new with the revue, thanks in part to the combustible pairing of Wendy and Lavita, and to the hint of stardom that glinted off the new girl, Rachel Wells.

Bill Smith

Georgia State University, Atlanta

April 19, 1972

B ill loved to lecture other people, so when he asked the crowd of thirty-one students, "How do you explain why you love someone?" he did what came easily to him. Rather than let one of them speak, he delivered a sermon without truly delivering the answer.

"Some say it is because of genes or dominating parents," he explained, though he couldn't explain why he was gay. "There are all types of theories, but one thing is clear, you are not sick when you can relate to a person for what he is inside, not for what sex he is."

He had been at the same cusp of freedom as some of the young gays and lesbians in the room, ready to embark on a new life when he began college. When he left home, he'd spent a first lonely year at the small Emory University campus in rural Oxford, Georgia. Atlanta called him with the twin lures of easy sex and the heady politics of the gay liberation movement; he left Oxford and enrolled at Georgia State as a political science major.

That day in April of 1972, he tried on behalf of the GLF to organize on campus, with a plan to eventually gain university recognition. The college's deans had asked the GLF to keep its presence quiet, to avoid public groupings on campus and to hold meetings in private apartments. Bill and the other GLF organizers laughed off the suggestion; silence would perpetuate the "ghetto environment" gays and lesbians faced when they remained quiet.

The GLF didn't want to keep quiet. It wanted political power. Just as Bill and Klaus Smith and Berl Boykin had descended upon Governor Carter's office the year before, the GLF went to Mayor Massell's office for a fifteen-minute session on a regularly scheduled "Little People's Day," and demanded a seat on the Community Relations Commission, a council that had no legal power but held sway as a mediator between citizens and a city caught in the throes of integration.

The GLF wanted to tap its power to draw more gays and lesbians to march in Atlanta's second Pride protest. Pride in 1972 would have specific legislative missions: a citywide gay bill of rights, and the reopening of Greenhouse Hill, a notorious cruising grounds that had been shut down for that reason. The hill closure dealt explicitly with only gay men, but Bill thought it would underscore the oppression all gays and lesbians faced: "Why should the area around the lake be left open—where blatant heterosexual cruising goes on all the time—and only the Greenhouse Hill be shut down? If Gay people can begin to see how they're being oppressed and discriminated against by political institutions, then—and only then—can they start realizing what effects that oppression has on their own behavior, how it makes them turn around and oppress other people by dehumanizing them."[1]

Pride organizers had no idea what to expect in terms of attendance. They wanted to reach beyond the echo chamber of radicals and find new followers—and to do that, they decided they would have to change their battle plan. They would have to recruit from the places where gays and lesbians gathered for fun, not for politics. They would need to take their protests to clubs like Frank Powell's Sweet Gum Head.

Rachel Wells

Lenox Mall and Lenox Road

April 1972

Just twenty-one, barely shaving, rail-thin, with a nearly hair-less body, John could show anything he wanted at the Sweet Gum Head and get away with it. Even so, applause was thready. Rachel Wells didn't have a following or even an act yet. She needed to be something more than just the new girl.

She had started from scratch at the Sweet Gum Head. The crowds from the now-shuttered Cruise Quarters hadn't followed her to Cheshire Bridge Road. Her early outfits were little more than tied-up T-shirts, halter tops, and hot pants with boots. She didn't know makeup. As she struggled, she kept her eyes open for a gimmick to set her apart, beyond her anodyne appeal.

Even as a brand-new performer at the Sweet Gum Head, Rachel made $25 a night, five or six nights a week. She could afford some nice clothes on her salary, maybe even a pet. She wandered the aisles of a Lenox Mall pet store until she came across Reba.

Reba was a six-foot-long boa constrictor.

She could be a cavewoman, she thought, like Raquel Welch in *One Million Years B.C.*, when she deserted her tribe and risked her life to follow Tumak of the Rock People. She even had the perfect proto-disco song to go with the look: the Chakachas' "Jungle Fever." One snake to go, wrapped up in a burlap bag, one more outfit shredded into pieces, and Rachel had her gimmick.

Rachel kept Reba a secret until showtime, mostly out of fear. She already panicked when she peeked in the bag and looked at a snake she'd never held. What would everyone else do?

"Jungle Fever" punted her into shock mode with its kick drum. Guitars jangled, and Rachel reached into the bag for Reba. They slid onstage together, to wild cheers from a crowd of a hundred or more. Reba had a rough night from there. Rachel put Reba's head in her mouth, and swung her by the tail over the bobbing heads unlucky enough to be in the front row. One last pose, a quick encore, and Reba's star was born. So was Rachel's.

Backstage, Rachel put Reba back in the bag and spat snake out of her mouth for the next few minutes.

///

Reba would be the woman in her life for years. Herman would be the man, though he trembled at the idea of a reptile living with him and John. When John saw Herman, he saw a confidant, a brother in arms.

They had met not long after Crystal Blue had left town, when Herman drifted in from Alabama with a convincing fake ID, a McCartney shag hairdo, and a Jim Nabors accent. Herman had worked with John in drag at the Lighthouse as Marlo, and shared a bed with him as a friend. They rented a squalid apartment together near Twelfth Street, dressed in identical pigtails and lipstick, pretended they had sent husbands off to war while they took drags off Winston cigarettes. They clung to each other and cried when they watched sad movies. Without much money and without many boundaries, they crafted an adventure from a scratched-out existence.

They shopped at Christian thrift stores and were asked to leave. They ran around in male clothing with light makeup on, to shock people. They wore full drag too. In March 1972 they drove Herman's one-headlight blue Maverick out of the zone where their female attire would cause no problems. When the police pulled them over they made Rachel and Marlo stand outside of the car.

"You're cold, aren't you?" The cop looked at Rachel's tiny dress. "You can get in the car if you take your wig off, Gaylord."

"I'm not taking it off," John spat, furious. He refused to stand on Peachtree Street without a mane, looking like a man in a dress. After ten minutes of Herman begging—"Please don't tow my car!"—the cop relented. Herman paid the ticket.

John could count on Herman to be the calm one, the proper one, the "we can't do that" friend, the fatherly one who worried about consequences. John's first instinct was to do or say exactly what came to his mind. John had become a more fearless version of himself as he became Rachel. His power in drag had infiltrated his life as a man. The two had started to resemble each other.

As he grew more like Rachel, he took more risks. He dabbled in drugs. Marijuana didn't deliver the high it did for others; it just made him effusively sad. John was quick to take anything he was offered. He was open to just about any new experience, except any needle drugs. He also was naïve.

Acid gave him his first nightmare. The orange powder he consumed tasted like children's aspirin. For half an hour he felt nothing and talked to friends. Then the world began to dissolve around him.

He went to the back bedroom and sat in the dark until Herman came in. By then, John had broken with reality. Herman started screaming at John, "How could you do this?" and while he bellowed, John saw Herman's face turn into a horned demon.

Someone with more trips under their belt heard the screams, and came to keep John calm. In an instant—or more than half the night later—John woke up, thirsty and achy. He apologized to Herman but never let his failures stop his experimentation. He wasn't fearless. He just knew he would fall, and knew he had to learn how to get back up.

Bill Smith

Twelfth and Piedmont, Atlanta

1972

Bill and Diane got closer to each other through drugs. They tripped on acid often, including the one time they had sex, at Bill's apartment on Twelfth and Piedmont, one of the half-dozen apartments he had lived in since he left for college. Bill fed Diane the Long Island Iced Teas that made her vomit the next day; she'd never been drunk before. Marijuana mellowed them both out, enough so that Bill would confess the darker moments in his life to her. Strychnine and acid together rendered the world in gorgeous saturated color but made their bodies ache for a week after. If they took only small amounts, it wouldn't kill them.

When they first began to date, Bill and Diane would see each other constantly. Then, early in 1969, Bill developed a habit of disappearing for a few days at a time. He would come back, then disappear again. He evaded their relationship while she ran headlong toward him.

When he came out that spring in a letter to her, she read the joy in his words, and it soothed the sting. He had become involved in the Gay Liberation Front, with the Metropolitan Community Church, with the Southeastern Gay Coalition. He felt relieved to find a group of people that accepted him without question. The excitement vibrated off the page in long, pointed, forward-leaning script. He had released a burden.

He found someone. Diane had flown out of town for a few weeks, and Bill wrote her excitedly about the Mustang from Hertz that replaced his green Porsche 914 while it was in the shop, about his ulcer diagnosis, about his grand plan to adopt an Afghan hound. He told her about Steve, the man who wanted to be with him forever. They'd had matching rings made, wide bands with rough textures offset with delicate lines. Diane was there to grieve with him when Steve left, and to plunge with him back into their familiar habits.

He now lived in a circus, he told her. In one apartment he shared with his drag-queen friends, they would lip-sync to the Supremes in front of the fireplace, singing into pretend microphones. When Diane and Bill saw the first production of *The Boys in the Band* at a small theater near his Midtown apartment, Bill smirked after it was done: "We could have sat at home in my living room and seen this," he told her.

They never went straight ahead. "We never go straight, Diane," Bill would say. "We go forward."

She took his advice when he chose her clothes. Her mother's Salvation Army finds turned Bill pale, particularly the black micro-mini dress with the red rose stitched at the bottom of its V-neck, where it drew attention to Diane's breasts. The first time Bill saw it, he tore the rose off. "It's ridiculous," he said. "Don't ever wear that again."

He longed for her when she was gone. "Trees get lonely and vines seem to be attracted to them," he wrote to her, leaving behind a mystery, which of them was the tree and which was the vine.

She knew he loved her, but she also knew he had no interest in sex with her. She wanted him anyway. They kissed. Bill told her they'd never have sex as long as she was a virgin. She told him that was no longer a problem. He blanched.

Bill knew she wanted to have sex to cement their bond, so they did. They both seemed to enjoy it, but he had to show her what he could not bring himself to say: that they needed each other to ground their lives; that they were more like brother and sister; that they had a loving and close relationship that could never be romantic. When he could not form the words, Bill got out of bed, went into the living room, and had sex with the hustler they had brought home earlier in the evening.

John Greenwell

The Sweet Gum Head

May 1972

The Sweet Gum Head and its oasis of profanity had become Rachel's harbor from morality.

John had learned from his cast mates the power of the possible: They could do anything and didn't know what they couldn't do until they tried. John fed off that energy and thrived in the permissive atmosphere.

John had learned early on that with Lavita and Wendy, performers had to expect the unexpected. They pulled off wigs and threw pies in faces without warning, deliriously slapstick and vaudevillian in their form of drag. They were pranksters, but Lavita and Wendy also challenged John to grow as an entertainer. His confidence bloomed; eventually, he clashed with more seasoned performers who hesitated and leaned on experience instead of inspiration. "Well, in Nashville we did it this way," drag performer Toni Duran would often say—until John told her one day in exasperation, "I don't give a fuck what they did in Nashville."

The Sweet Gum Head's fame had grown beyond Atlanta via performers and out-of-town visitors, so Frank Powell sent the troupe west to San Antonio on tour, with Allison, Lavita, and Wendy piled into one car. Rachel rode in another with her roommate and his boyfriend, with Reba in a paisley velveteen bag with a drawstring that kept her confined for hours on end. The troupe appeared at the Hypothesis nightclub, where local drag queens went agog over the big-time Sweet Gum Head act. The revue even won favorable reviews in the city's straight-laced *Express* newspaper—"If you can stomach the idea of big men, some with arms like dock wollopers, mincing about in sheer, black panty hose and high-heeled pumps, some of the acts are rather amusing."[2] But Texas crowds were small, possibly because on the first night Allison had dared Rachel to run from backstage screaming, with Reba held high. Some in the audience screamed with her—and ran out of the club.

They were paid little, but their first road show felt like fame. They set out for home with a little bit of money, and plenty of time for Wendy and Lavita to sketch out the grand spectacle they sprang on Rachel back at the Sweet Gum Head: a performance of all the music from *Jesus Christ Superstar.*

"You've got to be kidding," John said when they brought up the idea during rehearsals. He knew Wendy and Lavita had big ambitions for the Sweet Gum Head's shows, but a full-on musical? It sounded crazy. It also sounded like a step backward. He had worked hard to perfect the illusion of Rachel Wells, and now the other performers asked John to play a bearded man on a cross.

"I'm playing Judas because I'm Jewish." Lavita had worked it out, down to the theology.[3]

For the next month, Rachel bit her tongue and took direction from Leonard, a round-faced friend of Wendy's who'd appeared in a chewing-gum commercial. She listened to him, even when he drove her up the wall, because he had acting experience—and he helped her get better at performing. Rachel drew on a scraggly makeup beard. She learned all the songs to a musical she'd never seen.

When she took to the stage as Jesus, Rachel endured the whips and beatings of centurions, the crucifixion, all for the chance to be a star. She intoned her lines, nearly naked, hanging from a real cross inside the club's darkened space: *Father, forgive them, they don't know what they're doing.*

Wendy and Lavita hammered thunder and flashed lightning in perfect percussive time with the Sweet Gum Head's lighting and sound. The crowd drew still, and silently waited as the stage went dark.

When the curtain fell on the Sweet Gum Head's version of *Superstar,* the full house cheered through a long, enthusiastic standing ovation. John heard their cheers during their callbacks: "We love you, Rachel!"

The crowd left in a reverie. The queers and freaks had won them over with a show that had stretched the boundaries of drag, of blasphemy, and of the scrawny budget the club could afford for its shows. It had been a breakout performance. It had stretched John's idea of what drag could be, of what he could become.[4]

Frank Powell

The Sweet Gum Head

June 23, 1972

Frank's booming laugh filled the Sweet Gum Head on the not-so-busy nights, and it disguised his worry. He worried about money: He knew how much money a popular nightclub could make and how much it could lose, so he paid everyone discreetly in cash. He worried about some of the people who sat at the Gum Head's bar, night after night, as he played bail bondsman, therapist, and best friend. He worried that straight men wrote laws and straight police enforced them, so he sent a barhand to the parking lot with a flashlight, under standing orders to signal him when a squad car passed.

Frank knew how to make it all work, when to pay attention, when to turn a blind eye, when to keep quiet. He held a low opinion of those who put their homosexuality in the headlines. "Reputable gay people don't carry signs in the streets," he would later say. "I see those people on the news and they look like creatures out of a weird movie."[5]

The Great Speckled Bird, Atlanta's alternative newspaper, had told readers Frank believed homosexuality was a sin, and that his bars were sexist supermarkets, where muscled and lean white men were put on pedestals, where gay liberation was stifled. The GLF had said he carded women and Black patrons differently.[6] *How could gays and lesbians, already discriminated against themselves, discriminate against others for their race or gender?* they wondered.[7]

By Pride 1972, Powell had had enough of the longhaired rebels who railed against him in print. Now they dogged him inside his clubs, too. On the Friday evening before the second Stonewall protest march in Atlanta, Bill Smith and the small but vocal Gay Liberation Front entered the Sweet Gum Head and handed out flyers to promote gay meeting places outside the confines of the clubs.

"We don't want any of that radical shit here," Frank barked at the protesters. [8] At the Sweet Gum Head, they were simply ordered to leave, though no one touched them. At Frank's other bar, the Cove, GLF members were shoved out into the parking lot. Frank had tried to keep his clubs under the radar, but he had given shelter to the gay community, and that fueled the change that quickly blazed out of his control.

Bill Smith

Peachtree Street

June 25, 1972

B ill flaunted his pride as he sauntered down Peachtree Street, leonine hair rustling and bouncing in defiance, voice growing strong with every chant.

"What do we want?"

He had filled out, his face fuller, his eyes almost lost behind his glasses. In his white T-shirt, stenciled with the Greek letter lambda, adopted by the gay rights movement as its symbol, Bill marched backward down Peachtree, leading a call-and-response as they paraded down the city's most prominent street.

"What do we want?"

He yelled and cajoled other gay men and women until the coastal drawl in his high tenor voice went hoarse. He cupped his hands around his mouth, lifted his arms and brought them down forcefully to push more angry air out of his lungs, a human megaphone. He stared down, focused on his chant, not on the news cameras that faced him.

"What do we want?"

"Liberation!" the crowd answered.

"When do we want it?"

"Now!"

The mantra carried them toward Piedmont Park as police flanked their sides. This year the marchers had obtained a permit, but only after they answered anxious questions. A city official asked, "How close will the marchers be to each other?" The GLF's Charlie St. John wrote back with discomfiting wit: "Very close."[9]

On June 25, 1972, in the first officially recognized Pride parade in Atlanta, men in halter tops and bare midriffs and tight blue jeans openly held hands, stretched arms around shoulders, put hands on asses in playful rebellion. A woman marched fully wrapped in lavender sheeting to hide her identity. A man in classic redneck camouflage overalls, a huge beard, and a red bandanna toted a banner to champion his own cause: OUT NOW.

Bill and the marchers chanted their revolutionary slogan as they moved down Peachtree Street, in front of churches just finishing their Sunday prayers. Some churchgoers blanched in disbelief. Others smiled at marchers and flashed peace signs.

The parade of more than a hundred gays and lesbians and allies ended with a drag float captained by Kitty Litter and Lily White. Drag already had splintered into factions, and the so-called Grease Sisters were offbeat, outrageous queens who ditched the glamour-induced melodrama of the older generation. They wore flouncy tattered dresses and dirty ostrich feathers and waved to the crowds with their dirty white gloves. They were part of the community, but some of the other marchers in the parade still considered them freaks and wanted nothing to do with them.

John Greenwell

The Sweet Gum Head

August 1972

At night, behind the nearly anonymous doors of the Sweet Gum Head, dancers spun and swept through unabashedly erotic poses, caught in flagrante delicto. They cooled their sweat with tall strawberry daiquiris, spilled them, left the murky red carpet stickier than they had found it. They traded bills for pills, traded looks, traded numbers. They sampled every earthly delight, backed by the ripe beat of a new underground music that curled sinuous tendrils into their ears and sent tribal urges through their hips.

On the DJ's cue, they took their seats among the rows of tables that lined one side of the club, towered overhead in the back, crammed into every nook. Their laughter kept time with the patter of shoes as the oak dance floor emptied.

Before the Sweet Gum Head closed promptly at midnight, the final show began. Murmurs went quiet around the dark room. An ersatz Marilyn Monroe stepped into the light, clouded in white silk, tinged with despair. The oak stage warmed under a hot pyramid of light while John watched from the side of the stage, his head whirling in confusion.

Chairs scraped closer to the stage. Dollar bills emerged from half-empty wallets. A record popped as the needle dropped into a groove. A record spun in hypnotic circles on a turntable as John swan-dove into a dark recess in his mind. A baroque curlicue of strings swooped upward, liberated from the black vinyl: Shirley Bassey's "This Is My Life."

"This Is My Life" became an early drag anthem long before the Sweet Gum Head opened, but at the Sweet Gum Head it soared to perfection. A florid, orchestral telenovela of a song, it strikes defiant note after defiant note, from confessional verses to its triumphant climax. With her trademark floor-length sequin gowns, billowy marabou, and extravagant makeup, Shirley Bassey didn't just inspire drag queens, she resembled them—and they in turn resembled her.

Born in extreme poverty in the Tiger Bay section of Cardiff, Wales, Bassey was not yet thirty years old when she recorded the song. At twenty she had her first hit with "Banana Boat." By twenty-seven, she'd earned a fortune with the theme to the James Bond movie "Goldfinger." By 1968, she had divorced twice, and had moved to Italy to avoid taxes. There, she first recorded

"This Is My Life," in Italian and in English, translated from its original form ("La vita"). She owned it from the first performance, her troubled life fact-checking every verse. With its soaring melody and Bassey's trademark over-the-top delivery, it became her showstopper. She plunged so deeply into the song's melodrama, it proved almost impossible to overdo, and easy to lampoon.

On the Sweet Gum Head stage, Allison's performance of "This Is My Life" started with silence. In that pause, she would step into the light.

Outside the club in boy drag, Alan Allison's blond-brown hair framed movie-star looks with ice-blue eyes. His hairy legs stuck out from his usual uniform, the cut-off jean shorts he wore all summer long. Inside the club Alan became just Allison. When Bassey hesitated, then pulled down the crucial note, Allison would begin to cry, and make the lyrics her own:

Sometimes when I feel afraid, I think of what a mess I've made . . . of my life.

No one else cried when they performed it. No one else knew exactly why Allison cried from the first line. She lived life like a party, and the tears were a rare exception on her face.

Some in the audience mimed along with Allison. Most sat transfixed as she began to disrobe. The first audience to see Allison perform the song couldn't have known what to expect. First she removed her false eyelashes, one by one. She had glued them on like women did but with a man's hands, clumsy and big.

Her shoes came off next. Drag queens spent hours constructing their looks. Allison deconstructed hers—ripped it away, bit by bit. Then she slowly pulled off her wig, and dropped it to the floor as the first verse stepped through a march of strings. She cried radiantly as she unfastened her silken white dress, slipped free of its straps, and let it drop to the stage.

The dress fell to reveal a man, smooth at the shoulders but hairy-legged. An illusion had hung in the air, alive only between a few glints of the mirrored ball that spun above the room. Stripped down to his jean shorts, Alan stood at the center of the stage surrounded by crumpled dollar bills. He'd cried the whole way through, as the drag anthem became his story. It was all an act, but it lived in the same body as the truth.

Some in the audience cried along with him. Their tears were the condensation of pain. Just about anyone in the room could tell a story of how they had been punished, rejected, or discarded, how they escaped another life that refused to have them.

///

John had taken his place in the back row, where the tall girls always stood, in his white halter dress and a cloud of russet hair.

The song caught him off-guard; his mood sank, as it did when he took acid or smoked pot, or sampled female hormones. The song crystallized his confusion between his daytime self, the man he was, and the woman he became at night. What had he done to himself? What kind of man was he? The song had real power, as music does, to reveal a hidden sadness he thought he had left behind in Alabama.

The crowd chanted and whistled. Then they morphed and wobbled behind John's blurry tears. The first tears fell down his painted cheek just before midnight, just before he turned, and ran.

No one in the audience saw John disappear. Tucked behind the wall of marabou and makeup, the *Red, White & Blue Revue*'s ingenue had staggered offstage, slipped out a side door, and run toward the latest place he called home.

John stumbled and blinked as he hobbled across Cheshire Bridge Road in his women's shoes. He fumbled for a nonexistent key, left behind in his dressing room.

He sat on the curb outside his apartment and wiped his tears while he waited for the club to fall dark. A man's voice emerged from the dark.

"Are you all right?"

He recognized the voice. It belonged to a hustler he knew, and it comforted him. In the warmth of that late August night, the young man with a brilliant smile held John's hand, and stroked his back. He listened while John tried to put words to his anxiety. Almost everyone knew him as Rachel, the girl who loved animals and plants and antiques, who cruised flea markets in her day drag, who had no small ambitions, who wanted to find the purpose for her existence. Still, he knew himself as John. Popular and stunning, Rachel Wells threatened to blot out John entirely.

"I'm a man, I want to be a man," John told the humid August air. "I'm not Rachel; she's a character, and she's getting out of control."

Rachel Wells

Miss Gay Atlanta

September 1972

Delisa Darnell became the first Miss Gay Atlanta in 1970 at Chuck's Rathskeller. The pageant had been conceived as a way to bring in more customers on a slow night, but local performers took it seriously. In 1971, the pageant crowned pretty pixie British Sterling its queen, in what some thought was an attempt to undercut the racism in the gay community.[10]

John wanted to be the third to win the title. He had begun to accept the divide in his life, between himself and Rachel Wells, and had grown more sophisticated with his look and his act. He learned how to walk in high heels, how to pose for the judges, how to turn in a lavender chiffon gown and long white evening gloves with a book on his head. He learned how to live two lives, and came out with every introduction: "I'm John, but you can call me Rachel."

To win the pageant, he needed practice. He asked the Sweet Gum Head to sponsor Rachel in a trio of pageants, the first in a Florida bingo hall. Rachel chose "Jungle Fever" for the Miss Florida talent competition; the song fused its energy around a core of a repetitive dance beat that had emerged from underground clubs and had just begun to hit the mainstream. It didn't yet have a name, but its music had a few common elements: talented musicians, complicated rhythmic structures, and classically tinged melodies.

The new music took root in former Paris jazz clubs during World War II. In 1941, La Discothèque opened on rue de la Huchette; it played recorded music, and influenced clubs like the nearby Whisky à Go-Go when it gave postwar crowds a place to dance. The Parisian clubs inspired mimics like New York's Peppermint Lounge, a bar west of Times Square that became famous in the early 1960s for its celebrity guest list and its dancing. Gay men and women still could not dance as same-sex couples in public, but soon the private places they created and the music they played edged their way toward the mainstream. The line between the exclusive straight clubs and the underground gay dance clubs began to blur; promiscuous and ambiguous sex and drugs combined with repetitive looped music to create a new cultural moment.

The missing link between kitschy Latin lounge tunes and the deep bass dance music just hitting the airwaves, "Jungle Fever" alternated measures of sinuous, syncopated bass and burbles of muted brass with incomprehensible lyrics chanted by its Belgian auteurs. Rachel paired the song with her snake act, unaware that burlesque shows had put reptiles in the hands of temptresses since the days of Tex Guinan's jazz-age Manhattan speakeasies.

She swung Reba again, wrapped the boa around her neck, and soon she had the mostly Cuban audience wrapped around her finger. They pounded the tables in approval—but still, Rachel lost to another Atlanta queen, Tricia Marie.

Frank drove her to the next Florida pageant, Miss Dixieland. Reba wasn't invited. "If you bring that goddamn snake, you can take the bus," he said with a laugh.[11] Rachel finished second runner-up. Back in Atlanta, she competed in the Miss Gay Southeast pageant, the first one held at the Sweet Gum Head. She wore the same lavender outfit she'd worn in Florida, but performed to a new song, Barbra Streisand's "Space Captain." She lost to Wendy, but finished ahead of Allison, a pattern that would repeat itself time and time again.

In the 1972 Miss Gay Atlanta pageant, Rachel would be the only Sweet Gum Head girl angling for home-court advantage and for the attention of Buddy Clark, who owned the contest and ran it with military precision. Hyperactive and compact, Clark demanded that his twenty-five contestants knew he was in charge.

Clark made it clear no songs would be repeated by performers, so the twenty-five contestants drew numbers for show order. When it came time for Rachel to choose, all of the songs she had prepared had been claimed—even Streisand's "Space Captain," picked by Apple Love, a sharp lip-syncer from Tampa who wore a brace from childhood polio. From the time she was fifteen, Apple would go to a Tampa "chicken club" that only admitted those under twenty-one, and would sing to the jukebox while she sipped her soda. In her eye shadow and lip gloss, she was the only person who looked like a boy and wore makeup, and even the effeminate men in town looked down on her for that. She left for Atlanta in 1971 and promptly fell in with Lily White and the other Grease Sisters and joined them, as she gently realized that her gender was as much rooted in mythology as biology.

Apple's Streisand was good, so pageant organizer Clark took Rachel aside and with a wink, handed her "Maybe" by the Three Degrees, a song he had chosen specifically for her.

Pageant night fell on a Thursday. Wendy had put together a white outfit for Rachel, with a cross-over halter and billowy pants that flowed like a skirt for the evening-wear round. For the talent competition Rachel bought a spaghetti-strap red dress with lace-up sides. Silver chains held a white bikini together under a fluffy white bathrobe for her final sportswear look.

She had the costumes, but Rachel was having a hard time with "Maybe." A woman's lament before she reunites with a lover, "Maybe" starts with a three-minute monologue. The deceptively easy rhythm of the singer's patter and voice felt unnatural to Rachel. She practiced and practiced, but knew she couldn't deliver it perfectly. She would have to find a way out of it. She would have to trust herself.

Rachel shared John's competitive streak. She flaunted her evening gown, struck an exaggerated pose in her barely there bikini. She took the microphone for "Maybe," and after leading in with its first line—*"You know, girls, it's hard to find a guy that really blows your mind"*—she smashed the mic on the stage and fell to her knees, prostrate in love and lust. Rachel could read a crowd. She had quick instincts to make the most of a moment, especially the moments when even her stunning looks and body could only go so far. She fumbled some of the song's lyrical twists and turns, but the crowd gave her a standing ovation.

Rachel Wells won Miss Gay Atlanta 1972. Wendy watched with drag-mother approval. Allison handed her red victory roses, wrapped in a bow, and British Sterling placed the four-point crystal crown on her head.

Vice Mayor Maynard Jackson

Atlanta City Hall

October 1972

Burton Wolcoff toyed with the Atlanta mayor, who seethed while Wolcoff sat next to his attorney and calmly explained to the TV news camera that he wasn't the criminal.

"If anyone was a criminal," he said with a smirk, "it was the mayor's brother Howard Massell."

Sam Massell strained free of his press secretary and police bodyguard and charged forward, aiming for Wolcoff. "I think you are in the underworld and organized crime," Massell yelled, "and you are not welcome in this city."[12]

"You keep using the word 'think,'" Wolcoff said icily. "Aren't you positive?"

"I'm almost positive," the mayor cut back, enraged.

"Well, almost isn't good enough," Wolcoff deadpanned.[13]

Massell's on-air tirade peeled back the cover from his frustration with Atlanta's fight against organized crime. In a live television address on Monday night, September 25, Massell portrayed the battle with syndicates as a test of strength. "We either succeed in putting everyone on notice that organized crime is not welcome in our city," the Mayor told the city, "or we will be admitting we cannot 'get our thing together' down here and this prosperous, growing city is ripe for the plucking."[14]

Organized crime had infiltrated Atlanta more than a decade before, but it had mostly been ignored until 1972, when local interests began to give way to national syndicates through sports betting, loan sharking, and prostitution. They had slipped without any friction into Atlanta thanks to its myriad layers of city, county, and state law enforcement; some fifty-seven police departments governed the area, and would never stand to be integrated into one.

Massell's anger bloomed in tandem with his pursuit of the Wolcoff brothers, Burton and Robert, who had been linked to organized crime in Chicago, even to Al Capone. Police chief John Inman had sounded the alarm: "When hoods like these Wolcoff characters are so persistent in trying to set up shop in our city, the message is clear."[15] Atlanta police tried to keep tabs on the Wolcoffs by setting up a stalking horse, a vending-machine company that stocked bars with cigarettes and 45rpm records.

They also convened a grand jury that took testimony for nearly a week. Those called included a vending-machine operator, a home-improvement company owner—and Howard Massell, who testified for more than two hours before he slipped out of town, headed for Florida.

The grand jury also called bar owners. On October 11, 1972, the Sweet Gum Head's Frank Powell took his turn on the stand. When asked about organized crime in the city of Atlanta, he professed ignorance, as did many of the gays and lesbians who flocked to Atlanta's growing gay bar scene. Some of them suspected that some of Atlanta's gay clubs, like the Stonewall Inn in New York, had certain entanglements—and chose to ignore it. What other choice did they have? They either could spend celibate Saturday nights at home with Mary Tyler Moore and Carol Burnett, or spend it dancing on the edge of darkness.

Massell pleaded to the governor for help. In late October, Jimmy Carter held a press conference, called the Wolcoffs "a threat to the orderly structure of Atlanta and Georgia," and gave the State Division of Investigation orders to share any information they had with the Atlanta police.[16]

Wolcoff continued to taunt Massell on TV and in newspapers. He claimed to have a tape of Howard Massell "asking me to take the heat and stating that the mayor really appreciates it." He wanted that tape played for all to hear but did not produce it.

By late October, Massell's fury over his police chief's inaction blew through the stone walls of city hall. Howard had told Sam to name Inman his chief of police; now the mayor demanded Inman quit. "Are you protecting the Wolcoffs?" he shouted from his office at the chief, so loudly a reporter could hear the exchange. "Don't you know how to investigate?"[17]

Inman turned on the mayor, and told reporters his troubles with city hall began when he refused to lean on bar owners for a half million dollars in donations for Massell's reelection campaign. Then the chief took action: he instructed officers to begin to enforce the rules surrounding bar operating hours, rules that had gone slack in previous administrations. Bar patrons would no longer be able to drink until two in the morning. Last call would come at midnight.

The grand-jury investigation into bar licensing fizzled when the Atlanta Board of Aldermen, under Vice Mayor Jackson, elbowed prosecutors aside. Jackson had been happy to watch Massell twist in the wind. He had been frustrated by Massell's demands for absolute obedience. "I don't give that even to my mother," he riffed.[18] Under Jackson, the aldermen decided they would investigate the issue themselves.[19]

1973

///

WHO'S THAT LADY?

John Greenwell

The Sweet Gum Head

January 1973

"Why don't you leave today." Frank said it in a flat, drunken sneer.

John had tried to be nice about it. He had gone to Frank to explain why that night would be his last at the Sweet Gum Head.

The Red, White & Blue Revue had struggled after the murder of British Sterling in October 1972. Sterling—who was Robert Lyons, a Philadelphia native and graduate student—and her roommate Klaus Smith had met two AWOL soldiers at a party, and brought eighteen-year-olds Alfred Eugene Yarborough and his friend, Richard Allen Ford, back to their home. Ford and Sterling went to Sterling's bedroom, while Yarborough tripped on acid in the front room. Still under the influence of drugs, he had entered the room after them. He bashed Sterling's head in with a broken bottle and stabbed her in the chest. He heard Klaus in the hallway, groggy with sleep, and stabbed him with a knife he found in the kitchen. Ford and Yarborough ran from the house with a wallet and a stereo, and sped off in the night while Klaus and Sterling bled to death. Their other roommate, Gum Head DJ Tony Romano, found them when he returned home in the morning.

Rachel had loved British and the smart talent she put onstage. British had appeared in the Gum Head's production of *The Wizard of Oz*. Lavita overemoted as Dorothy, Allison hid behind her tail as the Cowardly Lion, and Rachel played the Tin Man in hateful silver body paint that took hours to remove. British played Toto, because the world could not yet imagine a Black Dorothy, even one who had been Miss Gay Atlanta. British stole the late-September show: She followed Dorothy everywhere during the play, panted like a dog, barked and whined, and turned a nonspeaking role into a star turn.

When British died it took away any sense of normal. The cast did their numbers and took their callbacks, but it felt wrong, and horrid, and—something it had never felt before—sad. It grew more tragic when the killers plied a gay-panic defense and only Ford went to prison, for voluntary manslaughter. Rather than bring the revue together more closely, the murders hollowed out the group and left a painful void at its core.

Maybe it would help to get away for a while, John decided. He went to Frank and gave two weeks' notice. He was cordial and quick, and went back to the dressing room to get ready for Rachel's next act.

Frank cornered him in the hallway outside the dressing room instead. Red-eyed with booze and angered by the perceived betrayal, he ordered John to get out by the end of the night.

"Ungrateful," he called him, and it stung.

///

The Sweet Gum Head crowds thinned when the *Red, White & Blue Revue* disbanded. The audience missed the familiar faces and the tightly choreographed production numbers. They missed British and Rachel and Allison, though their replacements tried hard to resurrect their acts. Neely Demann had adopted "This Is My Life" as her anthem, but it lacked the gravitas Allison had conjured. Neely only took off her wig; she was a hairy man, and her long-sleeved sequined gown kept that fact hidden.

The new performers tried to establish their own standards. A queen named Heidi played off a vague Julie Andrews resemblance when she performed at least one song from *The Sound of Music* each night. Tricia Marie replicated Agnes Moorehead with bangs, heavy lashes, and sequined netting that clung to her for dear life when she leaned back into the rapture of a chorus.

The Gum Head had a reputation for professionalism, but now it risked being the bawd. Mona March worked her long tongue when she danced to "Chain of Fools," and gave French kisses to patrons when they tipped. When John stopped by one evening and opened a broom-closet door, he found a performer giving head to a patron.

The Gum Head's show directors experimented outside the realm of drag, once with a young man named Wayland Flowers, from Dawson, Georgia. Slight and blond, the ventriloquist sat in the shadows while his wisecracking dowager puppet, Madame, told awful, dirty jokes. Frank fired him after one show and told him he'd never work again.

///

While it limped along, the Sweet Gum Head still proved a powerful draw for Cheshire Bridge Road itself. It had been born in an insular gay world, which had begun to expand around it. Apartments filled, restaurants and bookstores opened, and a new enclave of Atlanta gradually emerged—a happy, optimistic one where gay culture thrived and replicated, where gays and lesbians could forge their own community, one that did not see them as sinful or wretched or pathetic.

But the outside world wanted a look. The rising gay neighborhood gave permission to straight people to wander in the front door of gay clubs. These gawkers sampled a fringe America, where black-and-white gender assumptions rendered themselves in a more colorfully ambiguous palette.

The gay bars gave gays and lesbians a moment and a place where they could be a part of a community, possibly for the first time, but they also warehoused more than their share of pain. The patrons numbed it with drugs. An aquifer of drugs sat just under the surface of their oasis. A discreet word slipped into a phone-call order to one local pizza joint added a side of marijuana. Young people who looked a certain way never had to pay for uppers or pot or acid. Drag performers certainly didn't have to. Fans would give it to them, and they usually would take whatever they were offered, no questions asked.

Speed came in all kinds of pills and forms, with nicknames like quacks and black RJs. Pot became universal, a mellow way to take off the edge that alcohol couldn't touch. Acid blew out brains in transformative vectors, warping the obvious world and fragmenting it into colorful shards. Performers would trip on acid—and it would take their act to another level. They coupled the chemical high with the natural high of performance; their bodies responded to the emotion embedded in the music, writhing and pantomiming with extended arms, rushing across the stage, investing completely in the song itself. The audience followed along; they were often high too.

The most popular drug of all was methaqualone. A Quaalude could depress the body's anxious reactions and release inhibitions, especially sexual ones. Easily available from doctors with minimal fuss, Quaaludes created an army of zombie lovers who presented themselves in clubs as confident, relaxed, sexually free—and poorly coordinated, without total control over their arms and legs, or of their speech. They were the "wallbangers," the people who took too many pills to counteract amphetamines, or developed a tolerance to them, or drank and took more than a few grams then choked on vomit in their sleep. A Quaalude got people horny, but it tended to make sex difficult. The euphoria and sexual abandon it brought on made it highly coveted, but the Quaalude was a garbage drug, one both easily acquired and easily abused.

///

John had worked at the Gum Head until he was sad and exhausted. He had performed nearly every night for two years and needed time away. One day he found himself in a car with friends, headed to Florida, to a new life, but only made it as far as Shallowford Road before he asked to go back home to Atlanta.

Resolved to stay in his new home, he began to renovate Rachel Wells. He hunted down a new wardrobe, dyed his hair Rita Hayworth red, and leaned heavily on Bette Midler's latest album for new show numbers as Rachel Wells toured the South.

He made time once or twice to travel home to Kentucky, to visit his family after their return from a second stint in Germany. When he did, he spent all his time with his mother and his favorite sister. His father still lived at home, but John barely acknowledged him.

Retired from the army, John's father drank heavily every night. He began to have delusions. John's mother, Dolly, would try to water down his alcohol, then she tried to hide the bottles. John's father found them, and learned to hide his drinking. It made his son's visits home painful and brief and rare. When John did come home, his father would remain silent, even when he saw John's hair had grown down to his back, a crime against nature and against military code.

When they did talk once, his father alerted him in a quiet, paranoid voice, "Your mother's trying to kill me."

His parents had divorced when John was young, but Dolly remarried John Greenwell Sr. because her children needed a father. His drinking never stopped, even when she had her "second litter" of daughters. Not quite old enough to understand why, when they first divorced, John decided he'd never really had a father, and did not change his mind when the family reunited.

After a tense day or two in Kentucky, John would go home to Atlanta, where he could relax, where he could be happy, where he got to decide whom to love, whom to forgive, whom to hold on to, and whom to set free.

Bill Smith

Downtown Atlanta

Spring 1973

Bill shared a name with his father. They shared an intellect. They shared a sense of humor. Their conversation flowed easily when they ate lunch together near city hall, where they both worked.

Lunch gave them time alone, free from Bill's mother, Winnell, who ruled her home with genteel aggression. She swept her black-dyed hair into a beehive that made her appear tall and imperious. She served pound cake and sweet iced tea to Diane and talked about her social plans. She kept conversation light and superficial. She told Diane how happy she was that she and Bill were dating, but rarely asked about Diane herself, or her interests.

Bill's father stood for many things his son did not understand and could not tolerate, but he held him in high esteem nonetheless. Bill Sr. had been born in Atlanta during the first world war, had served in the second, and had retired as a Navy Seabee after twenty years of service. The Seabee motto "Can Do" was his own motto: Bill Sr. served for thirty years in the city's Motor Transport Department, where he took charge of all kinds of vehicles, from ambulances to police cars. He and his wife entertained mayors from William Hartsfield to Maynard Jackson. If there was a way to get something done inside the ornate Art Deco church of government known as city hall, Bill Sr. knew how to do it.

Bill's parents kept Sunday sacred and reserved it for Baptist church. They belonged to an even more conservative sect than the Southern Baptists that lorded over Atlanta politics and climbed its social ladders. Bill Jr. had affiliated himself with the gay-affirming Metropolitan Community Church, but kept it at arm's length. His parents' appetite for church had gorged him on doctrine until it made him sick.

His homosexuality was something the family had never dealt with before. There were times they didn't speak, times they cried, times they embraced. But at one point, Bill's father had told him, "No matter what you do or what you are or what you say, you can put your feet under my table." Over time, Bill felt his father had accepted him, and some family members began to ask openly at gatherings when Bill Jr. didn't bring male friends with him.[1]

Bill Jr. stood for causes and rights his father could not fathom. Bill Jr. wanted to be an elected official. He would not remain silent. He wanted to be the town queer—but that would have to wait. On February 6, 1973, Mayor Sam Massell made a slew of new appointments to the Community Relations Commission, inaugurated in the 1960s as a way to ease the integration efforts in the city and to address concerns at the local level. With the stroke of his pen, Massell reappointed all eleven commissioners already in place, and named eight new ones, including Charlie St. John, a six-foot-tall gay man and Detroit native with a cleft palate. St. John and Bill vied for the spot, but Bill didn't deem it a competition; they were brothers in arms for a cause, not Machiavellian suitors for a volunteer city slot. When Massell chose the more vocal St. John, Bill confessed his disappointment, but refused to sour on the cause itself. When people said Bill had founded the Gay Liberation Front, he demurred: No, that was someone else, he would remind them. When people said he founded the Metropolitan Community Church in Atlanta, he answered politely that, no, he supported it and helped it happen, but was not a founder and was not a member.

Bill didn't want to put any more stumbling blocks in the way of gay rights, and he believed he could still be of help, since he worked at city hall in the accounting offices at the Board of Education, a job his father had helped him get after Bill Jr. had graduated college in 1972. Bill's father had been glad to help, and showed great pride in his intelligent, charismatic son, even on the days at lunch when he may have barely recognized the young man who sat across the table—the same curly haired young man who looked at him from the portrait hung in the family home, a photo on a faux-oil canvas. Bill had been the quiet boy in horn-rimmed glasses who collected coins just a few years before; now he was the vocal young man known inside city hall for his vivid opinions, for what he had done for a community of outsiders without his father's help. For being gay.

Bill Sr. may have watched in amazement at what his son had become, someone so like himself but so starkly different. Bill Jr. wanted to give safe passage to all those like him. He wanted to create a road map for an existence that had no map, no route, no safe stops along the way. His father sat at his side, knowing he could only watch as his son went down a path entirely of his own making.

Rachel Wells

On Tour

Summer 1973

The Miss Gay America pageant drew near, just up the new interstate in Nashville, Tennessee. Georgia didn't have its own statewide pageant, so contestants could qualify with a win in any local pageant. Rachel decided her Miss Gay Atlanta title would do, and her mentor, Wendy, had convinced her that it was her civic responsibility to represent gay Southerners. She needed a sponsor, and the most likely source of sponsorship money was Frank Powell.

Would Frank forgive her? John wasn't so sure, but when friends negotiated a truce between them, he went to see Frank at the Cove. His former boss put down his glass and acted as if he'd never fired him. All had been forgiven, though neither understood who had forgiven whom.

With his entrance fee set, John chose an outfit, picked out a favorite Streisand number, then climbed into Herman's blue Maverick and headed toward Nashville, ready to compete against queens who would already know Rachel Wells from her work at the Sweet Gum Head.

Drag pageants filled bars on quiet nights and gave bar owners the chance to scout new talent. Owners would compare the pageant winners with the drag queens who got the most applause—then book the real winners. No one could resist the Carol Channing who made fruit salad onstage and threw it into the audience, while she sliced and diced and soaked the judges with watermelon, even if she didn't take home a title.

The first Miss Gay America pageant had taken place in 1972, in Nashville's major drag bar, the Watch Your Coat & Hat Saloon. Owner Jerry Peek had booked country acts into his saloon until he decided drag had a place in Music City outside of house parties. In 1971, Peek went to the Nashville police and asked the chief how he could have drag onstage and avoid the law. The chief held to his word: as long as Peek's queens obeyed the laws, they wouldn't have any problems. Gays made up early audiences, but soon enough straights and gays mingled; Mayor Beverly Briley brought his friends for what already amounted to a nationwide talent show. Peek canvassed clubs from Indianapolis to Chicago for acts to fill three shows a night, five nights a week. On the sixth day he hosted a sewing day so performers could make new costumes. On the seventh day, presumably, they all rested.

In 1972, Peek wrote to club owners across the country to announce the Miss Gay America pageant. All contestants had to be free of female hormone therapy or cosmetic surgery below the neck. Miss Gay America had to be a biological male, he decided; transgender performers were not allowed to compete. In the pageant's first year, club owners from twenty-two states sent entrants. The Sweet Gum Head in Atlanta sent a contestant who twirled batons lit on fire. Another performer brought a sprinkler and backup dancers while she performed to "Singin' in the Rain." The stage crew had to stop the show for twenty minutes afterward to mop the floor. Nashville's own Charlie Brown took first runner-up.

In Nashville for the second Miss Gay America pageant, fierce competitors again showed up with old-fashioned drag numbers in their repertoire, with big flouncy costumes like those worn by Shirley Bassey, with heavy makeup too. Carmen del Rio had tap-danced in Danny Windsor's Vegas-style show, and in Nashville locked herself in battle once again with fellow performer Roski Fernandez, who mimed during her traditional Filipina dance.

Rachel's experience proved more disappointing than exciting. She knew she was out of her league from the beginning, surrounded by seasoned entertainers, even if she thought they wore too much makeup and over-the-top costumes and looked too much like men in dresses. She was frightened to be out of town, even before Nashville police pulled her over and arrested her for driving without a license. She barely made it out of jail in time for her interview round, but she knew by then she'd already lost.[2]

The Lady Baronessa had simply outclassed all her competition. An ice-skater, a fabulous chef, and a history major from Chicago's Loyola University with only four years on the drag circuit, Baronessa wanted two things in life: to be Miss Gay America, and to be a mother.[3] With a stunning performance to "My Way," she accepted the crown that year from the first Miss Gay America, Norma Kristie. Baronessa won $1,000 and a new Pontiac.[4]

"As of right now, I'm a boy," the twenty-four-year-old Puerto Rico native told the Nashville press. "Eventually, I'm going for my sex change."[5]

Baronessa showed Rachel exactly what it would take to win the title. While fellow contestants placed a tiara on the winner's head, Rachel admitted to herself that she was hooked. One day, she wanted to win Miss Gay America.

Organizers had hoped that the pageant's prizes and glamour would garner it mainstream attention, but they were rebuffed when they offered to give some of their profits to charity. Jerry Peek said the United Givers Fund and the Kidney Foundation were not interested in accepting his show's donation. He said the Kidney Foundation thought "they would lose half of the organizations that support them" if they took money from a bunch of drag queens.[6]

Bill Smith

Piedmont Park

June 23, 1973

"*C*ome out, come out, wherever you are!"

The crowd streamed from the Atlanta Civic Center, past the Georgia Gay Liberation Front offices at 128 Pine Street, toward Piedmont Park and its greenhouses, the cruising grounds where gay men met in clandestine corners.

In the bright light of a breezy June day, almost 150 people marched, despite fear of police harassment and losing their jobs. Some took to the protest with bags on their heads to send a message: *Do you know who is under here? Is it a brother, a sister? A lawyer, a teacher, a priest?* Others risked exposure in front of TV cameras as the crowd marched from the Civic Center down Peachtree toward the park.

"*Ho-ho-homosexual, sodomy laws are ineffectual!*"

Twenty motorcycle policemen escorted the marchers past the steeple of the Basilica of the Sacred Heart of Jesus, toward the park and the rally on the hill. Most of the protesters went on foot, though some circled slowly around the parade on bicycles.

"Liberation now!"

By 1973, homosexuals faced immense oppression, but Bill believed that the ice had begun to break, that political action had begun to work. For the first time, the city's newspapers covered the event; the *Atlanta Constitution* informed its readers that the march commemorated the Stonewall riots, which were "generally marked as the beginning of the gay liberation movement in much the same way that the refusal of Rosa Parks to step to the back of the bus is seen as the watershed for the Black civil rights movement."[7]

The core of Atlanta's gay rights movement had formed by 1973, and Bill and other activists had worked hard to keep it intact. As a group and as individuals, they had put together a hotline that helped gay men and women resolve cases brought against them in the areas of child custody, police entrapment and harassment, and in establishing the rights of gay students to organize on campuses. They had invited all the mayoral candidates in the 1973 race to address the Pride rally at Piedmont Park, though none showed. The gay civil-rights movement had by now become a regular part of summer in the city, like the fireworks that exploded in a rainbow of colors over Lenox Mall every July, or the lightning bugs that glowed in gloriously random order when dusk drew, still and warm.

Few realized that behind the television-friendly march, the movement was drifting apart. Conflicts had arisen along all sorts of fault lines: between gay men and gay women, drag queens and those against drag, liberals and Marxists and Socialists, gender-affirmed and gender-fluid. Infighting wrought hours of heated rhetorical arguments and little action, accompanied by large doses of bullshit, Bill thought. He left GLF meetings uptight, exhausted, and angry. It was do-nothing politics at its worst.

The memories of Stonewall had fused a coalition that always had been fragile, and now its frailty was exposed. The more conservative gays and lesbians—the dinner-party-and-cocktails set—were the first to drift away. Then the movement lost the bar-goers, the drag queens. They'd never been active in politics, and when it became complicated or time-consuming, it became too much. The movement was left to the antiwar protesters, the extreme radicals, and those who just wanted to hear themselves speak. Then even *they* started to abandon the GLF. Bill blamed it on the quest for power: Even within the gay world, some wanted to be in control of it all, everyone wanted to be right. The facade crumbled, and the GLF began to consume itself.

It felt like a slap, and a step backward. Atlanta was not New York or San Francisco, but it was critical to the gay civil-rights movement. If the movement were to succeed in the South, it would have to succeed in Atlanta. Atlanta's gays and lesbians had made progress since 1971, but by 1973 the cohesion was gone. Four different organizations had banded together to stage Gay Pride Week, but the group disbanded shortly after the march.

The Gay Liberation Front itself had been in near constant turmoil since its first meeting in 1971. Though he still believed the struggle for gay civil rights was alive and well, even Bill had left the group in March, with a strange sense of relief. His resignation gave him the time to take a fresh look at the gay-rights movement, and to talk to people who'd never been a part of it. It gave him time to focus on his own potential as a leader. At one point Bill Smith counted a hundred people at its meetings, but only two had attended the last meeting of the Georgia Gay Liberation Front— on July 14, 1973, Bastille Day.

Rachel Wells

Atlanta Memorial Arts Center

September 1973

Rachel wore a long, white ostrich-feather coat and a Jezebel-red dress with thin straps that hung over her lean, defined shoulders. She matched the cool-white Atlanta Memorial Arts Center Building, with its cool-white modern take on the ancient Greek temple, and its lipstick-red Symphony Hall seats. The ballet fundraiser under way would prove a bust, and in its haste to abandon its first drag performer, it unwittingly sent Rachel Wells's celebrity into orbit.

Female impersonation had become big business in Atlanta, and the Sweet Gum Head had put drag on Atlanta's map. It kept gay audiences enthralled with inventive drag and attracted straight allies, and sometimes couples with drunk husbands who groped at the drags and tried to kiss them. Rachel's act was so convincing, she entertained offers to walk the runway as a model.

Excited by the idea that he could pass as a woman in public among straight people—something he could no longer do in the gay world, he'd become so well-known—John took a card from a stranger who approached him between shows at the Sweet Gum Head. He feared the man might be the kind of curious, rude stranger who wanted to know if Rachel was a woman. Instead, he was Gary White, the president of the Peachtree Modeling and Talent Agency.

Gary promised to work with Rachel on hair and makeup, and to set up a publicity photo shoot. He asked her to model for the Phoenix Affair II, a charity fundraiser to be held for the Atlanta Ballet.

Is this a joke? John thought, until Gary called the next week.

For the next few months, Gary groomed Rachel Wells for the runway. He made her over, had a pro shoot beautiful photos, taught her how to pose like his female clients. He printed her photo on a poster for the event, where she shared co-billing with the beautiful Mississippi-born Naomi Sims. Gary wanted the poster to be truthful, so he printed "Rachel Wells, presented by John Greenwell" under her picture.

Two weeks before the September 11 evening affair, organizers removed Rachel Wells from the program. She was deemed inappropriate, and Gary had been pressured to cut his "special attraction" from the event. He came to the Sweet Gum Head to apologize, but John shouted him down outside.

The *Atlanta Journal* reported on the fracas: "It turns out Rachel Wells is a he, not a she," the paper said matter-of-factly.[8] In an interview, Frank Powell said Rachel had won pageants and was upset over the removal, while bar-goers snapped up dozens of posters that had already been printed with Rachel's picture.[9]

The publicity changed nothing, John decided. Rachel would attend after all. A Symphony Hall seat would have to do.

Rachel took a star turn as she entered the hall. She stepped in the building on the arm of a male friend, in her white coat and red dress, toes poking through a red high-heeled shoe. She draped the coat over one shoulder, marched into the Symphony Hall's lobby, and struck the modeling poses she'd practiced with Gary for two months, blended with some she learned in Miami from Cuban female impersonators. Glares mixed with stares, and with a few warm greetings from some who were sorry that Rachel wouldn't be onstage after all. Some stood in awe.

"Oh my God. You look like you're real," a tiny woman told John.

"Well, I am real," Rachel said with a laugh.

The event failed miserably. Directors had likely hoped the

fundraiser would draw as many in the audience as it had the year before, when it filled the 1,200-seat hall with no charity tie-in. In 1973, the fundraiser seated that many only over the course of four shows: three nightly events and one matinee scheduled expressly for ballet guild members. The matinee had an audience of 110 people.

Gary thought the benefit had missed its opportunity to show-case Rachel and female impersonation in a sophisticated set-ting, somewhere well removed from its seedier Cheshire Bridge digs. John could have told him that, as successful as he could be onstage at the Sweet Gum Head, the world outside still wanted to see men and women as completely distinct creations—not one blended artfully together by their own hand.

In haste, Rachel told reporters her removal was discrimina-tion. "I am beautiful and I know it," she blurted, "and that's what it is all about."

"Nobody knew," Frank Powell would tell people at the bar. "She was that convincing. Then, she got into the papers, and every-one knew. They pulled her from the show, and it flopped. They should have left her in, because after that story, everyone in the city wanted to come out to see the drag queen."[10]

Mayor-Elect Maynard Jackson

Atlanta

October 16, 1973

Maynard Jackson's wavy hair had fallen out of place here and there, but his shirt remained crisp, and his suit remained suitably sober as he claimed victory.

"Like the phoenix, which is a symbol of our city," he said with a smile, "today we have arisen from the ashes of a very bitter campaign to build a life for all Atlantans."

Jackson's resonant tenor voice could sound remarkably like Jimmy Carter's in its measured pace and tone, but in his victory over Sam Massell, his voice grew louder and rang more clear with authority.

As vice mayor, Jackson could be a bull in a china shop—a "nice" bull who would respect the china, his wife Bunnie would say, but would turn it around, snorting on his way out.[11] He showed little of that gentility to Massell, whom he trounced in Atlanta's mayoral election on October 16, 1973. Massell had tried to convince voters that "Atlanta's Too Young to Die," to cast unsubtle doubt that a Black mayor could lead the city. Massell's bitter message passed through the electorate undigested. Jackson captured nearly 60 percent of the vote.

To the throng of overjoyed voters, Black and white, who greeted the city's first Black mayor, Jackson offered a civic homily:

"When people ask us what kind of city Atlanta is, we will not answer that it is a city divided by hate; we will not answer that it is a city trembling in fear; no, we will not answer that it is a city clouded with despair; we will answer that it is a city full of hope."[12]

He then made a promise he knew would be difficult, if not impossible, to keep: "We will move immediately to protect our city," he proclaimed, "against the vicious encroachment of organized crime." A cheer broke through the applause—*Right on!*—and brought with it laughter. Jackson's vow already sounded like another political promise that seemed certain to be broken.

Bill Smith

Atlanta

November 1973

While Jackson savored his election-night win, the editor of a newspaper for the gay community plastered congratulations over a prototype issue headed to the printer. The first issue of the *Atlanta Barb* laid out a wide span of editorial offerings, starting with a wish for the new mayor: "Congratulations! Honorable Mayor Maynard Jackson. A step in the right direction toward equality for all. Continue the Fight For Equal Rights!"

In its back pages, the *Atlanta Barb* claimed 5,000 copies would be in circulation soon, listed Barry White's "Love's Theme" among the biggest hits in Atlanta's bars, and posted ads for both the Community Relations Commission's Police Action Line and for the Sweet Gum Head, "The Showplace of the South!" Amateurs had written the copy and pasted it up on wax boards, but the *Barb* was more than an amateur effort: it was the signal that the gay community had begun to claim a new voice.

When he was in college at Georgia State, Bill had sniffed at the quality of the campus newspaper, calling it poorly organized and laid-out. This new effort for the gay and lesbian community didn't seem much more promising, and he didn't think it was very good, but he could see the paper as a way to reach more than just activists.

Bill filed away thoughts of the newspaper for the moment. He had other means to pull the gay civil-rights movement in Atlanta out of its stall. In November of 1973, before he was ushered out of office, Mayor Massell had appointed Bill to the vacant spot on the

CRC that had been left behind by Charlie St. John. Charlie had raised his voice often—once too often, when he filled the inboxes at his job at the *Atlanta Constitution* with flyers for the Gay Liberation Front. He was fired, and remained fired even though protesters picketed the newspaper on his behalf.

But that wasn't what cost him his CRC seat. St. John lost that position when police raided his apartment and arrested him on drug charges—charges his friends believed were trumped up to get him kicked off his position on the council and evicted from his apartment.

Though he was friendly with St. John, Bill stepped into the void left behind. Bill wanted to be a politician, and wanted to lead the charge toward equality. At times, he'd felt like a one-man show in the GLF. Now he had something truly powerful. He had a seat at the mayor's table. He had become part of the machine so many activists sought to destroy.

1974

///

ROCK THE BOAT

Rachel Wells

Sweet Gum Head

Spring 1974

Rachel wriggled into her costume and heard the cue for her next show drift in through her dressing-room door. She had paired a sequined dress with gold clip-on cabochon earrings. A beauty mark perched under her left eye, her eyebrows arched knowingly, her cherry lips turned up at the corners in a gentle smile.

She dressed in a private dressing room near the stage, the one reserved for the show director, where round bulbs glowed from a light strip, one or two already burned out. Her red hair billowed softly and closely around her head. Gowns and jewelry piled up on a low table scattered with cigarettes and a lighter, an ashtray, a framed mirror on a stand. She sipped a drink, pinky finger extended, and let the bangle on her wrist slip down. Her wardrobe had grown sophisticated and smart, like her character.

John had started doing drag with no money, and couldn't shop a lot, not even at thrift stores. One of the two outfits he'd brought to Atlanta was overalls. He wore them so often, the other drag queens teased him. Now he had the perfect sequins, the right heels, the good makeup. He still wore a painted rainbow ring onstage, one of his small luxuries, a reminder of good times to come. It was his good-luck charm, one he believed kept him protected in the tiny apartment he rented on Euclid Avenue in Inman Park, where Atlanta's few Queen Anne houses still stood, painted ladies preserved from the ravages of time.

The opening notes of an undanceable song signaled the crowd to take their seats. In the spring of 1974 the song that gave them their cue whirled to life in an updraft of strings as it wafted into the air: "Love's Theme," the number-three song in gay Atlanta, according to the *Barb*. She could hear the audience outside already, ready to chant her name.

As the show manager, Art Elliston had installed Rachel as the show director. Elliston came from St. Louis; his oval face, thinning blond hair, and blond mustache made him a ringer for Roger C. Carmel, the man who played the shrink in the transgender-themed bomb *Myra Breckinridge*. He became the bar manager in late 1973, when Frank Powell began to spend less time at the Sweet Gum Head, when Rachel had been performing elsewhere. Art wanted Rachel back at the Gum Head, and she wanted to be back.

During the first month after she returned, Rachel worked for another show director, Neely Demann, and mimed off a reel-to-reel tape of hits played straight through, without any spontaneity. The crowds had thinned and the club had grown more seedy. Sex happened all around her—frottage in the front, foreplay in the back—but Rachel was there to work. She had two costumes to change and three numbers to stage.

When Neely left the Gum Head and Rachel took over as director, the crowds returned, and the spark reignited in its cast. Rachel knew the Gum Head's stronger performers and how to blend them with the less experienced ones. Lavita could go on first, Rachel would write in pencil on a ragged sheet of paper. Lavita had perfected the art of stage patter. Next up, maybe the "evil eyes" of Satyn DeVille—or Satyn's wife, Teddy Bear Julie, who had been doing male impersonation only six months, but had talent. Allison could give the audience a Champagne bath during a rendition of "Hello, Dolly." Deva Sanchez could follow with a big-mama number.

Rachel left three slots for herself as the star of the show. She could shuffle through a deck of impersonations with ease. She could grease her hair back, don aviator sunglasses, and play a man playing a woman playing a man—perhaps Kenickie from *Grease*—with full lips and copious curly hair like a Botticelli babe. Or she could go all-in with full glamour, almond eyes drawn with dark smoke, a maraschino-red pouting lip, starburst crystals in her ears, gown down to the floor, leonine hair teased to heaven. It looked perfectly expensive, but she rarely spent more than $25 on a look, while others spent every tip they made on Calvin Klein fashions.

She could pull out the cavewoman look, complete with her pet snake, Reba, who frightened castmate Deva Sanchez. Deva had reached down near her dressing table one evening to get her makeup, but instead touched the slick head of the six-foot-long boa constrictor. Deva screamed, threw her two hundred pounds backward, and hurtled out of the dressing room.

Rachel could lean on her new favorite impersonation, one she'd learned as Deva listened to "Always Mademoiselle" from the musical *Coco*. Deva did it first, with the cast backing her up as models, but her Della Reese looks didn't match Katharine Hepburn's gravelly gravitas. With upturned hair and a jagged voice, Rachel created an uncanny resemblance to the Oscar winner. She practiced Hepburn's manners, her films, her shake, and had a costume designed for the role. She didn't want to bank another impression of an older woman, but couldn't deny its perfection either.

Rachel would move toward the dressing-room door when "Love's Theme" began its descent. The song soared across the tops of musical clouds, through heights of percolating guitar, sweeping strings, and resonant piano chords as it bounded to a light disco beat. Some swayed to the popular song, a song so perfect as an instrumental it needed no vocals.

"Love's Theme" would reach number 1 on America's Top 40 that year. It would be Barry White's masterpiece, though it sounded as if he was all but absent from it. The original track had surfaced during recording sessions as an outtake that White mulled over before bringing in the Philadelphia orchestra. White realized the song didn't need his voice; he knew he'd crafted a disco counter-part to George Gershwin's "Rhapsody in Blue."

From the other side of the door Rachel could hear the thun-der of applause that swept around the tables and swelled until it broke in waves across the stage. The DJ called her name but the crowd already had rushed to the edge of the stage before she made it out, sometimes before she even remembered what she'd chosen for her next song.

She had begun to look at drag as a new dimension of her life, as more than just a phase.

It overwhelmed her sometimes. She was an introvert and crowds made her paranoid. Out of drag, no one would have had a clue who she was, as John Greenwell, but onstage at the Sweet Gum Head John was Rachel Wells, drag superstar.

Bill Smith

Atlanta Gay Information Service

March 7, 1974

Bill spoke into the tape recorder and winced as regular shrill rings of the phone buffeted the magnetic tape. He talked eagerly with a reporter about the future of the gay community and about his own ambitions for the Gay Information Service he'd founded. Now, if only the goddamn phone would stop ringing.

Every time it did, the Gay Information Service lent a hand to anyone who came to town to explore gay life, or came to start life anew. The hotline could give them the location of the nearest gay bar, gay-friendly place to stay, or the number for an attor-ney they could call should they need one to defend themselves in court.

Gay civil rights had made considerable progress on a national level in the year after Atlanta's Gay Liberation Front died. A National Gay Task Force had been founded in New York City. The mental-health universe had decided that homosexuality was no longer a disease to be cured. Rumblings of gay-rights legislation were making their way through state chambers. The movement had begun to attract prominent supporters in the most unexpected places: William Safire gave voice to some libertarians and conservatives who believed that sexuality was not a matter for the law: "when we fail to give [gays] the equal protection of the law," he wrote, "then it is the law that is queer."[1]

In Atlanta, evidence of progress came in a census of gay places, led by a gay-bar scene that had grown exponentially. "In 1969 we had three," Bill explained to the reporter. "Mrs. P's, Joy Lounge and Chuck's . . . Now here we are five years later with 17, plus a bath and a gay theater."

The repression that had been practiced in Atlanta, moderate as it was compared to the surrounding South, had dissipated for the time being. Bill felt safe inside the city's Perimeter ring road, though he was careful to leave any impression that he thought all was well. He knew the city's law enforcement still could arrest drag queens, so he asked Chief of Police John Inman about the laws on cross-dressing. Inman, Bill told the reporter, said no city ordinance gave police a reason to arrest anyone in female dress, no matter their gender. A law enacted in 1951 to prevent the Ku Klux Klan from wearing hoods in public could be used against the drag queens, however.

"So if you're arrested for anything while in drag," Bill said, extending the last word almost out to two syllables, "and don't give your correct ID or identify your correct sex then you can be charged. That's not cross-dressing, that's masking. I've been stopped by the police on two occasions when the driver was in full drag."

Bill believed he could work with Atlanta's new mayor on behalf of the gay community, but confessed that it would have to begin with small initiatives.

"Right now we have nothing to go on with Maynard Jackson," he said. "He's been a strong civil libertarian. He is black. He was elected by a coalition of the black community and liberal whites. Hopefully he'll follow this line.

"It's just that gay problems are not his priority. The whole city government's reorganizing. . . . It's gonna be a while before we can get to this person and talk in depth."

Eventually, Bill wanted to put Georgia's sodomy laws down. "The laws in Georgia are incredible. Nobody can believe them," he said. "Unless you are married in the missionary position it's illegal. If the bed breaks during a sex act you have violated the felony statutes on the way to the floor."

Bill used that code to his advantage in opening the topic on gun-shy legislators. "I just look 'em square in the eye and say, 'look, this is the state law—have you violated the state felony statute?' Well, no man is going to admit, and we're dealing basically with straight men, that they always have engaged in sexual activity in the missionary position. They're a little bit more liberal than that. So I've got 'em over the barrel too. They've violated the state law same as I have."

Bill enjoyed the fact that he had something on them, and he was willing to use it to his advantage. So far he didn't have to: the police and other officials had been cooperative and thoughtful, he said. As long as Atlantans didn't press the gay agenda— as long as Bill didn't press it—the relationship could take small steps. The lesbian and gay presence in the city was large but its influence had been small, and tenuous. His CRC appointment had helped, but as he said, "everything is strictly at the sufferance of a liberal administration."

"Fortunately we're blessed with that," he concluded as the phones kept ringing. As a member of city government—an unpaid one who served at the whim of the mayor—Bill had access to power nearly no other gay person in Atlanta had. He now wrote a column in the city's gay newspaper the *Barb,* and could use it as a bully pulpit and to raise awareness too. But in the city of Atlanta, a lot of the hard work of politics still was accomplished in quiet, behind closed doors, with a lot of negotiation, and Bill had not yet learned that.[2]

Hot Chocolate

Sweet Gum Head

Spring 1974

L arry Edwards was tall and lean, with broad shoulders and a sweet smile that suited his outgoing nature. Under his first drag name of Tonya, in big hoop earrings and a ponytail, he had shown up at John's apartment door because he wanted to meet the most famous drag performer in the city. He'd stared at Rachel onstage, watched her reactions and her interactions with the audience, and learned from her. Now he sat on John Greenwell's couch and stared at him, smitten.

Larry had a family in Fort Myers, Florida, and a place in his family's grocery store, but he also had a clique of friends that hung out downtown in a cruisy area by the yacht basin. He got into his first gay bar, the Red Lion, because the owner liked young men.

He lived near his grandmother, and when she needed more attention Larry moved out of his family's home and in with her. He would sneak out and stay out all night long and sneak back in; Grandma let him do what he wanted. He ran to Tampa, where he tried drag in public for the first time. He found new idols, Roxanne Russell and Gilda Golden, and followed in their footsteps.

He left for school in Atlanta, not long before his grandmother passed. As a fashion merchandising student at Massey Junior College, Larry partied at the Sweet Gum Head, and introduced himself to its star. When the school had a fashion show, Larry asked John to be his date. "Oh my God, that's Rachel Wells!" All his friends in school seemed to know the most famous female impersonator in town. He thought they were more mainstream than that.

Larry would watch John tend to a small garden at his apartment; it was how John escaped the nightlife. When he began to perform and make money, Larry's refuge was shopping; he loved to find the unique outfits, hats and dresses, that would give him a more professional look. The Pointer Sisters were his inspiration, as he shopped thrift stores for outfits with padded shoulders that feminized his body.

While other queens performed to pop standards and slow songs, Larry took on high-energy numbers. He nailed a Gum Head audition with Gladys Knight's "I Got My Imagination" and the Staple Singers' "I'll Take You There," under his new stage name, Hot Chocolate.

Hot Chocolate stepped on the Sweet Gum Head stage first in a production of *Jesus Christ Superstar* as an angel. In one early performance at the Sweet Gum Head, Lavita and performer Satyn DeVille dressed up as honeybees and performed doo-wop backup to Gloria Gaynor's "Honey Bee" while Hot Chocolate changed her outfit three times during the song, to incredible applause. When she performed, the crowd surged toward her. They stuffed dollar bills in her costumes. They stuffed money in her mouth.

During another early performance, in a pageant, the stage crew lit two urns for Chocolate's performance, a piece choreographed to Paul McCartney's "Live and Let Die." The few performers who had lit fires used alcohol to get a quick tongue of flame. Larry wanted more—so he brought pails of gasoline. A stagehand put a match to one, and the flames leapt and licked the ceiling. While Hot Chocolate danced and mouthed the song, the Gum Head filled with acrid black smoke. Fire extinguishers spat white foam at the stage while the club was evacuated. The judges nearly passed out from the fumes.

She earned low scores that evening at the Sweet Gum Head, but her legend had been assured. Hot Chocolate immediately became a threat to the existing drag order. She was someone for Rachel to admire as a friend, and someone to recognize as competition.

Rachel Wells

The Atlanta American Hotel

May 5, 1974

On the stage, a performer in a Liza-style black bob and a short jumpsuit, long black leggings and rhinestone choker, bright-red lips, and blue eyeshadow held the crowd in thrall. Behind the stage, a room full of female impersonators preened in white flowing gowns, fixing their makeup, applying a new layer of lipstick, squealing and spilling tea in a scene indistinguishable from a Miss America pageant.

Outside, an earnest news reporter held court in front of the Atlanta American Hotel. The Miss Gay America 1974 competition had taken over the evening news, if just for a minute and thirty seconds.

"How do you end up at the point," the reporter asked the Lady Baronessa, "where you decide you want to dress as a woman?"

Baronessa, the winner of the previous year's pageant, put on a bemused look for her answer. Her simple white gown, its beaded collar, her drop earrings, her high-arched eyebrows carried off a simple answer with a regal tone matched by a slight bemused smile, *Mona Lisa*–esque. "Well, it's not ending up at a point where you want to dress as a woman," Baronessa chided the reporter. "It's a job for me. . . . If you look good and you make money at it, it's a good field, it's an entertaining field. And I like to entertain people."

Flailing, the reporter turned to Baronessa's drag sister. "Do you earn your living at this?"

Wrapped in lavender marabou that discreetly covered her midsection under a deep V-neck and an enormous bouffant wig studded by a rhinestone crest, the unnamed performer answered the question: "No, I don't," she responded in a thicker Southern drawl. "I have another job. I work eight to five every day, and do this on the weekends for extra money."

Inside again, a fan dancer jiggled in a bejeweled bikini that barely covered her ass. She brushed her feathers aside and fanned herself to the Broadway version of "If My Friends Could See Me Now" from under a pearl-white wig, while the crowd hooted.[3] Organizers had lobbied hard to attract the interest of television networks, with some success.[4] For much of Atlanta, this was their first peek into the world of drag.

By 1974, pageants had become a lucrative place for drag artists to show off their skills. National contests still were rare, but the 1974 Miss Gay America pageant awarded nearly $7,000 in prizes. The winner would get $4,000—enough to pay Rachel Wells's rent for a year. Even if they didn't win, performers booked gigs out of town thanks to Miss Gay America exposure. It gave them the chance to gauge their own skills. They could meet the people whose names preceded them as they toured, or reconnect with those they'd met before, and judge their costumes and talent against their rivals.

Rachel knew the Miss Gay America field of contestants had a few ringers, but she would take no chances. She had often performed "I Don't Know How to Love Him," her favorite song from *Jesus Christ Superstar*. Swathed in the Magdalene's robes, it lent itself to a dramatic display.

She had played Jesus in the productions, down to a fake beard, since she barely had to shave twice a week. What if she played them both? Would it offend the judges? Would she be able to pull off the timing? She tried it for the first time at that year's pageant, and earned a standing ovation from a crowd that included a noticeable contingent of what appeared to be heterosexuals.

Despite the applause of the hometown crowd, she left downtown Atlanta empty-handed. Jesus had gone over well, but her interview question had not. When asked whether she would answer questions about her sexuality, Rachel gave a blunt and unpolished response: she promised she would answer the question, and vowed to say, "Yes, I'm gay, and that's just the way I am. Thank you." When only a few people clapped, she knew her pageant was over.

Shawn Luis took the crown from the previous year's winner, Lady Baronessa, who seemed reluctant to give it up. John had made the top ten, barely. Rachel Wells wasn't yet ready for a major title, but she was on her way.

John Greenwell

The Sweet Gum Head

June 1974

The DJ was at it again. It thumped in the Sweet Gum Head's dressing room, vibrated the dressing tables, shook the floor.

Rock the boat, don't rock the boat baby.

He could strangle him.

Before John joined the Sweet Gum Head troupe, he'd fought with the DJ, who looked like an unlikely praying mantis perched behind two turntables. He couldn't believe he'd been hired. TomTom was repetitive, down to his name. He'd play too few songs too many times in the same week.

Rock the boat, don't tip the boat over.

It rang for hours in John's head long after he'd left the club. Maybe the DJ's instincts weren't wrong. His job was to keep people happy with turntables and long-play versions of popular songs that flowed effortlessly into one another.

"Rock the Boat" sounded a resonant chord, no matter how many times it spun. The Hues Corporation's first major hit, "Rock the Boat" pushed disco toward its perfected form—but it set up conflicting messages with its beat and its lyrics, something that eluded Gum Head dancers who snapped their fingers and swung their hips at one of the 1,500 discos estimated to be in the United States in 1974.

It was unlike "Jungle Fever" or other proto-disco songs that almost eliminated lyrics. "Rock the Boat" wove complex interjections of male and female voices with punchy brass in gospel-tinged counterpoints to the honey-toned lead tenor. Disco synthesized powerful social mores—integration and equal rights for women—and "Rock the Boat" did so with an irresistible hook, a catchy and tight interpretation of soft calypso and shaggy reggae chords, and a Latin backbeat. It even had a complex lyrical notion, of a man begging and pleading with his companion to stay in what comes off as a troubled relationship.

The Hues Corporation at that point were Fleming Williams, Hubert Ann Kelley, and Bernard St. Clair Lee. The group had been named ironically, a dig at the extreme wealth of Howard Hughes; it won attention with its three songs on the *Blacula* soundtrack. Hues released the song on their first album in 1973, but it went nowhere—except in gay clubs, which mixed and remixed it to its danceable form. Their label, RCA, sent out a mixed version in early 1974, and the song shot to number one on the Billboard pop chart that May.

"Rock the Boat" inspired a flood of new music with the trademark heavy 4/4 beat. It was disco before the name stuck, and it long out-lived the band in that form. Williams departed not long after the song reached the top of the charts, and the group joined legions of others with another kind of honor: the one-hit wonder.

John didn't want to rock the boat, but he was in charge now, and he didn't want to hear that goddamn song again. One day he went to the Gum Head early to rifle through the hated DJ's record collection. He spotted the classic RCA orange label and grabbed the disc, tipped up the dropped ceiling panel over the DJ booth, then flung the 45rpm record into the void. He had to do it four or five times in a month before TomTom forgot about the damn song for good.

Bill Smith

Atlanta, Georgia

Summer 1974

A thick goatee slightly muffled his drawl as Bill spoke at a news conference held before Atlanta's 1974 Pride gathering. The city's gay groups had splintered so completely, there wouldn't even be the usual march.

"We are saddened," he said to the camera coolly, "on the eve of Gay Pride Week by the sudden and unprecedented number of arrests and instances of harassment of gay citizens occurring during the past few weeks."

Bill's hair had grown even larger, as if to balance out the rigor implied by his plaid tie and sober, dark suit. He was no longer just a citizen. He was the gay community's voice inside the city of Atlanta's bureaucracy, their channel to slow the onslaught of petty arrests that clogged the courts and put a new burden on them.

The bars were no longer easy targets for the police. As of spring 1973, they could stay open well past midnight—until four a.m., thanks to new rules. It was the city's parks where the police hunted gay men that spring.

Police had conducted an inquisition against gays in Piedmont Park during the spring of 1974, sending many to jail, sending others into a legal and personal hell. Police focused on the Sears store in Buckhead as well as Winn Park and Piedmont Park in a sting laid out in the *Barb*: "The mode of operation according to these reports is for two older vice division officers to openly cruise a third younger vice division officer. After the suspected gay joins the scene (or some unsuspecting straight flees to report homosexual activity) the two older officers leave to allow the third to solicit the suspected gay person."

It was as if the city had turned back the clock to the 1950s, when Atlanta police planted sex decoys in libraries and marched men out of the building under arrest, then published their names in the newspaper, effectively exiling them.

During the two-week sting in May 1974, more than 150 people were arrested for lewd behavior, assault, and battery, which could be an infraction as minor as a verbal insult yelled at the police.

When he appeared on television before Pride Day in 1974, Bill still glowered in anger. He had been a city commissioner only for a few months, but it was time to rock the boat. Bill had pressed his fellow commissioners in April at a three-hour meeting for a resolution that would prevent discrimination based on sexual orientation, and won it with unanimous approval. That same month, the CRC officially asked the city government for enforcement powers for anti-discrimination codes—but didn't yet have them.

Bill hoped he could now press gay civil rights through both the CRC and through the *Barb*. The newspaper had become a community touchpoint. If bad drugs circulated on the street, the *Barb* wrote about them. When venereal diseases were spreading out of control, the *Barb* reported on it—all in columns laid out next to stories about Mayor Jackson's efforts to woo the gay community, and reporting on the federal Equality Act proposed by Bella Abzug and Ed Koch on May 14, 1974, which would add protections for sexual orientation, gender, and marital status to the Civil Rights Act of 1964. Those protections had been added to the original act as a poison pill by lawmakers who wanted to see it defeated, then were removed before it was enacted.

Gay leaders demanded a meeting with Police Chief Inman after one of his officers said they would not meet with "those kinds of community leaders" to discuss the arrests.[5]

Jackson had struggled to fire Inman since he became mayor, and had maneuvered to get rid of the chief who had carried over from the Massell administration. Blocked from other remedies for the moment, Jackson installed a Morehouse College friend, A. Reginald Eaves, as public safety commissioner above Inman.

Even then, it took the threat of a stand-in by gay church leaders to win a meeting with the newly minted mayor on July 18, a meeting brokered by Bill. Jackson calmed the group first with an explanation of the city's actions against Inman and became visibly frustrated when talking about Inman's rogue actions. Jackson told the group that, without question, his administration was for equality for every Atlantan, including gays and lesbians.

Gay leaders made sure the mayor knew how uncomfortable the police had made life for their constituents. They asked Jackson to have the police trained only to use "gay" and "homosexual" and "lesbian" when they felt the need to refer to someone—instead of the repulsive words they often used. Before the meeting closed, Jackson agreed to order the police to do so. Bill pressed the mayor directly for his support of an Atlanta gay-rights ordinance. Jackson said he had reviewed the CRC recommendation and was waiting for specific language to proceed.

For the moment, Bill believed his first official meeting with Mayor Jackson had gone well, but the immediate problem of gay harassment still loomed over Piedmont Park after dusk, one of Bill's favorite cruising grounds.

The police and the Mayor's Office would be forced to wage a court battle over control of the city's police department. That battle would not be resolved until the Georgia Supreme Court ruled in the mayor's favor. Only then would the sting taper off.

///

Between public service pieces and photos of the paper's "Stud of the Month" flexing his muscles in a bikini bathing suit, the *Barb* published its own version of a guide to gay life, one that instructed gays on how to respond when they were hassled by the police. "Be courteous; the police officer holds all the cards in the deck," the paper said. "Volunteer NO information. In court, ask for a continuance in order to obtain an attorney. If you cannot afford an attorney ask for the continuance anyway and request a court appointed attorney at your second hearing."

Bill took deep umbrage at the justice system's treatment of gays and lesbians. He found the city's municipal courts full of unethical and inept judges, open to perjured testimony that cost gay citizens hard-earned money and livelihoods. He wrote of cheers in courtrooms when vice squad officers couldn't bring enough evidence to convict gay people of what he considered unjust charges. The pursuit of gay men in Piedmont Park filled him with righteous anger.

He took pride in his unusual position of having one foot in the world of rebellion, one foot in the door of city hall. He believed with an almost religious fervor that it would lead one day to equal civil rights for all people, and he used Atlanta's own past as a weapon. The civil-rights movement had given the gay civil-rights movement its road map: Both Blacks and gays were subject to violent and systematic oppression. Both Blacks and gays were told they were morally and genetically inferior. Both Blacks and gays knew what equality was, and knew they didn't have it.

For gay men and women to claim their equal rights, Bill

understood, they would have to put in the hard work that the heroes of the civil-rights movement had endured. "If you want the equal protection of the law, if you want a law that protects your ability to maintain a job, housing, and public accommodations you must ask for it, work for it," he wrote. "No one gives a share of the table to anyone. It must be taken with the dignity and pride of personhood."[6] Bill knew freedom would be achieved only through difficult work and painful sacrifice. He knew that the movement would make enemies.

Rachel Wells

Miami

July 1974

Rachel and Hot Chocolate checked into their room in Miami's Fontainebleau Hotel, the grand curved Morris Lapidus fantasy in white stucco. They had to wait for the bellhop to bring up the pieces to the cross Rachel would use during her talent performance: Airline baggage handlers at the Miami airport misplaced the two-by-sixes she would drag as Jesus down the pageant runway.

When the airline had finally tracked down her Jesus drag and delivered it, Rachel and Chocolate went to the rehearsal, where a dazzling array of nationally known female impersonators convened. The contest would be covered in depth by *David*, the gay magazine that sponsored it, and the perfect evening wear or talent performance could spawn a year of publicity and bookings.

For the evening-wear category of the Miss David pageant, Rachel had borrowed a friend's black-velvet gown with long sleeves and a deep neckline. For the talent portion she leaned on Jesus yet again; poor Jesus had to be tired, but most of those at the Miss David pageant hadn't seen her still-developing illusion of the savior and Mary all rolled into one. Rachel thought she had a shot at redemption from her lackluster Miss Gay America performance.

Rachel posed perfectly for her evening-wear segment, then went back to the hotel room for a few hours to avoid the crush of performers that crowded backstage. She snuck downstairs in a robe and slippers to see a favorite performer's flawless Marilyn Monroe impression, then began to transform herself.

She had kept her savior a surprise. She gooped rubber cement on her face and placed a flowing beard to her lip and chin. Focusing on herself in a mirror, she tried to get into the right frame of mind while she first put on her religious garb, then covered it in flowing white robes. She headed down on the elevator with a cross slung over her shoulder and made her way to the wings.

Perfect stillness greeted her. Other drag queens stared at her, agape. No one spoke to her as she stepped through a stand of rival queens in lamé gowns and layers of makeup, unintentionally hilarious stand-ins for the Roman soldiers who spat on and beat Christ in the musical.

Rachel moved to the stage in step with the first mournful notes that whistled and the first guitar chords that strummed to open the song. The same still wave passed over the audience. A Gum Head DJ had edited the song down to the time Rachel was allowed for her performance in the pageant, and she had blocked it out, step by step.

She had chosen to re-create the Gethsemane scene and as Jesus began to pray to God, to ask why she should die. Have I taken it too far? she thought to herself. She couldn't read the audience.

A peal of thunder rolled out on the tape. Rachel leaned forward on her knees, hid herself almost inside her hair, and then flung off her robe as lightning flashed. In a matter of seconds, she had transubstantiated into the Magdalen, in a flowing white tunic. She reached toward the crowd in an emotional rendition of

"I Don't Know How to Love Him," discovering a deeper meaning in the lyric: *In these past few days when I see myself, I seem like someone else.*

The crowd stood and applauded. They wouldn't stop. Rachel could barely hear the music through the remarkable reception for her performance.

The audience clapped as she walked behind the curtain. She gave a thumbs-up to God. The audience clapped more while she reapplied her makeup. Her conversion stopped the show for ten minutes. It guaranteed her a spot in the finals and a place on the stage when the host announced the winner:

"And this year's Miss David is . . . from Atlanta, Georgia, contestant number twenty-eight, Rachel Wells!"

Maybe there was something to this pageant thing after all.

Thank you, Jesus.

Bill Smith

The Barb

September 1974

The Sweet Gum Head's drag shows and drag artists had inspired a raft of rivals by late 1974, and Atlanta's new gay newspapers and magazines trumpeted their arrival. The *Chanticleer* covered the opening at Peter Winokur's new disco, Mother's, in August. It also touted another club, owned by a mother and son from Florida: a club already open, known as the Sting, though the hand-lettered sign in the window dubbed it the Yum Yum Tree.

In the *Barb*, gays and lesbians could read about Burt Reynolds's latest movie, *The Longest Yard*, which had been filmed at Georgia's

Milledgeville state prison, complete with the help of nine inmates who appeared in the movie in drag, dressed as cheerleaders. They could read gossip on Phyllis Killer—Atlanta's own drag legend Billy Jones, a self-reported very close friend of Joan Crawford—and her upcoming Oscars awards program, complete with nominees for best drag performances in clubs including the Sweet Gum Head. They could discreetly order glossy magazines filled with photos of attractive young nude men, or an address book by Bob Damron that listed all the gay destinations in cities across the country.

They could read what appeared to be an abject about-face from Bill Smith, who extended an olive branch to the Jackson administration for perceived slights in the *Barb*'s reporting on the mayor. Bill admitted he had been one of those who was quick to criticize Jackson, and he laid praise on Reginald Eaves, the new public safety commissioner. Bill thanked the mayor for the progress he'd already made, and had promised to pursue.

"Our city has often been called the 'city too busy to hate,'" Bill wrote. "I believe that if your administration continues to move openly and aggressively as it has indicated that it can move over the past nine months, we can add that while our city is too busy to hate, it is not [too] busy to care!"[7]

Bill hammered the keys of his typewriter in eager reparation, then set the column himself, cutting it and waxing it down on the page sent to the printer. Bill might have done it all some months; he had begun to take over the *Barb* in his usual fashion, by insisting on his opinions and tackling more than his fair share. He had joined the paper in March of 1974, when publisher Ray Green gave him a monthly column. Within months, Green gave him control over the paper's business operations. Then Green gave Bill Smith a big chunk of the ownership of the newspaper itself and a potent platform, while he turned and headed for the door of the money-losing operation.

John Austin

Sweet Gum Head

Fall 1974

Bob Jones University's 1951 yearbook gave fair warning to Frank Powell when it quoted an obscure Christian writer: "The generations crowd each other off the stage of time in swift succession." Frank had christened the Sweet Gum Head and it had bought him a thousand friends. He earned the mantle of granddaddy of the Atlanta gay bar and drag scene along the way. He even got in on the act when he put himself into an elaborately beaded gown and referred to himself as Catherine the Great.

Over time his interest in the Sweet Gum Head had waned. Competition grew stiff, and receipts dwindled. Bars usually made their best money in the first few years after they opened. Frank knew he could sell a club while it still was hot, before the liquor-license renewal came due, and he could pocket a small profit. The Gum Head's attendance had revived even in the year of Watergate and recession, but its overhead still loomed large. The Sweet Gum Head's performers and bartenders and costumes could cost Frank double what it cost to run his other clubs.

In October of 1974 he gave it all up, rather abruptly. He told Billy Jones he needed a vacation from his bars, from show business, and from men. By the end of the year he'd sold the Cove; then he sold the Sweet Gum Head to new owners, who installed bartender John Austin as the new manager.

A stocky, smiling blond war veteran, John Austin had been

born in Missouri on June 25, 1946. His father hosted a CBS radio show that toured the country. John took dance lessons in fourth grade with his sister, and went on for years after she dropped out. He worked with the St. Louis Civic Ballet, and danced as an extra in the Ballets Russes de Monte-Carlo. He studied visual arts in college, but with too few hours enrolled, he went to his draft board in 1968 and enlisted. He spent his Vietnam War tour entirely in the United States, as a part of the medical corps in Fort Jackson, South Carolina.

He hadn't yet acted on his feelings, but John knew he was gay when he entered the service. While he served the army, he came out to his parents, and it did not go smoothly. His parents asked if he needed psychotherapy. When he went, his therapist preached acceptance: John was perfectly normal.

He sold suits for Sears after the army, but a one-night stint as a barback at the Potpourri gay nightclub in St. Louis ended that. His boyish smile and his muscular military build earned him more money than lifting kegs and washing glasses. The Potpourri's owners hired him, and in a year sent him to Atlanta to work as the head bartender, then the manager, of the Sweet Gum Head.

When he took charge, Austin applied the discipline and self-reliance he'd learned in the military to his bar schedule. He woke up at eleven in the morning to work out at the gym and to tend to his house. He would stop by the bank when needed before he set foot in the Sweet Gum Head, where he made sure the bar would be ready to go for the night, fully stocked and organized, its stage lights set to shine. After a two-hour nap, he would be ready to handle anything: to talk down angry patrons, cover for sick bartenders or security, to design a set backdrop for *A Chorus Line* or for the Miss Gay America pageant, or to block a group of stoned street people from getting inside the club.

Other nightclubs tried to match the Sweet Gum Head's popularity. New hot spots sprouted across Atlanta, from downtown to

Midtown and along the Cheshire Bridge boomerang. Austin nurtured his all-star cast and kept his club behind a firewall. On the other side of that wall, the friendly competition between rival bars grew more intense. In the shadows of the safer space of the Sweet Gum Head, danger lurked.

1975

///

THE HUSTLE

Rachel Wells

The Sweet Gum Head

1975

"How many of you had a good week?"[1]
Lavita Allen stood under a colossal blond wig, sequins at her eyes, and in a turquoise dress. The show's host had already performed "We Belong Together," and brought the crowd close with her stage patter.

"How many of you people had something better to do than watch TV?"[2]

The mirror ball glinted dots across the stage and around the bar. Like manmade fireflies they alighted on straight couples who packed the Sweet Gum Head for $2 apiece, and mingled with the gay men in tight jeans and T-shirts and the lesbians who cheered the drag queens.

"A gay person will spend his last dime in a bar," the doorman said loudly over the clatter inside the doors, "but the straights usually come in to catch the show and see how the other half lives."[3]

The Sweet Gum Head scene spun wildly to the pulse of hits and deep dance beats, downers and trucker-grade speed. Its scent clung to T-shirts and blue jeans in notes of perfume and sweat and chemicals. It etched itself into memories with brief glances exchanged, with highs experienced and senses overloaded.

"Wait till you see Rachel," a twenty-four-year-old blond department store clerk told her boyfriend. "She looks just like Raquel Welch. She's *beautiful*."[4]

Rachel slinked onstage. She would rehearse for weeks, working to capture the emotions in a song like Melissa Manchester's

"Easy," plotting out how she wanted the audience to react. When the song began, she walked the stage and sought out the best positions for attack. She used the stage, the floor, the spotlights. She used the crowd. She teased them, aroused them with her beautiful body. She lured them, and they were captivated.

///

When he got back to his dressing room after a show John Greenwell could relax, smoke, unwind until his next show, or just go home to the apartment he shared with his friend Herman, who waited tables at the Gum Head while John performed.

John had moved back in with Herman in early 1975, to an apartment across the street from the Sweet Gum Head. They dolled the place up, painted broad orange and brown lines around the living area to pull it together with the brown carpet.

In the apartment they called home, John and his friends played hours of cards with one another and with other drag queens. John could make corned-beef hash from scratch for everyone, or Herman's boyfriend could cook up the country food they all loved. Or they could eat at the Eggshell Grille next door, where their favorite waitress, Frances, tipped her cigarette dangerously close to their food. She let it burn so long, the ash constantly perched on the edge of calamity. John walked everywhere; when he had to use a car, Herman had a new blue Pinto that he let anyone borrow.

John could breathe more easily now that the war was over. His draft number had never been called. If he'd had to serve, John had decided, he would have gone in full drag, just like the Corporal Klinger character on the CBS TV show *M*A*S*H** who paraded around Korea in the hope of a Section 8.

His existence became rather easy. John worked five nights a week and spent much of his time planning his next act. Three or four days a week, he practiced with the group, and he spent a lot of time listening to and learning music. He could try out new songs at the Gum Head during the late shows on Sundays and Mondays, when the late liquored-up crowd would forgive the flaws and bugs. He led a happy and interesting life, on his own but not alone.

The Miss David victory had given him the freedom to travel and to play new clubs, where he could recycle material he'd perfected in Atlanta. He always had a place to call home—with Herman and across the street at the Sweet Gum Head—in the little universe he had carved out for himself. He had come to Atlanta after living in fear, but now he lived on Cheshire Bridge Road in a sweet sort of triumph.

Bill Smith

The Sting

April 1975

*T*he Wizard of Oz played in the background in his apartment on Easter Sunday in 1975, unwinding its tale of a fantasy world with a dark underbelly, as Bill became the *Barb*'s editor and publisher with the flourish of a pen.

Bill hadn't started the *Barb,* but before it had been in business a year, he *was* the *Barb*. He had spent much of the year prior working for the paper, spending his own money on it, assembling its office files, working on its financial records, rewriting its news stories. In November 1974 he had become its business manager; soon after he owned 40 percent of the paper and became editor.[5] After just a year with the paper, founder Ray Green moved to Memphis and handed over full control.

Now a self-proclaimed journalist and an entrepreneur as well as an Atlanta city commissioner, Bill promised no change in the paper's editorial tone. "WE WILL continue to confront the issues important to us as gay women and men," he wrote. "We will support and criticize the sacred as well as the profane as the facts and our judgement lead us to."[6]

Bill added another set of hands to the newspaper's staff in Richard Evans Lee, who became an associate editor when he moved to Atlanta in 1974. From Savannah, Lee was nineteen years old and wanted to be a part of the gay revolution. He had found a book about gay destinations at a bookstore, and found a phone number for Bill Smith, and called him on a long-distance line at his job. From what he understood, Smith was the person—the only person—to call in Atlanta about gay rights. He met Bill as soon as he made it to Atlanta. Lee moved in with Bill to a townhouse at the city limits, then to a three-bedroom house in Midtown, at 375 Fifth Street. Bill couldn't pay him; they weren't romantically involved. All he could offer Richard was a place to sleep.

Bill claimed a circulation of 15,000 copies monthly for the *Barb*. Its monthly run came from the largesse of J. Lowell Ware, who printed it on the same press as the *Atlanta Voice*, a progressive paper first published in 1966. The free paper depended on Ware, Bill's own money, and all-nighters to survive. Bill and Richard would type copy, then cut and paste it onto board, standing up at worktables all night long to prepare twelve- and sixteen-page issues from Bill's manifestos and movie and music reviews, all intermingled with bar ads. Drowsy from the lack of sleep once the paper was ready, Bill and Richard would jerk themselves out of brief seconds of sleep over patty melts at a nearby diner.

The *Barb* survived by selling ads to nightclubs like the Sweet Gum Head. Bar owners expected to be paid back in coverage: Bill and a handful of unpaid writers would devote column inches to the clubs, and Bill would make sure the coverage kept the bar owners happy. He gave free rein to Phyllis Killer; Billy Jones, the vain but funny old queen who made everyone laugh, wrote a column about the nightlife each month. Bill deferred to Billy, despite Phyllis's untrammeled fondness for multiple exclamation points: "WELL HELLO, MY TOOTSIES!!"

Without the aid of Ware and his paper, the *Barb* would never have been born. One night the dependence almost killed it. Bill and Richard drove proofs to Ware's presses one night and found the doors locked. Bill made a few phone calls to friends in city hall; shortly after that the doors unlocked, the presses spun back to life, and the *Barb* was back in business, in bundles of fifty issues of newsprint folded in quarters, bathed in the intoxicating smell of ink and fresh pulp.

As Bill's assistant, Richard drew no salary, but only worked a few frenetic days each month when the newspaper needed to go to the printer. The paper had its fringe benefits: It proved to be a great way to meet people, especially men. Bill's friends dropped by unannounced, and sex would happen on short notice. "Nice to meet you, wanna trick?" It gave them a calling card at the night-clubs, where Richard found Bill to be overly aggressive, with a personality that turned men off. Richard ignored it, thrilled to be in gay bars, backed by the beat of disco music, and submerged in just enough darkness to take advantage of drugs and sex.

Bill and Richard lived together, but never became close. Bill portrayed himself as the leader of the gay civil-rights move-ment. Richard thought Bill's CRC post required very little of his time and seemed mostly symbolic. He had his friend Diane, who worked at a community crisis center as a psychologist; he had no romantic life that Richard knew of, and a lot of insecurity when it came to attractive men. Bill didn't seem to have a lot of power over his life—and he didn't seem to have much fun.

///

Bill went alone to Mama Dee's Yum Yum Tree—her name for the bar that still had "The Sting" as its name on the marquee—one early April evening in 1975, on a mission to sell ads for the *Barb*.

Mama Dee was Elizabeth DeBoard, who wore a broad smile and squared-off glasses and gray hair that contrasted to her tall blond son Robbie's blond-surfer good looks. She came from

Winston-Salem, where she and Robbie's father had run grocery stores. After the family moved to Florida, DeBoard divorced her first husband and took Robbie to Cocoa Beach, where they ran more grocery stores, straight bars, even a hotel, until they could afford to buy their own business: a gay bar in Daytona Beach they christened the Yum Yum Tree.

Mama Dee knew her son was gay, and got tired of seeing him beaten by rednecks, called "fag" and "queer." She opened the bar as a place where straight and gay people could mix together. The Daytona bar led them to open a second bar by the same name, in Pensacola. Health problems forced DeBoard to sell the Daytona club in 1972, but the Pensacola bar had been a big success. Mama Dee and Robbie had been approached many times with offers to sell it.

Then, in July 1974, fire ripped through the Pensacola Yum Yum Tree on two consecutive nights. The Yum Yum Tree's insurer refused to pay out on DeBoard's claim, citing arson. DeBoard sued, but a Florida court ruled the fires had been set intentionally.[7]

She then moved to Atlanta with Robbie, where she opened the Locker Room bathhouse in a former ladies' day spa, complete with a whirlpool, and bought the bar she would also call the Yum Yum Tree, where she sat with Bill Smith on a very crowded night. The Atlanta edition of the Yum Yum Tree was a hit with the gay and lesbian crowd, and DeBoard was talkative and eager to anoint herself the new mother of the gay nightclub scene.

It was only the second time Bill had met her in person. He didn't know her sense of humor. She sounded confident that the Yum Yum Tree would be one of the most successful gay bars in town. She wanted to take over Atlanta, and as she leaned in to Bill, she made him understand that she would take over, one way or the other.

"I'll either own all the gay bars in town," Bill heard her say, "or they'll all be burned down."[8]

Mayor Maynard Jackson

Atlanta City Hall

Spring 1975

On April 24, 1975, apartment residents near the Cabaret After Dark nightclub reported the sound of glass breaking. A car sped out of the parking lot as fire swept through the club. Fire trucks screamed to respond to the club at three in the morning, and when rush-hour traffic thickened hours later firefighters still battled the blaze.

Glitter turned to ashes. The fire had destroyed the building, leaving only scars on a brick facade. The club had been poised to open that night, taking over an abandoned space on Monroe Drive that had once been home to Chuck's Rathskeller. Police said almost immediately that the fire had been intentional, but did not say whether the arson was revenge from former employees or a firebomb lit by someone who hated gay people. The nightclub never would open as the Cabaret After Dark.

The fire fanned whispers of a "gay bar war" in Atlanta. Atlanta's gay bars never claimed as much in terms of injury or property damage, but they were victims of fire quite frequently. The *Barb* made sure to note that the fires weren't necessarily due to arson: Old bars often applied a fresh coat of paint and changed their names to become "new!"—and construction crews left materials all over the place, Bill wrote in the paper. Paint and lumber made for fine fuel too.

The *Barb* omitted one detail from its coverage of the Cabaret After Dark fire. On April 23, 1975, Mayor Maynard Jackson had vetoed a liquor license for the club. Jackson's veto came after the license bureau ignored a classic red flag: the same owners had been involved in California clubs that were under investigation for underage drinking.

A few months after the Cabaret incident, another suspicious fire would scorch Mother's, a nightclub at 2110-B Peachtree Street, owned by Peter Winokur. Someone had poured gasoline inside Mother's and lit it on fire, but the city's arson investigator said the building's sprinklers had snuffed it out with only $6,000 worth of damage. No one was prosecuted. The club was said to attract a tough element of the homosexual crowd, hustlers and prostitutes and their pimps.[9]

City officials had gone out of their way to dismiss the idea since Mayor Maynard Jackson was inaugurated the year before, but the *Great Speckled Bird* questioned whether Atlanta— which had never had more than a provincial level of organized crime—was in the midst of a Mafia takeover. The paper claimed that under the Massell administration, organized crime had infiltrated the city through government and the business community, and had established itself in gambling, prostitution, and nightclubs.

The *Bird* wrote that the 1972 grand jury that studied organized crime had been a setup to make the city look tough, and reported that Police Chief Inman now controlled it all, from liquor licensing to vice arrests. As a result, by 1975, law enforcement had become "a decidedly selective matter in Atlanta," according to the alternative weekly newspaper. It warned that "nightclub owners with the right connections and the right money are not busted, while those with the wrong connections are," and that "the free flow of drugs is reportedly untampered with."[10]

John Greenwell

Bardstown, Kentucky

May 1975

His mother's voice wavered over the phone. "I need you to come home." She pleaded with him to head to Kentucky as soon as he could.

John dug in. His father was an angry, insane, abusive drunk. Even his mother hated him. "I don't want to come home, Mother."

She calmly answered from the hospital phone, "Well, I need you to come home. I need you to do it for me, not for him."

John bought an airplane ticket and flew over the hundreds of miles of lush green hills that took him from Atlanta to Kentucky, where his parents had moved after their second stint in Germany, where they had three more children, where his forty-seven-year-old father had drunk himself to death on Mother's Day.

His father's sister fetched John at the airport and attempted the small talk that would fill the ride into town. "So what are you doing now?"

"I'm a female impersonator." That shut her down for the remainder of the trip.

He fumed through the arrangements at the funeral home. While his mother studied caskets, John rushed her along coldly. "Get the cheapest one you can get."

He marched to the front of the church, an odd mix of Greek Revival pillars outside and pointed Roman arches inside. His funeral garb seemed engineered to enrage his father back to life: long extensions in his hair, tall platform shoes, wide bell-bottom pants in plaid. He sat in the front of the church and tried to compress time with anger. "Let's just get this over with."

When the short service ended, pallbearers carried John Richard Greenwell Sr.'s casket outside for full military honors. The few other mourners watched John with generational suspicion as he marched after his father's body, impatient, huffing, turning around to see what was keeping his mother and sisters. When they lingered at the front of the church, he stomped back to them and ushered them out, pushing them out the door: "Get your asses up, come on, we got to go."

At his father's grave, he showed no emotion, despite the lonely sound of "Taps," even as they lowered the casket into the ground.

John lived in fear of being like his father. His bigger fear was that he would blame John Sr. for the way he had turned out, for everything that had happened in his life, and that he would forget all the good he had created for himself. When the funeral was done, he left for Atlanta, where he could open all his familiar wounds again, try to close them back up, wait for them to heal anew.

Weeks later his guilt over his behavior had not receded, so he put together a performance just for his father, an act of forgiveness. John went to the back patio of his apartment and sat on a ledge while his cigarette burned a hole in the dark and made a path for his angry sobs. He forgave his father for being an asshole, for losing his fight with alcohol, for damaging his family in ways he thought would never be repaired. He wept bitterly, sending his hate into exile with his tears. When he was done crying, he forgave all, his father, his pain, himself.

Bill Smith

Piedmont Park

June 1975

On warm spring days, gay Atlanta relaxed on Piedmont Park's verdant hills, sat in the soft, thick grass by the park's greenhouse, and kept watch on the constant flow of faces, in the hope of finding a familiar one, or at least a friendly one.

At night, the park became a nightclub of a different kind, populated by men hidden in darkness, given away by the flicker of a match that glowed enough to outline their naked bodies as they coupled.

The newly open version of gay life that had emerged in Atlanta still occupied strictly defined spaces. Straight people lorded over the churches, the fancy malls, the finest restaurants in Buckhead, the swanky country clubs—but Atlanta's gays still kept Piedmont Park as their public space: their backyard, their tanning booth, their play space, their cruising grounds.

Neighbors pushed back, and demanded the police clear the queers from the park, which sat next to one of the city's bigger high schools. Straight boys from the suburbs did their part: they feigned interest in or simply chased after gays in the park, then beat them up. A Methodist minister likened the gays to insects: "Just like blight has killed the elms and the chestnut trees, the beetles are boring into the pine trees, now the homos are gnawing at the church doors."[11]

Police checked licenses at the park, sent undercover men in the bushes, forbade parking, and arrested just about anyone they suspected of having sex in the park. Two men killed themselves after they were caught in the sting.[12]

Being gay still was illegal in Georgia, after all. Its sodomy laws, which now were used to prosecute gay women as well as men, could be used against those who had consensual sex in the privacy of their own homes. Sodomy laws made every unmarried person a potential felon. They gave cover to those who thought homosexuality naturally attracted organized crime, drugs, and prostitution. As Gore Vidal famously wrote in *Esquire*, laws against sodomy dated back 1,400 years, to the emperor Justinian, who felt that there should be such a law because as everyone knew, sodomy was a principal cause of earthquake.[13]

The state legislature saw an attempt to repeal Georgia's laws against sodomy in early 1975, but the bill died in committee, and the persecution continued. One wet and warm day in the summer of 1975, Atlanta vice cops arrested eighteen people in Piedmont Park and in Midtown under a new idling and loitering ordinance, which gave the squad the right to detain anyone seen talking to more than two people.

Bill had tried for months and failed to get the city council to repeal the loitering ordinance. He filled a notebook with names arrested under the rule, and went to court to see how vice officers prosecuted their case. "I've sat in that court so many times," he wrote, "watching drunks, prostitutes, rapists, murderers, shoplifters and gay people marched through this travesty of justice."[14]

Bill had no power to change city ordinances alone. The Community Relations Commission had empaneled a special sodomy committee, which he chaired, but the CRC itself had just survived a motion by a councilman to disband it. He tried through the Atlanta political machine to press for change, but the city's machinery still imposed consequences on anyone who ran afoul of the law or the system of anti-gay policies that turned every public act into a suspicious one. Bill's friend Charlie St. John had suffered the consequences: Charlie worked like hell in Atlanta, Bill wrote, and "in return for his efforts he was fired from his job, thrown out of his apartment and harassed by the police."[15]

Little had changed when, for the sixth year in a row, Atlanta's gay community gathered in the park in June of 1975 for the anniversary of the Stonewall riots. In some ways it had been an encouraging year. Civil rights hero Rep. John Lewis had sponsored a Gay and Lesbian Civil Rights Bill, implicitly linking the struggle of Black America with the emerging war for gay recognition and equality. No parade marched down Peachtree for Gay Pride Week, but an estimated 600 gays, lesbians, transgendered people, and their allies gathered on Piedmont's grassy hills in a sign of solidarity.

Atlanta was still safer than anywhere else in the South for gays, Bill reasoned. "Either a gay person comes to a place like Atlanta," he told the Atlanta paper, "or he stays in Opp, Ala., or Palmetto, Ga., and becomes the town queer."[16]

But in the park, day or night, the police still arrested gays for sodomy, then convinced them to plead guilty to loitering and to pay a fine rather than be convicted of a felony with grave consequences. Pride or no, in 1975 Bill had to admit that gays and lesbians in Atlanta had made almost no progress in their quest for equality.

Dina Jacobs

The Sweet Gum Head

August 1975

Dina Jacobs swam in the green-blue radiance of the Pacific and adored the scent of hibiscus as a child. The Hawai'i-born Latina was one of six children raised without a father, along with her brother and four older sisters. She learned how to be feminine; though she played second base and knocked in home runs in after-school baseball, she believed she was a young girl, about to become a woman.

Then her mother caught Dina having sex with a boyfriend.

"I'm not doing anything wrong," Dina pleaded when her mother kicked her out of the house. "I'm just living my life!"

/ / /

Dina longed to perform in Honolulu's nightclubs. Born Cliff Montalbo, young Dina thought she didn't look feminine enough yet as a teenager in the 1960s. Still, she went to an audition and sang and danced—in Hawai'i, performers did not pantomime—and got the gig. On her debut night, she climbed the stairs from the club on the ground level, past the apartments on the second floor, to the top.

In the dimly lit cabaret on the third floor, the Clouds, she saw a woman light a cigarette in the back row. From the glow of the match she made out the familiar face of Emily Montalbo, and Dina ran, just as she was being introduced. She was not ready to reunite with her mother.

Dina's sister brokered a peace between the two women. "Mom just wants to talk to you," she said.

"I hurt her, and she was always good to us," Dina said.

"Do you ever regret giving birth to me?" Dina asked when they eventually came back together.

"No. Never," her mother answered.

Soon her mother would hush the people who talked when Dina came onstage. "Shut up, that's my son up there singing!"

/ / /

Dina toured Honolulu's nightlife and became an emcee, then booked dates at mainland clubs. At the famous Jewel Box Lounge in Kansas City, she met Roby Landers, who eventually hired her to work in Chicago.

Dina went to Atlanta late in the summer of 1975. John Austin fell for her talent and her sharp wit; he offered her a job on the spot, and they became roommates. Their incredible apartment had so many rooms, Dina would get lost. It had been carved out of one of the Coca-Cola family mansions on Peachtree Road, and was blessed with high ceilings and festooned with pretty woodwork in its thirteen rooms. Austin told her not to worry about anything; in other cities performers might snatch bits and pieces of other performers' costumes, even steal their tips, but in Atlanta and especially at the Sweet Gum Head, you were with family.

Dina won over the discriminating Gum Head audience from her first performance as Tina Turner doing "Acid Queen." The audience was enraptured when she sang her own version of "My Way." She took her callbacks with powder dabbed on her nose, as if she'd done cocaine offstage. During another performance, she came out topless with magic marker circles on her chest, mocking another performer's new implants.

Dina knew right away she'd made a good choice in coming to Atlanta; she was reinvigorated. Under the direction of Rachel Wells, the Gum Head's shows had gone hard for laughter and joy.

The Gum Head's troupe had built a reputation for increasingly complex shows, with professional polish. They hustled to put them together: They sewed costumes, built staging, and designed their own choreography.

That year, the popularity of the movie *Jaws* gave them an idea for a show. It sprang from innocent lunch talk, as the girls ate sandwiches from the deli across the street, dissecting the movie, its more effective scenes. It would make a perfect target for parody, they decided, but how could they make it funny? They could make the shark a giant, toothless catfish from the Chattahoochee River: *Gums*.

The parody developed rapidly as Lavita Allen set up recording equipment. It would take place on a raft in the muddy river near

Atlanta, during the city's annual river-raft race. The drag queens would pantomime to their own voices on the big Gum Head stage. Lavita would play Gums, the giant catfish; Hot Chocolate would tell the story; Satyn DeVille would play the scientist, in a full wet suit, and Lisa King would be the sheriff. Rachel would be the beautiful girl eaten in the first scene, of course. The cast came up with the ideas, but John Austin was the one who made sure they had the money to build sets and sew costumes and the time to choreograph this show and others. Most clubs didn't spend anything on those luxuries for their shows.

Dina Jacobs would play Mayor Maynard Jackson. Jackson was notoriously touchy about his image. He didn't like being teased about his weight; he dressed like a dandy and coiffed his hair perfectly. He wouldn't tell people the size of the floral trunks he'd worn to box Muhammad Ali in a charity bout earlier that year. The Sweet Gum Head could safely mock him, though. There was no chance he would be seen there, or that it would get back to him—or that they would hurt his feelings. The Gum Head was a place of forbidden pleasures and earthly delights, but its denizens knew Mayor Jackson was the best ally they had.

Out of drag, wearing a spiffy white suit, Dina was a dead ringer for the mayor. It was Dina who would come out and reassure the entourage that everything was all right, even after Rachel had fallen off the raft and had been eaten by Gums.

One by one, while the performers moved cardboard cutouts of waves in vaudeville fashion, they were eaten—first Rachel, then Satyn, then Lisa. Lavita ate them all, except for Hot Chocolate, who delivered the campy end to a purely camp skit with the last line: "He who rafts last, rafts best!"

Dina got thunderous applause as the Mayor. Jackson wasn't in the Sweet Gum Head that night, but Dina convinced some in the audience that he had been. On the Gum Head stage Dina *was* the mayor. Her eyes even shimmered in the same shade of green.

Bill Smith

Midtown Atlanta

August 12, 1975

In the summer of 1975, the *Barb* published its first ads for Young-man, an escort agency that promised polite, attentive, young, and attractive companions. Bill published the quarter-page ads from the business, which Richard E. Lee of 742 Monroe Drive in Atlanta, had incorporated on August 12, 1975, "to conduct a modeling agency and to engage in all kinds of lawful business for pecuniary gain in any place in the world."[17]

The escort agency belonged on paper to Richard Evans Lee, Bill's assistant, who brought the idea home from a visit to Fort Lauderdale. He'd gone to drum up advertising for the *Barb*, and to meet with the owner of a local rentboy service called Party Boys. Nothing like Party Boys existed in Atlanta, and its owner asked Richard if he'd like to open a franchise in Atlanta. The owner wouldn't have to do much: get the word out, take a phone call, send over a handsome and willing young man, and pocket his share of the proceeds.

Richard presented Bill with the proposal. He didn't have the place or the money to start it on his own. Richard assumed Bill would turn down the idea and they'd go back to writing political screeds and hounding bar owners for every cent they could get.

Bill liked the idea. He liked hustlers. He liked the idea of bringing in more money when he had so many ways to spend it—on his apartment, on the *Barb*, on the office he'd rented for his gay help line. But he didn't want some guy in Florida to get any of his business. He paid a lawyer $500 plus legal expenses and incorporation fees to start Youngman.

Bill would keep his distance on paper. Youngman would be separate from the WESJIR Enterprises business Bill named in each issue of the *Barb* on the masthead, an enterprise with no track record in Georgia corporate registries. But Bill would take the calls from customers to place orders, sometimes for men, sometimes for women, sometimes for both, sometimes for as much as $500 apiece. Bill's cut funded the newspaper.

Expenses had to be paid—and Bill's freewheeling attitude toward sex didn't leave much room for self-critique. Neither did his love for hustlers. In the years before the *Barb* he'd fallen in love with a hustler and formed a casual relationship with him. They met, they dated, they had sex, but Bill never paid. Jimmy was married, and would return to his family after a few days of working Atlanta's seedier streets.

An escort agency seemed an easy, victimless way to make money. Escorts performed a service that was negotiated by phone, conducted discreetly in homes or hotel rooms, and was often paid for by credit cards. Bill showed few moral qualms with controlling an escort agency: he set up its phone line in the Midtown home he shared with Richard and with other roommates. Everything happened at the house, including screening of the people they sent on escort calls. Most of the men they hired were employed in other jobs and took clients before or after work, whether they were a commercial artist or the assistant manager of a K-Mart. Drug and hygiene problems were nonstarters, but even then, the applicant pool never ran dry of middle-class, mainstream men who were more than willing to take money in exchange for mostly gay sex.

Bill's friends warned him. "Are you crazy?"[18]

He would scold them, but he knew they were right. He didn't care. He had come to understand that his power as an unelected city commissioner would always be limited by his homosexuality.

He ran a money-draining gay newspaper, and lent a voice to a gay civil-rights movement that refused to emerge from its own carefully constructed shadows. He gave in to every impulse. He dove into each one pell-mell. He refused himself nothing, because the world had refused to move quickly enough.

Burt Reynolds

The Sweet Gum Head

September 1975

The Sweet Gum Head turned four years old in 1975, old by gay-bar standards, but still perched at the core of a budding gay neighborhood along sleazy Cheshire Bridge Road, ignored by those who closed their blinds to it in the tract homes that sat just a few hundred feet away.

The straight neighbors had little choice but to accept its late-night crowds: gay clubs had cropped up all along the road, a former dirt path that cut through a Confederate soldier's farm. Cheshire Bridge had become a wider thoroughfare before World War II; the GI Bill brought hundreds of new families to the freshly paved streets that flanked it with quickly built ranch homes. The interstate plowed through in the '60s, and brought the exit ramps that led directly to the first liquor stores that Georgians from dry counties could find just inside the Fulton County line. When the neighborhood shifted toward the louche, gays and lesbians reclaimed it, bringing with them their doctors and teachers and lawyers, the gay newspaper, the gay bookstores, gay churches, a gay massage parlor or two, and a half-dozen gay bars, including the Sweet Gum Head.[19]

Gay bars had become bright, showy places that attracted larger crowds than ever: "Gay people like to be awed by their own numbers," Peter Winokur, the owner of Atlanta gay bar Mother's, told *Time*.[20] The Sweet Gum Head counted as one of the 10,000 discos that had opened across the country by 1975, but not one that spent thousands on sound systems, luxurious bathrooms, and valet parking. The Sweet Gum Head relied on talent—$25-a-night drag performers and lots of hard work. A single revolving mirrored disco ball would be joined by a second one, both reflecting blips of light across the dance floor.

During the week, small late-night crowds gave performers the space and time to try out new numbers and to refine their act. Anyone who watched a show at two in the morning was either too drunk to leave, or had nowhere else to go. Drag queens tested the waters with experimental long-playing disco tracks between the favorites that raked in tips.

On weekends, people crushed to get into the club, built to seat only about three hundred people. The Gum Head had become an A-list event in a B-list town, a magnet for visiting celebrities who themselves became transmitters of gay culture. It attracted pop singer Melissa Manchester, who had met John Greenwell after she gave a concert nearby; she dove over the stage railing to stuff tips in Rachel Wells's bra. Karen Valentine, fresh from a national TV series, stumbled in and begged to perform as Tammy Wynette: "I want to do a drag number," she slurred through a half-empty glass of white wine. Rachel and Satyn DeVille obliged and slathered her in ostrich feathers, long eyelashes and a long dress, carmine lipstick and a blond wig, and cued the DJ to play "Stand by Your Man." The flamboyant pianist Liberace waltzed in grandly and had only moments before a performer fired at him, point-blank: "So cut the crap. Are you gay?" He vanished in a flourish of his trademark cape.

Among the regulars, comedian Paul Lynde took a seat in front of the stage. Frank Powell often said he and Lynde had gone to school together, but how that was possible he never made clear:

Lynde came from Ohio and attended Northwestern in Chicago, while Frank had left rural Florida for school in South Carolina before he came to Atlanta.

One evening in September, Rachel prepared for the show in the tiny dressing room she shared with Satyn. The crowd had been loud all night, but grew louder as Herman leaned in the dressing room door.

"You're not going to believe who's sitting in my section," he sputtered. "And make it quick, I'm losing money as we speak. Burt Reynolds!"

Rachel went back to her makeup. Sure, she thought. Like he would come in here. The biggest box-office star around.

Reynolds had been a fixture in Georgia since he filmed *Deliverance* in the white water of the Ocoee River. A football player from north Florida, Reynolds had gay friends, went to gay clubs, cultivated a gay audience, even aped the Castro-clone look of mustache and jeans popular among gay men. He fed his own universal appeal with plenty of non-gendered flirtation, like the infamous *Cosmopolitan* photo shoot in which he posed nude, barely tucking his manhood from view. He had acted brilliantly in *Deliverance*—a film where the rape of a man quickly became a punch line for off-color jokes—but Reynolds believed his *Cosmo* centerfold and his sexuality had kept him from being nominated for an Oscar.

Inside Rachel and Satyn's tiny dressing room, the noise turned into a din.

"Could be," Satyn mused while spraying her hair into submission.

Rachel put on a robe to see exactly what was going on, then needled her way past the DJ to an immobile clot that surrounded Reynolds. It was him. On a break while filming *Gator* down in the Okefenokee Swamp, he had come to Atlanta and decided to check out the biggest drag-show bar in America.

"Oh my God! You are Burt Reynolds!" She managed to get closer through the throng that swelled around him before she had to zip into her next dress. "Hi, I'm Rachel Wells. I'm in the show here." Then the crowd swallowed him again.

She got ready for her next number when she heard a knock at the dressing-room door. "It's getting a little crazy out there," John Austin said as he brought Burt into the tiny room at the front of the club. "Can he hide out in here?"

And there he sat, dark hair tousled in the excitement, mustache brushed askew, friendly, warm, and witty. Rachel worried about the dressing room, which smelled of cigarettes and beer and had drag outfits scattered all over, but Burt seemed oblivious and charmed her for the next fifteen minutes, until he left to go on to Mrs. P's leather bar. Rachel couldn't remember a thing he said to her, but she didn't have to. It wouldn't be the last time she saw him.

Mayor Maynard Jackson

Atlanta

October 1975

A slim cylinder had begun to rise downtown, destined to be a seventy-story hotel that would put Atlanta on the architectural map and would provide an unmistakable physical monument of Maynard Jackson's reign as mayor.

The Peachtree Plaza signaled the city's new boom times, but to the *Advocate* it perfectly depicted the Atlanta paradox. In a decade, the city had gone from "sleepy little Southern farm town" to a polished, fast-moving city that mingled "farm boys with their warm southern hospitality and cornbread good looks" with "slick, sophisticated smooth-talking big city boys."[21]

In his story "Atlanta, Atlanta, Atlanta," journalist Charles

Morel argued the Southern city never was intended to be a great city, but somehow had stumbled into that clique. By 1975 it had nearly 2 million people, most of whom came from bigger places. It had lured corporate headquarters, it had begun to build a new airport, and it was building a new subway system like the ones that ran below New York and San Francisco and even the nation's capital, though with only a pair of tracks that intersected as they ran from north to south, and east to west.

For a town still stitched together from big backyards filled with tall grass and the chirp of crickets, Atlanta had its share of big-city outré delights: discos that ran all night long with unisex eroticism, leather bars with toy boutiques, and chic restaurants where the butterfly flitting of waiters and patrons created a hot-house effect. Atlanta had drag bars in incredibly large numbers, and had no trouble finding talents; the biggest bar in town had a Christmas show that featured a drag Tina Turner and *Jesus Christ Superstar.*

Atlanta still had discrimination too—and the *Advocate* laid the blame for the oppression of gays and lesbians at the feet of Maynard Jackson. The mayor and his administration should have sympathized with the gay civil-rights activists, the paper argued, but "not only are they not sympathetic, they publicly discriminate against gay people in an apparent attempt to win the popularity and votes of the white middle-class."

Jackson took the *Advocate*'s charges seriously. He and other civil-rights leaders had intended to lower prejudice against gays— and Jackson felt he had begun that shift and had reached as far toward the gay community as he could for now. His fury at the accusation scorched across the letter he sent to the *Advocate* in response: "As mayor of Atlanta I have continually pledged my personal support to individual civil rights of all people," Jackson wrote. "Gay people are no exception to that pledge."[22]

Bill Smith

Atlanta

November 1975

Bill handed Atlanta city council president Wyche Fowler a bundle of paper with hundreds of signatures, and waited for his next move.

Bill often used the *Barb* to float trial balloons for political positions and as a means to attack the positions of city officials. He leveraged his spot on the CRC to the same effect. In late 1975, he had managed to get the group to issue a report that said the city's loitering and idling ordinance was "not in keeping with the spirit of the City of Atlanta and does not appear [to] service any lawful purpose." His petition had been carefully crafted to put the council on the spot. Fowler had written many of the city's ordinances, like the one on loitering that had led to more than a hundred arrests over the summer. Bill's petition had more than five hundred signatures.

"I don't operate by petition," Fowler told Bill, and tossed the paper back at him.[23] The public had a right to be protected from being accosted by prostitutes and homosexuals on the street, he said, and added, "I have a responsibility to the total city and the image of the city."[24]

Rebuffed in his constant calls for change, Bill realized Atlanta would not let him live out his political aspirations, so he tried to take his fight to a national level. Activists including Dr. Howard Brown, Martin Duberman, Barbara Gittings, Ron Gold, Frank Kameny, Nathalie Rockhill, and Bruce Voeller had formed a National Gay and Lesbian Task Force in 1973. When they began to see the value of establishing a presence in more large cities, they looked to Atlanta. And when Voeller came to Atlanta, Bill was the person he turned to for a tour of the town, and for an introduction to its equality movement.

"The National Gay Task Force has been instrumental in bringing about some of the most important breakthroughs for gay civil rights," Bill observed in the *Barb*. "Very simply, one person or even three people standing alone are easily picked off. One person standing with the resources of twenty million gay people or even one million would be invincible."[25]

On November 13, 1975, upon his return to New York, Voeller wrote Bill and thanked him for his hospitality, "for all the good talk, the pleasure of getting to know you and the pains you took to see that I saw Atlanta and its gay rights leaders. You were great and I'm much indebted. . . . give Richard, Diane and the others warm regards from me."[26]

In return, Bill wrote Voeller and sent him a copy of a letter he'd written to Congressman Andrew Young, recently elected from Georgia and in his freshman semester in the House of Representatives.[27] The letter asked Young to study the Equality Act, which in Bill's words would provide explicit legal protection for gay citizens.

Bill saw the potential in becoming a part of the national movement. It might help Atlanta's disorganized equality movement get in lockstep with the bigger organization. It would help the profile of the *Barb*. It would give him a seat at the table of national gay politics, with the likes of Voeller, Gittings, and Kameny. Bill wanted to be in on the ground floor, to see it built out in stages, like a familiar gay-friendly church.

In December, he suggested in a letter to Voeller that the National Gay Task Force adopt a new structure. He wanted it to organize on regional and local levels as the best way to propel progress in places like Atlanta.

The risks couldn't be dismissed. Personalities might clash and they might not be able to move in unison toward a common goal. But Bill saw the success of the civil-rights movement in Atlanta, and thought the NAACP made for a good role model, as well as the ACLU and NOW. The South was ready for a local front in the fight for gay civil rights, he wrote Voeller. He steeled himself to lead it. Bill Smith, he decided, was going to be an important part of gay and lesbian history.

1976

///

DISCO INFERNO

Mayor Maynard Jackson

Atlanta

January 1976

The 723-foot Peachtree Plaza tower stood nearly empty, but civic pride flooded it when it opened in January 1976. The tallest building of any kind in the South, Peachtree Plaza had cost $55 million.[1] It contained the tallest hotel in the world, a Westin with 1,100 rooms. Its seven-story lobby atrium had its own manmade lake. Twin 90-foot tapestries by a Peruvian artist hung near three brass pieces by a Belgian sculptor. The *New York Times* said the terraces and plants and pools of water at the entry formed "one of the grandest displays since the Gardens of Babylon."[2] Mayor Jackson, along with the governor and the architect, had poured a symbolic final bucket of concrete on the tower's roof months before it opened.[3]

The glassy blue-gray cylinder had been built to put the world on notice: This was a new Atlanta—sleek, towering, titanic, international. The city had been hurt in the recession that descended on the country during the final throes of Watergate, just as it embarked on a massive construction boom. Thousands of hotel rooms and condos and office buildings were in progress; the mayor's administration had lobbied hard for and won a new $500 million midfield terminal at the city's airport; explosives tunneled under the city in preparation for its coming subway. Atlanta was on the move, but it limped while it waited to reignite the growth it had seen in the late 1960s and early 1970s. The Peachtree Plaza held the hopes of the city in its slim, skyline-piercing form.

It had the usual teething problems, like a leaky lake, but it had some more insoluble and intractable flaws. Architect John Portman had designed the Plaza's public spaces to confuse people. Ramps and elevators were scattered across its ground floor, and hotel guests had to go down a level and back up just to exit to Peachtree Street. The obfuscation created the illusion of constant human motion. Swarms of guests would be lost or inconvenienced, but they would fill the public space with the movement of a bustling city street relocated indoors, where it was safer.[4]

At ground level it looked isolated, defensive, a little naked, but the Peachtree Plaza offered a ray of hope. Once guests got past the twentieth floor, they could see an expansive view of Atlanta like no other, a framed view of an unfettered horizon, flocked by a leafy canopy and a smattering of high-rise buildings, a canvas ripe for imprint. The view would have shocked some visitors who still expected to see the cornpone city of a decade before. Atlanta was becoming something, even if its own citizens were unsure of what that something was.

Peter Winokur

Atlanta

February 1976

Arsonists had tried to obliterate Peter Winokur's club, Mother's, once already. On February 14, 1976, they tried again. Three men rushed the building and held three carpenters at gunpoint while they set it ablaze. The club burned halfway down, but it would remain open.

The rumor mill swirled like a drag queen's gown. Mother's, it was said, attracted a lot of "street trash," including hustlers and pimps. One fire was an accident, or maybe bad luck. Two fires were a vendetta.

The vendetta began over Gloria Gaynor, the disco diva who had recorded a hot track, "Never Can Say Goodbye," in 1974. It took a year, but the song gradually became a staple in discos and gay clubs—not in small part because of a nineteen-minute mix of the entire first side of the album that gave DJs a break from the booth for whatever they need to get rid of, or take more of. Gaynor had been booked to perform at Mother's on January 8. Shortly after Winokur confirmed her, Robbie Llewellyn from the Yum Yum Tree hired Gaynor to perform at his new club, Union Station, on January 6 and 7.

Llewellyn claimed an exclusive to Gaynor and took Winokur to court. The club owners fought bitterly over which club would host her performances in Atlanta—and Llewellyn lost. Gaynor performed at both venues, doing her scene-stealing hit each night, first at the expensively built Union Station, which had already begun to show signs of slowing down despite the wads of cash Llewellyn and his mother Mama Dee threw at it.

Club owners had fought in the press and in person, but for the most part, Atlanta's gay scene had been built around a community of friends. Bar owners hung out at one another's clubs during big events, let performers work freely between them, even shared interests in some venues. The arrival of discos changed that dynamic. Discos were temples and palaces, hugely expensive endeavors to start, some costing in the millions to imbue them with a distinctive look, whether it came from extravagant lighting, ground-shaking sound, or kitschy themes, as Union Station had been, fashioned as it was from old train cars abandoned in a gritty railyard. Discos opened with significant debt they had to pay off, and pay off quickly, before they grew stale and crowds moved on. For some clubs, big-name recording artists guaranteed a quick fix of foot traffic and big tips, and club owners elbowed one another aside to lock down exclusive appearances. Friends were friends—but money was money.

On February 18, Peter Winokur disappeared. He had come to Atlanta with no money, but within a year he owned 100 percent of a successful nightclub.[5] Police said his aggressive business tactics had built Mother's into a crowd-pleaser, but pointed out that the crowds came paired with club-opening debts as high as several hundred thousand dollars.

Winokur had gone to the Florida Panhandle to lease a new car, and had left Fort Walton Beach on February 19. Police recovered a 1976 Lincoln Continental Mark IV in East Point, near Atlanta's airport, on February 21. The mileage on the car indicated it had likely been driven from Florida to Winokur's home, then to East Point.

They also discovered that Winokur, age thirty, had opened his home to nineteen-year-old Keith Lawrence Stamm and seventeen-year-old Floyd Dempsey King. Winokur knew Stamm through family. King had been due back in Milledgeville at a youth-development center after his weekend pass expired. The teenagers were also missing.

"We're pretty damn well sure they're dead," a policeman said in late March.[6]

Mama Dee and Robbie

The Locker Room

Early 1976

Mama Dee and Robbie had bought their way into Atlanta's nightlife with the Yum Yum Tree, but it sat off in the Peachtree Battle shopping center, far from the gay nucleus of

Cheshire Bridge Road. They opened Union Station near the train yards under the new interstate, but its moment in the limelight would come and go quickly, leaving Mama Dee and Robbie in the hole for $300,000.

In 1975 Mama Dee had opened the Locker Room bathhouse. It sat in the elbow of a strip mall formerly occupied by the My Fair Lady salon, kitty-corner from the Sweet Gum Head. Once Mama Dee and Robbie took up residence on the corner of Lavista and Cheshire Bridge Roads, they realized a second club—another drag-show bar—could lure crowds from the Sweet Gum Head. It could take over the Cheshire Bridge nightlife.

As business slowed at the Yum Yum Tree and Union Station, the straight bar next to the Locker Room baths ran into trouble with fights and lots of broken windows. Mama Dee and Robbie took over the space, and opened Hollywood Hot on April 9, 1976. They had hired perennial drag-pageant threat and Sweet Gum Head alumna Roski Fernandez to program new shows. Fernandez lured away some Gum Head performers, including Hot Chocolate and Lily White, and from the start, Hollywood Hot staged big production numbers to rival those of the Sweet Gum Head.

The next evening, a freak fire destroyed the new club's dressing room. The Sweet Gum Head held a fundraiser night and donated $2,500 so the rival club's cast could get back into costume, but at least one performer wouldn't return.

The fire underscored a feeling Hot Chocolate couldn't shake. She was a close friend of Robbie's, but felt a darkness at his new club. She worried that Robbie would not like it when she decided to go back to the Sweet Gum Head.

The Gum Head had been uniquely immune to trouble until a fire swept its dressing rooms that spring. Rachel and Satyn ate breakfast across the street and saw fire trucks pull into the lot as their sirens blared. The fire had begun in an upstairs dressing room. Firefighters decided it wasn't intentional, since everyone who used the room smoked.

Lavita Allen and Satyn DeVille

The Sweet Gum Head

February 1976

On Mondays the Sweet Gum Head sold mixed drinks for seventy-five cents. It sold a lot of them in 1976. The club throbbed with people. It might be nearly full even on a Monday, with a crowd split equally between men and women.

Lavita Allen could have the crowd tipping heavily by the time the second show got in full swing, with her rendition of Tammy Wynette's "Stand by Your Man." She had the forehead for it. She paid perfect attention to detail. She would paint her face with makeup that matched her gowns, sometimes changing her eye shadow three times in a night.

She amused crowds with tongue-in-cheek performances of hits like Anne Murray's "You Needed Me," by taking a bread-kneading pun to excess, bowl of dough in hand, flour everywhere, shaping lewd loaves and letting them fall over limply.

Lavita would do a "grazing water buffalo" look when she got bored, pull her glasses down and her ears out, and pretend she chewed cud through a jutting chin while her eyes rolled to the whites. She would do it out of boredom while practicing before shows, and still stay in character and get the routines down pat.

She still had hope of becoming a professional actor, and would put together theme nights like "East of the Sun, West of the Moon—Eldorado," an ode to early country-and-western music, staged as slapstick.

"You know what would be funny," Rachel told Lavita during

her summer fling with twangy tunes, "is if you went out there with a fan, in chiffon."

When the strings swirled and Gogi Grant's "The Wayward Wind" blew in from the Gum Head's speakers, Lavita marched out onstage with a box fan in hand, an extension cord trailing behind like a snake. During the chorus, Lavita put the fan on a customer's table, turned it on high, and held a deadpan face while the wind whipped her hair and dress into a froth. She knew how to make herself the center of attention, and how to get the audience to laugh.

///

Rachel had left the Sweet Gum Head before, in short spurts, either in grief or in transition. This time, she made the choice to tour for financial reasons. Rachel's Miss David title brought in big offers from clubs around the South. She craved the challenge of keeping her act up to date. She would miss the steady money from the Gum Head and her fans, but knew that a tour would also let her fans miss her a little. She played clubs from North Carolina to Florida, where her forty-five-minute act required a scrim so she could change into different costumes in decency.

John Austin replaced Rachel as show director with Satyn DeVille, who'd worked at the club for two years. Satyn was a natural performer with a quick wit and a wicked sense of humor. Satyn was Clay Hester, who had been in medical school and had excelled, until he decided to drop out to do drag.

Satyn had been trained in drag by a popular queen named Ernestine Brown, who gave her the stage name after her darkly drawn "evil eyes," and her ability to cut a look while she tossed off droll commentary with ease, like the jokes she made about being burnt at Mother's. Her dark features and eyes lent themselves to songs like her go-to, Crystal Gayle's "Don't It Make My Brown Eyes Blue." She dubbed herself the "daddy of drag" and the "papa of paint."

Bill Smith became one of the most visible leaders of Atlanta's gay civil rights movement, first as a protest leader and then as a city commissioner. *WSB Newsfilm Collection, University of Georgia Libraries.*

Maynard Jackson was elected vice mayor of Atlanta in 1969 and mayor in November of 1973, when he immediately faced calls to meet with Atlanta's gay community leaders over harassment. *M004_2258, WSB Radio Records, Popular Music and Culture Collection, Special Collections and Archives, Georgia State University Library.*

Rachel Wells emerged in bits and pieces as a character dreamed up by John Greenwell; by 1974 he had perfected the illusion of her. *Kathy Novotny.*

The Sweet Gum Head's weekend shows brought out standing-room-only crowds and audience favorites, like a wisecracking, stage-diving performer dubbed Bertha Butts. *Susan W. Raines.*

The blowback to Anita Bryant's "Save Our Children" campaign came into full view in Atlanta in 1977, when Gay Pride Week drew more than a thousand protestors, from allies to drag queens alike. *Jerome McClendon*/Atlanta Journal-Constitution *via AP.*

Anita Bryant's victory against gay rights had been a warning shot. When she preached at the 1978 Southern Baptist Convention in Atlanta, the gay community fired back and moved up Gay Pride Week to protest her visit. *Calvin Cruce/* Atlanta Journal-Constitution *via AP.*

Bryant's Atlanta speech electrified the Atlanta gay community. More than two thousand people would march on the Georgia World Congress Center while Bryant sang "The Battle Hymn of the Republic" inside. *Calvin Cruce/* Atlanta Journal-Constitution *via AP.*

Alan Orton longed for an acting career, but his fame in Atlanta would come in drag as he transformed himself into Lavita Allen, a Quaalude freak who emceed shows for nearly a decade at the Sweet Gum Head. *Susan W. Raines.*

Atlanta Gay Pride had transformed from a movement into a well-attended ritual by 1979; that year, Pride raised money for protestors to attend that year's National March on Washington. *Calvin Cruce*/Atlanta Journal-Constitution *via AP.*

An attractive woman onstage, Clay Hester married Teddy Bear Julie, a woman who had been performing in male drag at the Sweet Gum Head. Julie joked that Clay only married her because her father sold used cars, and Clay could drive a different one anytime he wanted. When Julie and Satyn had a daughter of their own, they would perform as Sonny and Cher, and bring out their daughter as Chastity. Clay had a daughter and a wife, and he identified as a gay man, one who cruised the club between numbers, on the hunt for a patron that would buy Satyn a shot of Wild Turkey.

Few performers put themselves together like Satyn did. A perfectionist, she kept her wardrobe and makeup in impeccable order. She called Rachel's teased hair a rat's nest: Satyn thought her own smooth black hair had the sheen and stillness of the hairdo of Lynda Carter, the former beauty queen who had just begun a run on CBS as Wonder Woman. One long night after her show, a hungover Satyn told Rachel and Lavita they wouldn't believe what had happened to her the night before. She had driven home in costume, only taking it off when going to bed. Fast asleep, his daughter woke him up with a start: "Daddy, I just saw Wonder Woman go to the bathroom."

Clay was more political than some of the other drag queens and had an idea of the change about to descend on the gay community.

"The gay community is a vital force in this city. When you are talking in numbers of 200,000 [gay] people or more, you are talking about a very dynamic force. It's hard to get any group that large behind any organization, but if you could just tap a resource that large and get them going in one direction, we would soon get known as a force to reckon with in this city.

"Consider how far Atlanta's black community has come! We have a black mayor, director of Police Services, and many other city officials are black. For a city in the very heart of the South, that's quite an accomplishment. If the black community can do things like that when they organize, just think what Atlanta's gay population could do."[7]

Peter Winokur

Fulton County, Georgia

April 27, 1976

O n April 27, a hitchhiker stepped between the sweetgum trees in the woods near Cascade-Palmetto Highway in south Fulton County, far from the heart of Atlanta. At about four thirty p.m., he stopped to nap and smelled an odor that led him to search the woods.

He stumbled across three badly decomposed bodies. They had been there for more than two months. Police identified them as Peter Winokur, Keith Stamm, and Floyd King.

Police determined the killer or killers marched the three victims into a steep ravine, through a barbed-wire fence, then over near a creek.[8] The younger men had been bound with electrical cord. Each man had been shot in the back of the head. Winokur and one of the other men had been shot a second time. One of the bodies stuck out, facedown, only partly buried. The ground had been too hard to break.

Bill Smith

The Sweet Gum Head

May 4, 1976

T he Sweet Gum Head's stage lights dimmed for a brief moment before the show started. The buzz leapt from the lips of the people clustered tightly around the tables on the mezzanine upstairs to those who crowded down the side of the club to those who gave their drink orders at the oval bar in the middle of the room to those who lit fresh cigarettes at the VIP tables huddled near the front of the stage. The disco music stopped, the microphone stand came out, and Phyllis Killer dragged herself onstage for the May 4, 1976, edition of the annual Phyllis Killer Oscars.

"WELL, HELLO THERE, TOOTSIES!"

The Oscars—trademark be damned—evolved from drag pageants that mirrored the Miss America pageant Bert Parks hosted every year from Atlantic City. Phyllis had wanted to give out awards that honored all the drag performers who put on distinctive acts, even whole shows, everything from live versions of *The Wizard of Oz* to *Purlie*. Her awards show handed out statuettes for Atlanta's performances and performers, for direction, even for the bars and their staff. The Gum Head's regular cast was on hand, and many were up for awards: Lavita Allen would win over Satyn DeVille in the top performer category.

The special event would be capped by a very special award— the Cecil B. DeMille trophy, given each year to the biggest friend to the gay community. When the votes were tallied, Phyllis exclaimed the winner—"it's the mayor!"

At the Oscars, Bill Smith took to the stage. He accepted the award from John Austin on the mayor's behalf, and read a letter of thanks from the mayor's office, citing Jackson's commitment to the civil rights of gay people. Jackson had beaten one other nominee for the DeMille trophy that year: Bill.

Jackson wasn't there himself. He had tickets to see Tony Orlando and Dawn at the Omni that evening.[9] There was almost no chance he'd be seen in one of the city's gay bars, not in the year before an election.

Instead, later that week, John Austin took the long walk through the ornate bronze doors of city hall, up the elevators to Mayor Jackson's office to present the trophy in person in a brief ceremony arranged by Bill Smith on May 11. Austin dressed for the occasion; the mayor's dapper dark suit and paisley tie were nearly matched by Austin's wide-lapeled suit and his military stance at attention. Mayor Jackson greeted him warmly and had encouraging words for the crowd that had gathered at the Gum Head. "We have problems," he admitted. "The process of change takes time . . . but we are committed in this administration and they know it."[10]

Bill had to be content with the presentation at city hall he was able to arrange. It signaled the mayor still considered the gay-rights cause to be a just one, and an important one—and that Bill could be the mayor's point person. Now in his third year of writing in the *Barb* and on the Community Relations Commission, Bill had helped steer Mayor Jackson's office to become more sensitive to the treatment of gay men. "Do you remember the paddy wagon raids on Winn Park and the old Chuck's Rathskeller in the late '60s or the massive idling and loitering crackdown of last summer? Paddy wagon police raids do not occur in Atlanta. Vice squad officers do not sit in gay bars luring would-be felony assaults. The CRC alone did not end these tactics but nothing else had a larger voice," he wrote.[11]

But Bill worried that his influence had waned before it waxed. The CRC budget had been cut, and it could barely function. The head of the commission publicly worried it would be abolished while Jackson contended with crippling finances, a rebellious police chief, and the complications brought by hiring an old college friend, Reginald Eaves, to slot in above Chief John Inman. By hiring Eaves as Inman's superior, Jackson could regain control of a police department that some thought had gone rogue. None of those political headwinds kept Bill from voicing his concerns loudly, and in impolitic ways.

Bill had plenty to contend with that spring as well. He spent his days earning a living in the Department of Education, tracking the spending of the city's schools. He had to keep up appearances on the CRC and be present as often as it met. He had to answer to new calls for involvement from New York, and spoke out on behalf of the NGTF he'd joined. He had to spend nights at bars like the Sweet Gum Head to cultivate relationships, where he scored the ad dollars the *Barb* spent in increasing amounts.

He had to find someone for sex. The Gum Head was a particularly rich place in that regard. "Most gay men who act butch are bottoms," he told a friend. "If you want to get fucked, you have to find a drag queen."[12]

Bill's personal tastes began to work their way into the newspaper in increasingly graphic ways. He wrote about the political fortunes of the gay community, and wrapped those missives in the lascivious stories gay audiences seemed to want. In 1976 the paper published its first fully nude photo of a young man, fully erect. The young man was one of the Youngman escorts Bill sent on nightly trysts in his other life. Phyllis Killer touted the service in the column she wrote for the *Barb*: "For the girl who has everything and wants a little more I'd suggest you call Youngman Incorporated, Atlanta's Elite Escort Agency. Where personal attention is given to so many little personal things. If you're just visiting Atlanta my dear, you are sure to get lost so call the agency for your own guide. He'll lead you right."

Friends would warn Bill to be careful about what he said about the agency. Bill berated and chastised anyone who questioned his decisions. His life was built on contradictions, but he was thin-skinned and wouldn't listen. No one could tell him what to do.[13]

"Running a newspaper is a crazy proposition," Bill wrote in his editor's column. He may have felt stretched too thin, but he wore an air of invincibility by the summer of 1976, when all his worlds revolved around one another at respectful distances, one never disturbing another, one never sending another out of orbit.[14]

///

Richard Evans Lee had been absent from the home he shared with Bill for a few weeks, on a visit to North Carolina. When he returned home, a straight couple—old friends of Bill's—had moved into another bedroom in the house they shared.

Their arrival coincided with an abrupt change in Bill's mood. He grew hostile toward Richard, who never understood why. It felt as if Bill had flipped a switch. Richard could not tell whether he'd offended him or hurt his feelings. He only knew Bill's mood had changed and gone abruptly dark.

Bill did not hesitate to use people. Everyone did it, he thought, and it was fine to use people as long as they weren't abused.

Richard worried that Bill had used him to start the escort agency, and now had power over him. It was Richard's name on the agency's incorporation papers, not Bill's. It was Richard who could be arrested, not his roommate. Bill didn't just have friends in city hall, he worked there.

Richard didn't stick around to find out why he'd been shut out. He left the home he shared with Bill and left Bill in control of the Youngman harem.

Bill never mentioned or spoke to Richard again. It was as if he had ceased to exist.[15]

Heather Fontaine

The Sweet Gum Head

Summer 1976

Heather Fontaine survived her mother's divorce from a man who cheated. She survived the man her mother married next, barely.

She was ten years old when the alcoholic navy veteran came to live in her home in Huntsville. The soldier took a look at the child dressed in boys' clothing, and pushed her against a wall.

"I'm going to make you a man if it kills you," he grunted.

"Well," she replied, "I guess I'm going to die."

///

She nearly did. Her stepfather would drag Heather out of bed to beat her. Everything she did seemed to drive him into a rage.

Military boarding school in Tennessee had been no different. The captain in charge of Heather's dorm would apply corporal punishment for slight transgressions. He would wake up the entire dorm in the middle of the night to paddle each and every cadet. Heather begged to come home, and her mother finally relented, but not before Heather realized she was more like the women in her life than the men.

When she got home, Heather's stepfather picked up in lockstep with her military instructors. She began to plan her escape, and the life she wanted to have after she was free.

Heather felt alone in the world surrounded by seemingly conformist teenagers in high school. She studied theatre and fell into infatuations with the boys around her. One night in late 1973 she planned to meet three other high-school students at a place called the Palace. When she arrived, she realized it was a gay bar, and that her new friends were drag queens. She went to their apartment, and talked for hours.

The next Saturday, Heather's friends put her in drag. She knew then she wanted to start to live as a woman, like the pretty ladies with the updos and knee-length skirts who sat under the dryers at her parents' beauty salons. She asked God to make her a beautiful woman, like them.

Her parents sent her to therapists, who asked her when she began to feel like a woman. They told her they could change her into an assertive man. Heather stopped treatment. Her grandmother would ask if she wanted to be a boy or a girl, and the answer was obvious. Her grandmother took her to a Birmingham endocrinologist, then took her to her parents and convinced them to sign a consent form.[16] At sixteen, Heather began to take hormones. She began to set herself free.[17]

///

Drag queens in Huntsville, Alabama, knew the Sweet Gum Head. It was the biggest show bar in the South; it was where Toni Duran "funneled"—she spun around in a long dress or a cape until she bloomed like a flower, or a whirling dervish.

The police in Huntsville knew Heather's parents, and knew Heather too. They would pull her over, put her in the backseat of their car, and threaten to take her into jail for wearing women's clothes, until an officer with compassion for her plight told her to wear boys' underwear and to put two socks in her bra.

In nearby Birmingham, where Heather tried to perform, vice would go undercover to roust anyone in a gay bar who even touched another person. In between drag shows performers had to sit behind a metal railing so they couldn't touch the audience members. They could accept tips, but had to grab the bills just-so, to avoid skin-to-skin contact, as if they were diseased.

Heather just had to go to Atlanta, she decided. She knew Atlanta would be better.

///

Heather's beautiful face got her booked immediately into the Onyx drag bar in downtown Atlanta, but when she heard about auditions at the Sweet Gum Head, she went, and she won a spot in the show.

The Sweet Gum Head was always packed. Heather was not yet eighteen, but she had already begun what she thought was her dream job, in a room filled with ecstatic fans who wanted to see her perfect Marilyn Monroe illusion.

Since she was a new performer, she'd have to follow Rachel

Wells. Rachel would already be back in her dressing room, but the crowd still would be clapping for her, even when Heather's music had started, even when she'd stepped on the stage. She was young, and she didn't care.

The first time she met Rachel, she was nervous even to talk to her. Rachel had the audience in her grasp. Heather would study Rachel's looks and her connection with the crowd as she walked down the steps at the back of the room, from the dressing room upstairs.

At the Sweet Gum Head, Heather forgot how she had sat at the dinner table in her mother's clothes, how her stepfather had ordered her to stop and had her shave her head. How she had become Catholic when she was eight years old, and had to ask a priest how she could change her baptismal records and her communion to reflect her real name. How her mother and father and stepfather had sent her money to live in Atlanta, to keep her away from home.

At the Sweet Gum Head she met all the performers she had heard about, from the moment she confirmed herself in her teens. She met Wayland Flowers and Madame; they would sit right in front, and Madame would give Heather her tip.[18] She performed "Diamonds Are a Girl's Best Friend," her favorite song from her film idol, to exquisite perfection.

She would linger around the upstairs dressing room, which sat opposite the men's restroom. Most of the performers were looking for boyfriends, and eligible men figured out they could linger up there, too, and meet the performers that aroused them. They waited between the pinball machines, lined up against the wall, some of them the straight men who wandered into the Sweet Gum Head in an open-minded gesture that opened their minds to more than they dreamed. It was the happiest time of her life. It was all an experiment, all an illusion. It was Oz.

Mayor Maynard Jackson

Atlanta City Hall

June 1976

"I did not proclaim Gay Pride Week, as you incorrectly stated," the mayor intoned in his weighty voice. "I pronounced a Gay Pride Day."

Mayor Jackson could not have been clearer when he called into Atlanta's local conservative talk-radio show with host Neal Boortz on Friday, June 18, 1976. The talk-radio host had alleged that Jackson had taken things further than he had. Boortz had also made what some considered to be disparaging remarks about the mayor, about the need for such a declaration—which simply stated that "all citizens deserve basic legal rights regardless of race, sex, age, religious beliefs, economic status, national origin, or sexual preference."

The mayor would have none of it. He told people on his team that he would not be like some Black leaders who got scared to use their power once they attained it, because they didn't want to rock the boat. He could be the first Atlanta mayor to come out as an ally of the gay community—and he would be.

Jackson clarified his stance. "The proclamation has not yet been signed," he said. Then he signed it, while on the air.[19]

///

Jackson broke with a long tradition of Atlanta mayors while he acknowledged the city's growing gay citizenry. He campaigned for votes among gay people, and began to appear at gay community events. More than a year away from a reelection campaign, Jackson expressly courted the gay vote.

The city council took umbrage. In April, councilman Hugh Pierce demanded the City Council strike "sexual orientation" from the Community Relations Commission charter. He aimed his distaste directly at Bill Smith. In return, Bill wrote in the *Barb* that readers should hammer the phone lines at the City Council and urge members not to vote for the amendment, which Pierce quickly withdrew.[20]

When Jackson signed his Gay Pride Day declaration on the city's most popular AM radio station, he promptly faced the wrath of a group of seven Atlanta businessmen who called themselves Citizens for a Decent Atlanta. The group bought ads in the Atlanta papers and called the proclamation a travesty, in extreme bad taste. Letters of condemnation flooded the mayor's office. The businessmen went to Fulton County court to try to force the mayor to put a stop the planned Pride proclamation.[21] Rev. William Self of the Wieuca Road Baptist Church said the mayor needed to repent or resign.

Jackson refused to withdraw the declaration.[22] Instead, he took a nuanced position on his declaration and explained it in a release, the day before Pride.

"The city's proclamation does not condone homosexuality," he wrote. "It supports the rights of a group of Atlanta citizens, the gay pride planning committee, to seek public discussion and legislative action on the issue.

"Georgia law is very specific in prohibiting homosexual acts, and the city of Atlanta shall enforce that and any other laws we are bound to enforce. Police and other city officials, however, will not harass gay people who are not engaged in illegal acts.

"I am a lawyer who has fought for human rights and civil liberties too long to turn my back on an issue of civil rights just because it is highly controversial, he said. "I feel absolutely obligated to protect the rights of all Atlantans and ALL Americans to free speech and free assembly."

Too radical for some, not radical enough for others, Jackson practiced pitch-perfect politics. The calculated stance proved quickly to be an unpopular one for the popular mayor, and he would begin to walk it back almost immediately.

///

With Gay Pride Week on the docket, the *Barb* printed full-page ads for the celebrations for "Christopher Street South," which would include panel discussions from gay churches and from other organizations, culminating on Saturday, June 26, at one p.m., with a rally from the Civic Center to Piedmont Park.[23]

Bill's paper was the best way to find out what Pride in 1976 meant. He was a taproot for information on gay and lesbian life in Atlanta; he had directed his Gay Information Service while he also collected money for a British Sterling Memorial Fund and now sat as a director on the National Gay Task Force.

In 1976, Bill rented space on Fourth Street near West Peachtree to be used as an informal gay community center, one that offered counseling and discussion groups and political forums for candidates in upcoming elections, forums organized by Bill's friend Gil Robison, a wiry young man with more than a passing resemblance to Frank Zappa. The rented space sat near Cypress Street, where the city minted new hustlers with every bus that opened its doors and brought newly out young men to Atlanta from across the South.

///

"Out of the closets and into the streets!"

A sweltering day was nothing out of the ordinary in Atlanta in June. The sight of hundreds of marchers making their way down Peachtree had even become more common, as Atlanta celebrated its seventh Gay Pride Week.[24] A pair of smiling men held hands to lead it.

"Fags," one service-station attendant spat as the parade passed his pumps.

In the public forum of the city's papers, readers wrote to defend the gay-pride proclamation. They voiced the rational arguments of the gay-rights movement in ways that would echo through the decades to come.

"As a straight, Christian, post-graduate, liberated individual . . . this was a most progressive move on the part of the city as well as the mayor," said Ann Herrell. "I moved here because it had been indicated to me that this was becoming the cultural and intellectual mecca of the South. For the most part this is true."

"It's about time," wrote activist Vic Host. "We work, sleep, play, pay taxes, live, breathe and die just like every one else. If we choose to stay hidden, we could. But I thank God that we now realize that we have a right to our life–to live it as we see best."

Evangelicals expressed concern over "basic questions of inconsistency produced when a narrow, ultra-fundamentalist interpretation pronounces the judgement of God . . . but fails to also denounce the eating of catfish, ham, and the wearing of red dresses, which are also condemned," while it added that the New Testament offers no mention of homosexuality by Jesus.[25]

Bruce Voeller of the National Gay Task Force called for a boycott of businesses that sponsored the opposition group, and wrote that "only a few years ago, one suspects, the Citizens for a Decent Atlanta would have written similarly against blacks, claiming that intermarriage of the races is 'against the moral law of the Judeo-Christian tradition.'"[26]

With the mayor's proclamation in full effect, Pride 1976 went on without incident. The march swelled to about 500 people as it moved from the Civic Center to the traditional rally at Piedmont

Park. The mention of Mayor Jackson's name in speeches at the park drew cheers.

"A group of seven men, through intimidation and pressure on the mayor and in the courts went into court and four times they failed," Bill told the crowd gathered on the park's hill. "The mayor and the courts refused to give in to the bigotry and prejudice of these seven anonymous men."[27]

"They're not hurting anybody, are they?" asked a woman in thick makeup from the doorway of a nearby bathhouse.

Even the gas man relented. "I guess those people got a right to march, if they want to."[28]

Bill Smith

The Barb House

June 1976

Bill had tamed his huge hair and put on a black suit for the television cameras that filmed him in his office, where he sat behind a massive desk in front of a respectable brick wall pierced by respectable diamond-pane glass windows. For all the world he might have looked like some company president, save for the pencil sketch of two men locked in an embrace that hung on the wall. He lived in two different places and led two very different lives, and tailored his appearance to match the moment.

"The law in Georgia is incredible, and it is incredibly specific," he lectured. "A married couple, if the bed broke on the way to the floor, they would break several Georgia statutes concerning their sexuality. It's incredible that a state would make a law, that anyone would make a law to govern the private acts between two consenting adults in the privacy of their own home."[29]

When the Supreme Court failed to overturn a sodomy conviction against two gay men in Virginia in 1976, he saw it as a setback, but not the end of the gay-rights movement.[30]

"I think it's unfortunate. I think it's an abomination, as Frank Kameny, one of the leading gay activists in this country, has said, the court has just simply sidestepped one of the very important social issues that's confronting the United States today."

Flamboyantly knowledgeable about the ins and outs of sodomy law, Bill saw it as the ultimate invasion of privacy. The intimate negotiation of new gay relationships put at least four or five people in any given bed, once the police, the church, and the law slipped under the covers too. Bill set his sights on the sodomy laws in his usual unquiet way. He had long ago given up the refuge of a secret life when he grabbed his first protest sign and shouted his sexuality down Peachtree Street. He prayed his fellow gays and lesbians would do the same. They had to.

Black Americans had no choice but to marshal change. Gay people had a choice, Smith wrote. They could stay and let others decide for them—or they could go to the polls and be heard.[31]

If they chose to stay quiet, they could be punished for what the straight world saw as decadence, and they would have no control over what the punishment would be.

///

Bill walked into the After Dark bookstore in time for yet another interview. It was the biggest and most profitable adult bookstore in Atlanta, built into an old bakery at 1067 Peachtree Street, tucked between empty lots and storefronts on the stretch that used to be the center of the Strip.

Inside, the lighting emulated a strip club, with pulses and loud doses of hard rock played in the background. Racks of adult magazines lined the corridor that led to booths with locks on the inside, and handsome young men circling them, waiting for a perfect match in an erotic game of concentration.

Owned by an ex-NASA engineer, the bookstore had a pinball room and pool tables to cater to the nearly ten thousand people who walked through the door each week. The store had been harassed by police, not because it sold pornography but because it catered to the gay community. Police in plainclothes regularly came to the store to entrap people.

The owner dubbed relations with the police department "strained, but improving." He pointed out that the new police regime had made a point to listen to the store's concerns, and that the crime rate had fallen.

"Mayor Jackson is also doing an excellent job and has a strong following among the gay community," the owner of the store, who asked to be called Ron, added.

Why had he started a dirty bookstore? the reporter asked.

"When the space program fizzled out, I just had no job," he said. "I looked all over the country for a job that was equivalent to the kind of money I was getting at NASA, and could find nothing. A dead end. Well, I decided at that time I'd get into a business that I could enjoy, being gay myself."

As a city commissioner, Bill thought nothing of walking into After Dark and speaking with a reporter who was interviewing the store's owner.

"In a heterosexual environment, you can meet people to go out with, to have dates with, go dancing with. It's perfectly natural for a man to ask a woman in the office, or in church, etc., etc., to go out," he said. "But gay people, you know, can't do that. If they do that in their office they may lose their job. So you have to have a way so you can meet somebody that you actually know is gay without fear of repercussions."[32]

///

At his home, the home of the paper, and the home of Youngman, Bill laughed with everyone else as a hustler dropped his pants, bent over for the crowd with a pout, and said, "Look at this!"

The hustler's ass was bright red. His latest client had asked if he was a spanker, so the young man assumed it would be his hand put to work. The man who paid for his time had other ideas: the hustler got spanked instead, and took his money but wasn't at all happy about it. The crew at the Barb House gawked and howled.

The *Barb* had moved to 40 Peachtree Place earlier in the year. The house had been home to a community crisis center where Diane worked, and before that, a hippie commune called the Heathen Rage—something of a collective that included many of the writers for Atlanta's then-dying alternative newspaper, *The Great Speckled Bird*. Bill turned it into a sort of anything-goes gay fraternity house, one that blurred the lines between all the lives he lived, where he hustled from activism to hedonism in a syncopated rhythm that could not be sustained.

All the facets of Bill's life commingled in a few Day-Glo-painted rooms, where his great, easy laugh echoed from one room to the next. Straight friends would mingle with hustlers who came and went on their errands, where anyone could pick up a joint and smoke, where people were always coming and going.

Jimmy, the straight, married hustler would come by on occasion. He was the true love of Bill's life. Bill fell for Jimmy's combed-back, dirty-blond hair, his masculine edge, his athletic features, the darker aspect that accompanied it all.

Diane would come by and they would do as they always had done, eat out and come back to his apartment to talk, and to dance, in the rooms decorated with peace symbols and bright pastels, to the latest disco songs, including their favorite Vicki Sue Robinson song, "Turn the Beat Around."

Bill took care that Diane never met the escorts. Though he sometimes shared details of their dalliances with her, he tried to protect her from everything tawdry in the world. Bill would take agency calls from downtown when she visited, a request for a male escort, or sometimes for a man and a woman. On one of her visits to the *Barb* house, Bill told Diane someone had called and offered to pay a thousand dollars apiece for an evening with a man and a woman. He nervously asked if she wanted to engage that client with hi—

"No," she said emphatically, cutting him off.

"Oh, thank God," he said. "I was so afraid you'd say yes."

Mayor Maynard Jackson

Atlanta

July 1976

Mayor Jackson's black Lincoln Continental limousine idled in traffic on Peachtree Street while he fumed. He just wanted to get home from city hall after yet another long day of work, but the car hardly moved.

The three women in the local massage parlor appeared in a doorway of their building wearing very bare outfits, visible from Jackson's car. One pulled her panties down before she realized the mayor of Atlanta had witnessed the whole scene.

"Hey, Maynard!" one of the women yelled out to him. "Hey Mayor, come on in!"[33]

By some counts, the city "too busy to hate" had a good reason for being otherwise occupied. More than 7,500 prostitutes and escorts worked inside city limits, most making at least $400 a week. Bathhouses and "love tussle" emporiums more than tripled in count in the year prior, from four to fifteen. According to the head of the city's vice squad, prostitution brought in at least $150 million a year, a swollen untaxed river that made its way down the economic stream to the drug trade and other illicit businesses.

The triangle north of Baker Street, where the mayor's car inched forward, was one of two main districts for the sex trade, the other running from Ponce de Leon Avenue to Fourteenth Street, into the heart of the old Strip neighborhood, up to the fringe of Piedmont Park, where a woman known as the Piedmont Pig would lift her skirt like a vaudevillian female impersonator and clang beer cans together to advertise her wares.

Jackson had not been able to stem the tide of prostitution. He had been unable to cut off the flow of drugs that had swept the city under Mayor Massell. Members of his own administration smoked pot, after all—Jackson didn't, and his aides wouldn't tell him that they did. He believed that an altered mental state would get in the way of performing his duties, and Jackson had been raised to believe his job mattered more than anything.

His focus on work likely had some role in his pending divorce. He had separated from his wife, Burnella, in the spring. The couple kept the divorce particulars under wraps, though Burnella told *Jet* magazine she didn't know if there was a chance for reconciliation. "I wish I could say more," she said, "but if I did I might get my wrist slapped." At thirty-eight, Jackson was about to be single again, cast into the dating pool.

Jackson filed for divorce late in the summer of 1976 after a decade of marriage. He had moved out of the family home, agreed to give his wife custody of the children and $1,750 a month in alimony and child support. Jackson had visitation rights and would be responsible for their health care and college tuition. His administration had begun to show some wear; his personal life was in a shambles.

He could do something about the hookers, though. After his brief ride through the wilder side of Atlanta, he got on the phone with his new public safety commissioner, Reggie Eaves, and barked an order: "Clean it up!"[34]

John Greenwell

The Biltmore Hotel

August 1976

John let the steel ball bounce across the pinball machine table and smacked the buttons with both hands—*slap-slap-slap*—at Ms. Garbo's lesbian bar, another one of Frank Powell's places. He was welcomed during the day by the women who pressed dollar bills in his hands at night. The lesbians loved the beautiful Rachel Wells, even when she was out of drag. He had racked up thousands of points on the pinball machine when the gay community's new *Cruise* magazine caught up with him on Rachel's return to the Sweet Gum Head.

Rachel had been away on tour, and had returned to a club that cruised through the night at the zenith of gay Atlanta nightlife, a star in its own orbit. Five years into its run, the Sweet Gum Head had never drawn bigger crowds. Every time Rachel had left before to tour, or to run away, the crowds had dissipated. This time, the crowds had remained, and the cast had hardly changed.

Rachel was more famous than ever in Atlanta, and could only pass undetected in public as John when he dressed as a man. He took in his share of drugs and had more than his share of encounters with anyone he wanted, but he stopped at the threshold of hormones and surgery. Other performers let themselves be injected with silicone in their faces, and shared needles. Some lived as women and wanted to be physically changed to become themselves. John kept his cheekbones sharp by avoiding food.

Rachel Wells was one of the most famous names in drag in America, thanks to tours like the one John embarked on across the Southern circuit that ended in late summer. Rachel had thrived on the small stages in intimate clubs in Birmingham and Knoxville; they reminded John of the nights spent honing his drag persona in the dank, old, and long-forgotten Cruise Quarters. None of those places were like the Sweet Gum Head, but they had all prepared him for it. The Gum Head had the good lights, the good sound, the big stage—and it held the key to sponsors for that year's Miss Gay Georgia pageant.

John wanted a major pageant win to cement his status among the most popular drag queens of the day. Held at the Biltmore Hotel in Atlanta, the 1976 Miss Gay Georgia pageant crowds watched Rachel choose a handmade gown sewn by a fellow performer for the evening-wear category, then a skimpy new bikini that might match a brand-new tiara for the swimwear competition—and her old friend Jesus for her now-familiar rendition of "I Don't Know How to Love Him." After the waves of applause had died out, she'd lost out to the tap-dance brilliance of the Onyx's star performer, Vicki Lawrence. It didn't matter. Rachel—John—still was one of the most accomplished and famous female impersonators on the circuit. And he was home.

Bill Smith

New York City

October 23, 1976

Bill sat at a conference table with the other colonels of the resistance at his flanks: Voeller, O'Leary, Gittings, and Kameny. Bill sat in their orbit, on some level amazed by what he had engineered in order to take his place at this table, on another level bored by the formality and process that the National Gay Task Force had been mired in on even the smallest issues.

The NGTF held meetings in New York a few times each year for their board of directors. Bill had missed the first that happened in his official term, on June 12. Four months later, the NGTF still hashed through some of the same topics it had tabled at its summer meeting: draft resolutions for new policies, major donor efforts, and direct-mail campaigns.

The organization had been founded in 1973 with the same principles in mind as a dozen other pro-gay organizations. It sought to be the agency for change, a group of advocates that would appeal to government and to America's collective conscience to end discrimination against sexual orientation. The NGTF took particular interest in how gays and lesbians were portrayed in the media, in everything from newspaper stories to episodes of *Kojak*.

Bill had been given a pass for his first absence. The NGTF ran on a shoestring budget, and because it couldn't afford to pay for all travel expenses, directors often had to pay in part to attend New York meetings. In 1976, Bill already had rent to pay on two different apartments, and on business offices for the newspaper and agency, apart from his usual living expenses. He always seemed to have money, but friends thought his father secretly supplemented his meager income from the city.

The task force's agenda filled pages and took nearly two days of lengthy discussion to digest. The episode of *Kojak* occupied those at the table with its portrayal of a child molester as gay; an episode of the *Nancy Walker Show* had been noted for its negative characterization of a gay male secretary. The NGTF had won an audience with *Walker*'s producers; it had also been promised that a controversial episode of *Police Woman* would be yanked from syndication for anti-gay messaging.

Bill eagerly dove into the discussion. He wanted to receive Atlanta's media alerts so as to act on them sooner, and asked if there was a packet of dos and don'ts for gays and lesbians who appeared on TV; to him, it appeared that all gay people interviewed for the news were nervous and chain-smoked, and newscasts played that stereotype up by focusing on jittery hands.

The participants talked much about the wording of their statement of purpose. For an agitator who eagerly protested and picketed, the meeting bore all the hallmarks of talking and not doing—the bane of Bill's existence. He sat in meetings all day long for work, often for the CRC too, and they took up more and more of his time when he could have been out doing something positive.

Then the executive directors peered into the abyss of the NGTF's finances. Membership had crested at 3,000 people, and revenue from donations and sponsorships was up, but so were expenses. The nonprofit would need a lot of help and luck to break even for the year. The most prominent gay-rights organization in the country was running on fumes. For Bill, it was an uncomfortably familiar situation.

President James Earl Carter

Atlanta

November 1976

The tough questions came up quickly, and good Christian soldier that he was, Jimmy Carter's honesty got the best of him.

"Would you appoint judges who would be harsh or lenient toward victimless crimes," the *Playboy* reporter asked, "offenses such as drug use, adultery, sodomy and homosexuality?"

Jimmy Carter had traveled over 50,000 miles, visited 37 states, and delivered over 200 speeches before any other candidate announced that he was in the race to succeed Gerald Ford as president. His strategy worked, for a time, and he won the Democratic nomination on July 15, 1976. Then *Playboy* called.

"Committing adultery, according to the Bible—which I believe in—is a sin," he said. "For us to hate one another, for us to have sexual intercourse outside marriage, for us to engage in homosexual activities, for us to steal, for us to lie—all these are sins."

Carter tried to modulate and steer the interview back on message by reminding the interviewer how as governor in his home state of Georgia, he had seen the state cut penalties for pot smoking, how his administration had tilted away from prosecuting "victimless" crime.

"Almost every state in the Union has laws against adultery and many of them have laws against homosexuality and sodomy . . . Do you think such laws should be on the books at all?"

Carter's answer: America had emerged from Judeo-Christian foundations, and those moral standards were at least some guidance on how laws should be conceived and written. First he equivocated—"You can't legislate morality"—and then he lit a fire: "If there is a conflict between God's law and civil law, we should honor God's law."

Homosexuality made Carter nervous, he admitted. He didn't have any personal knowledge of it, he said, and his religion made homosexuality seem foreign and strange. He had digested the implications of laws he would now have to square with his deeply held beliefs, and confessed that he had little refuge other than to consider sodomy the same as sex outside of marriage.

Then he said: "I've looked on a lot of women with lust. I've committed adultery in my heart many times."[35]

Carter realized his mistake quickly. He hadn't understood how uncomfortable he was with his own sexuality, and stumbled through the discussion with schoolboy naïveté. He could do nothing once the interview went public in the fall of 1976. He had agreed to give the interview just as others had done, including Gov. Jerry Brown, Walter Cronkite, and Albert Schweitzer. Later, Carter expressed regret.

"But they weren't running for president," he said, "and in retrospect, from hindsight, I would not have given that interview had I to do it over again." Duly chastened, Carter promised, "If I should ever decide in the future to discuss my deep Christian beliefs and condemnation and sinfulness, I'll use another forum besides *Playboy*."[36]

The disastrous interview with *Playboy* would not derail his campaign in its closing days. Though rising stars like Ronald Reagan had begun to swing the Republican pendulum farther to the right, all the suitably chaste and sober Carter had to do was defeat the man who had pardoned Richard Nixon.

Carter had amassed a wide lead in polls during the summer, and in the morass left behind by the threat of impeachment and pardons and war, Carter glided into office on a bare majority of votes, winning 297 electoral votes to Ford's 240 votes. Endorsed by Atlanta mayor Maynard Jackson, Carter became the first commander in chief from Georgia, despite the murmurs of him being a closet progressive, despite nearly squandering his electoral lead with a string of mishaps, including the interview with *Playboy*. With Carter's election, millions of voters had sent the message that America was fundamentally still a Christian nation, that it was fundamentally unchanged, and that it needed someone with a fundamental streak to cleanse it of its political sins.

Bill Smith

40 Peachtree Place, Atlanta

Winter 1976

The final issues of the *Barb* in 1976 showed a Bill Smith on the ragged edge of professionalism. Some of Youngman's escorts were listed on the masthead of the paper as office and production assistants. Bill appeared in photos taken at nightclubs; at the Onyx Lounge, he posed for a Miss Tacky contest in a blond curly wig and a halter-style dress, complete with his glasses and beard. He promised a new section in the paper dubbed "Blue Notes," and disclosed a new 50-cent price for the newspaper. The *Barb* would no longer be free.

Youngman ads continued to run, but they ran smaller, even though the agency's very existence was a barely clothed secret. The gay community knew about the agency, and some shunned Bill for it. He continued to run it nonetheless, nearly out in the open, though he still was not its legal owner. If he'd wanted to hide it, he could have. He knew from his early closeted days how to hide his tracks well. He saw the future of gay politics for a thousand miles, but couldn't see the chaos he had welcomed into his life.

In the *Barb*'s December issue, the staff posed for a Christmas photo dedicated to its readers. Bill wore a blond wig again, styled by Phyllis Killer. Writers circled around a desk. A naked man squatted atop the desk, posed for Bill's delight.

"*The Barb* staff takes time out from their busy schedule," the homily read, "to pose around the Christmas Bush."

At Christmastime in 1976, Bill Smith was second vice chairperson for Atlanta's Community Relations Commission, a director of the ACLU of Georgia, a gay-rights activist who praised the work of others like him, such as Philadelphia's Mark Segal, and a gay confidant to Atlanta's powers that be. But in the eyes of the law, he was a pimp.

Charlie Brown

The Sweet Gum Head

December 1976

Charlie Brown grew up happy in the rolling country of Tennessee as Charlie Dillard, surrounded by a loving mother and father, and by an aunt he thought was the jolliest person on Earth. Aunt Mary made him laugh harder than anyone. He observed her wisecracks, and mimicked them. He narrated commercials with funnier dialogue to entertain his family.

Charlie's father also had a sharp wit and a sage view of the world. "Laugh your way through life," he told Charlie. "It will go so much easier, so much faster."

Dillard graduated from high school and went to Nashville for business school. During one summer, he took a job at the Watch Your Hat & Coat Saloon. It was a gay bar, and Charlie worked sound and took on some small roles as the male lead during his first six months. Before long, the rest of the crew dubbed him Charlie Brown. When the club had its regular "turnabout" night—the crew and managers would get into costume for the performers—the nickname stuck. He would be Charlie Brown, in and out of drag.

It didn't hurt that he had a male name, because the Nashville police turned away from the drag clubs as long as the performers made it clear they were men, doing it for a laugh. Artists had to put on their makeup in the club, and smuggle in their wigs and dresses.

His first performance came when he was twenty-one, and of legal age. He performed "Maybe" by the Three Degrees, the same song that won Rachel Wells her Miss Gay Atlanta title in 1972. Nashville was full of country queens who did Tammy, Loretta, and Patsy. Charlie stuck out as a white queen performing a lot of songs owned by Black women.

His act pushed the boundaries of what the clubs would allow. He'd learned the art of burlesque from EZ Ryder, a stripper and neighbor who worked Nashville's Printer's Alley, a dirty side street with a half dozen clubs that raked in fistfuls of cash every night. Ryder, a transgender woman with enormous breasts, taught Charlie how to strip. He would do his drag act, then run down to Ryder's club to watch her perform, and to learn. They became close friends. Charlie wore her head pieces and shoulder pieces and tail pieces. He stripped all the way down to a T-back, underwear that barely covered the letter itself.

His parents didn't know about Charlie's husband, Fred, whom he had met when dressed in full drag. They didn't know about his career. They lived more than an hour away from the city. They only knew that he'd begun to look different and to act strange. When Charlie went back to Nashville to perform at a supper-club show, the publicity traced him back to his drag shows. It was rough for a while; his family had old missionary Baptist roots, but they eventually accepted it all—save for one of his brothers, who never would treat Charlie the same again.

Charlie only grew more famous in Nashville. Then through a chance meeting, he booked his first out-of-town gig at the Sweet Gum Head in 1973, the year after he had finished first runner-up in the first Miss Gay America pageant. Atlanta frightened out-of-towners with its reputation as the capital of drag. The Cheshire Bridge clubs were the upper class on the scene, compared to the scruffy venues in Midtown. They were close together, held more people, and banded together to create their own clubby atmosphere. They had seven or eight girls onstage every night, three or four male leads. They did big, major dance productions. They rehearsed four, five days a week, to make sure the weekend shows ran smoothly.

The Gum Head amplified the fear in visiting performers. Its faded cabaret could seem like a Roman arena. Other clubs were carved out of empty warehouses and abandoned spaces. The Gum Head had a narrow entrance. First-timers stepped in through a pair of doors with feet stomping in the chairs overhead, surrounded by crowds, challenged by the bar that split the club across the middle, daunted by the golden-oak stage and its bare, unforgiving light, preceded and followed by performers with huge names. Charlie watched Lavita Allen put the crowd into tears of laughter, saw Diamond Lil sing and polish her legend. He saw Rachel Wells sweep the stage with absolute natural beauty that pictures couldn't capture. It scared Charlie like hell, but intrigued him all the same.

For his first Gum Head performance, Charlie pulled on a low-cut gown, light blue and sleeveless, split up to the crotch. The DJ cued up a real bar-burner, "You Came a Long Way from St. Louis," by Della Reese. Charlie climbed on the bar and stalked across it while he channeled Della's soulful interpretation. He kicked over glasses and shattered the crowd. He tore the house down. The club managers hired him on the spot.

He moved in with Deva Sanchez, wide-eyed to the advanced drag that the Sweet Gum Head drilled into its performers, so different from what he knew in Nashville. He remembered the advice his momma and daddy had given him long before: "Watch before you make a step." He watched and learned from performers who became his teachers.

Then he stepped into the light. "Charlie Brown is my name, fake pussy is my game," he said onstage. "I look like Mommy," he intoned in a higher voice, then swung into a basso profundo, "but I'm hung like Daddy."

He performed "This Is My Life"—eventually hundreds of times. Charlie peeled off his wig and his eyelashes, wiped off his makeup with a towel. It made him hundreds of dollars in tips. The right song could do that. It could pay the rent in one night.

Charlie played the Bitch of the South onstage. To the other performers at the Sweet Gum Head, he would be the same kind-hearted Charlie Dillard who never left his family in Tennessee, or the one he made on Cheshire Bridge Road.

By Christmas of 1976, Charlie had become a regular, and narrated the Gum Head's holiday show under John Austin's direction. Dina Jacobs had taken over as show director, and Rachel Wells had returned to the all-star cast, along with Lavita and Satyn and Julie, who brought their small daughter to the club when the cast celebrated the holidays and exchanged the original gift, that of family. They all gathered under the bright lights at the Sweet Gum Head, the old supermarket space with the sticky red carpet, the noisy drag-show bar behind the tire shop on gritty Cheshire Bridge Road, the oasis where they all had paused on the journey to places unknown.

1977

///

STAR WARS

Bill Smith

Atlanta

January 1977

On January 20, 1977, a bright twenty-eight-degree day in Washington, DC, James Earl Carter Jr. stood outside on the East Portico of the U.S. Capitol and took the oath of office as the thirty-ninth president of the United States. He broke with tradition and refused the usual ride to the White House. Instead of clambering inside the thick glass and armored metal of the presidential limousine, Carter took his wife Rosalynn's hand and they walked, humbly, down Pennsylvania Avenue for a mile and a half.

Carter had left an Atlanta fundamentally different from the one he moved to in 1970. By 1977 the story of Atlanta read more like an encyclopedia of cultures instead of a single culture's monograph. Its population boomed. It had elected its first Black mayor. Its gay community had grown larger and more vocal; a gay man, Bill Smith, was second vice chair of the city's Community Relations Commission. Mayor Jackson had nominated him for a second term, which he accepted. Bill was confirmed on January 5, 1977.

Bill told readers of the *Barb* that he was reluctant to take on the post for another term. The newspaper required a lot of time, and often conflicted with his city role, but he could not refuse Mayor Jackson's request for him to serve again. "I can think of few politicians that have a stronger commitment to gay rights than Mayor Jackson. It is an honor to be appointed and I feel it is also a strong indication of Mayor Jackson's continued commitment to gay people."[1]

Atlanta had quickly caught the fire of the gay civil-rights movement. Just ten years before, city aldermen called gay men "perverts" and actively plotted ways to bar them from public places
like Piedmont Park.[2] By the mid-1970s, Atlanta's gays could mix
amongst themselves, or mix in with the straight world with rela-
tive ease inside city limits.

Gay bars were now the hubs of distinct gay neighborhoods, the
biggest of which was Midtown, which used to be known as the
Strip. Three-quarters of the neighborhood was composed of single
men, compared to about a third of the rest of metro Atlanta. Half
the businesses in Midtown were owned by or serviced gay customers. About half of Atlanta's bars took up space in Midtown.

Six gay churches opened their doors in the area, split among
Catholics and Episcopalians and Lutherans and Evangelicals;
homosexuality knew no theology. Pols canvassed for votes in gay
neighborhoods, and sought the backing of gay groups like the
First Tuesday Democratic Committee. Gay softball leagues were
sponsored by gay businesses that banded together in a gay chamber of commerce. From humble roots, Atlanta's loose gay nucleus
was now a focused, thriving community, and Cheshire Bridge
Road was one of its hubs.

Along the way to organizing as a community, many discovered
a truth: the gay and straight world had more than a few things
in common. The Kinsey Institute found that homosexuals ranged
widely in appetites and attractions and lifestyles, but mostly
fell into the same archetypes as straights. Some preferred close,
long-term relationships, while others were active singles who frequently pursued new partners. Still others were asexual. Most
had come to terms with their orientation and were integrated
into the world as well as their heterosexual counterparts were.
Gay men and women were thriving, in remote mountain regions
and in the Bible Belt alike, in stable relationships, leading happy
lives. They hadn't just created themselves, sui generis; they had
always been there.

///

On January 11, 1977, Atlanta police pulled over a black Cadillac Eldorado convertible with a vanity plate that read "Robbie" on Peachtree and Fifth Street. They pulled Locker Room owner Robert Llewellyn out of the car and arrested him for the murder of Peter Winokur.

Earlier in the day, a Fulton County grand jury had charged Llewellyn with two counts of arson and three counts of murder. The case had stalled for eleven months until just before Christmas 1976, when a nearby county sheriff received a tip from an anonymous caller. Earlier that day, police had also arrested Robert Larry Schneider and Daniel Neal Millirons, while a nationwide alert went out for the arrest of a third hired hit man, Michael Sherwood Day.

In the next issue of the *Barb*, printed in late January, Bill warned that Llewellyn's indictment was not a guilty verdict, and that the police had arrested another suspect who later was released without charges. He reminded readers that eleven gay people were murdered in Atlanta in 1976, and that police needed cooperation in the community to help solve the crimes. In a defensive tone, Bill wrote that people who said they knew Llewellyn was guilty all along should be ashamed for allowing hit men to roam free for eleven months: "How many people are guilty of remaining silent?"[3]

In a final note, Bill handed over the editorial duties at the *Barb* to Gary W. Poe, whom he had recruited from Memphis while at a gay-media conference. The move would free up Bill's time to cruise the bars at night and to pressure club owners to take out more ads. The paper always had struggled; now it was imperiled.

Soon, in March, the murder trial against Robbie Llewellyn would begin. John Austin from the Sweet Gum Head would take the stand to testify. So would Bill. He would have to tell the court under oath that Mama Dee said she'd burn down every gay bar in town.

Robbie Llewellyn

Fulton County Courthouse, Atlanta

April 1, 1977

Robbie Llewellyn's trial began without drama at the Fulton County Courthouse in Atlanta in a flurry of paperwork and pretrial motions resolved. Then prosecutors sprang into their attack. They set out to prove that Peter Winokur's club, Mother's, had cut into business at Llewellyn's Yum Yum Tree, and, in turn, that Llewellyn had opened the Union Station disco as an attempt to cut into Mother's business. They hoped to lay out an iron-clad case against the thirty-six-year-old bar owner, whom they said had paid twenty-four-year-old Robert Larry Schneider $900 to kill Winokur.

Prosecutors also contended that Schneider had split the money three ways with the other defendants, Day and Millirons. In the course of the crime, the men had killed Keith Stamm and Floyd King, the two men found with Winokur. All three defendants were notified of a possible death sentence if convicted.

Llewellyn's defense was led by Harold Karp, the attorney who had filed the incorporation papers for the Sweet Gum Head in 1974. Karp's team told the court that Winokur had been a ruthless bar owner who let people deal drugs in his establishment. They hinted he may have torched his own bar for insurance money. Dozens had motives to kill him, they argued—and Schneider wanted to frame Llewellyn in exchange for life in prison instead of the electric chair.

Llewellyn's lawyers implicitly connected Winokur's homosexuality with the drug trade in his club. The judge allowed the jury of nine men and three women to consider whether Winokur's personal life and business dealings exposed him to people and conduct that put him in danger. They put homosexuality on trial.

///

Mama Dee had been in and out of the hospital for her nerves and for exhaustion, but made it to court to testify to try to save her son.

She had fancied herself the matron saint of some of the city's most popular gay discos and nightclubs, a counterpart to the avuncular Frank Powell. She had opened her heart long before to the cause of gay rights; she believed gay people should be able to live in public, to face the straight world as equals. She also believed they should mix in social places, so that the straight world would realize how much they had in common with their gay counterparts. She vehemently opposed gay-only spaces. How could gays, lesbians, and transgender people ever end their own discrimination if they discriminated against others? she asked.

Called to the stand to testify for her son's innocence and likely for his life, Mama Dee said her son had known Peter Winokur from Pensacola, and that they had been friendly, though the Pensacola papers had suggested their friendship had dissolved in rancor. Mama Dee insisted Robbie had nothing to gain from murdering Winokur or burning down Mother's, which was already losing customers and had been closed to remodel when the fires hit. She alleged that Winokur's murder arose from a drug deal gone bad. She said plainly that she had never told Bill Smith anything about burning down any gay bar in Atlanta.

"Now, Mrs. DeBoard, have you ever made the statement to anyone that you would either own all the gay bars in the city of Atlanta or you would burn them out?" asked the prosecutor.

"No," she said flatly from the witness stand. "I deny it."

///

The prosecution preemptively pummeled Llewellyn's defense that Winokur allowed drug use in his club from the start of the trial, with an armory of documents and a fusillade of witnesses, including former employees that said Winokur had successfully banned pill dealers from Mother's when they were caught. Prosecutors were prevented from using a key piece of evidence in court; the judge ruled that a slip of paper found in Llewellyn's office scrawled with Winokur's home address had been obtained improperly. But the prosecutors were able to show that Llewellyn had purchased airline tickets to Washington as an alibi to use after the arson and subsequent murders. He and an acquaintance had left town by plane—but returned the morning of the murders on a passenger train.

The lawyers who sought to put Robbie on death row put together a fact-filled narrative for the jury: Llewellyn cooked up the murder-for-hire scheme and manipulated Schneider, who owed him money. Schneider, Millirons, and Day had gone to Winokur's home, expecting him to be there alone. When they found three men at the house they kidnapped them all. Millirons and Day drove the victims in Winokur's Lincoln to the site where they murdered them. Schneider shot each victim in the back of the head; Millirons followed behind him for another shot at each victim, missing once.

As for Mama Dee, prosecutors said she gave Schneider $200 before the murders, and that Robbie met Schneider at city hall to give him the remaining $700.

///

The prosecution called witnesses who could establish Atlanta's gay bar scene and its economics, and give the jury some insight into how the underground world revolved. First they called John Austin, who told the court he counted between twenty and thirty gay bars in Atlanta. He noted that at the Sweet Gum Head, the number of straight people had almost turned the bar into a heterosexual haunt: "In my business I have probably 60 percent gay and 40 percent straight people now."

Austin explained that the gay-bar world was much bigger than some of the straight jurors might have expected. Gay bars had done well in the months between Peter Winokur's murder and Robbie Llewellyn's trial. He estimated that two-thirds of the clubs open in early 1976 were still open the next year, with the exception of Winokur's.

When the questions turned directly to the bars owned by Mama Dee and Robbie Llewellyn, Austin declined to call them direct competitors. "They operated on a different program than we do. Theirs is a thing—theirs is a disco bar, which specializes in dancing. We specialize in shows and female impersonation shows. . . . They appeal to the younger crowd, I would say. . . . Our clientele was an older clientele who preferred the shows."

Austin said the Sweet Gum Head had more in common with Llewellyn's Hollywood Hot.[4] Both offered drag shows, and the clubs sat diagonally across from each other at Cheshire Bridge and Lavista Road. A new club like Hollywood Hot wouldn't necessarily lure dedicated patrons from a single bar, but it could draw away a younger crowd that flocked to new places and would leave just as abruptly for the next popular spot.

Winokur and Mama Dee and Robbie competed directly with each other, Austin testified. Their bars had different audiences, but both were discos and put marketing money into luring dancers. New clubs opened all the time, Austin reported, and like new movies and new restaurants, they usually created customers rather than stole them.

When attorneys asked about violence in the bar scene, Austin revealed that he had been threatened—never directly, but he said that he'd heard rumors. They weren't serious enough to change the way he did business, but he had received them about eight to ten months prior, around the time Hollywood Hot opened.

"You ever had any problems with Robbie Llewellyn?" the counsel for the defense asked.

"No," Austin answered, and left the witness stand.

///

Bill Smith took his place next to the judge, facing the jury, and facing Robbie Llewellyn. He confirmed that he served on the Community Relations Commission and that Mayor Jackson had recently reappointed him. He identified himself as publisher and editor of the *Barb* for the past three years, and testified that he'd written a column about the case in the newspaper.

Bill had struggled with how to cover the Llewellyn murder case in the *Barb*. Robbie had done much for the gay community, from fundraisers to entertainment. Bill found it difficult to remain objective with someone so close to the community. In news stories and columns, the *Barb* portrayed the Llewellyn case as a decade-long grudge between old rivals. Bill described the vast and mostly peaceful gay nightclub scene in Atlanta as evidence that the Llewellyn murder case was not part of a larger "gay bar war."

He did not explain why more arsons occurred after Llewellyn went to prison—including one at the former Hollywood Hot, now renamed the Locker Room Disco, which Robbie's family ran for him while his trial was under way. Smith chalked up the "gay bar war" to a figment of media imagination, but the figment refused to die.

In his editorial on the Llewellyn case, Bill had chastened readers for any rush to judgment they might make. He confirmed that he had seen Mama Dee on his way into the courtroom; he repeated his allegation that, in April of 1975, he had a conversation with her about fires at gay bars.

"Do you remember what Mrs. DeBoard might have told you?"

"Yes, I do."

"What did she tell you?"

"We had a conversation that we had at her bar, The Sting. At that time, she made the comment that she would either own all of the bars or they will be burned down."

Bill assumed she referred to the gay bars in Atlanta. He said that DeBoard had been a longtime advertiser with the *Barb,* and said until that time, he wasn't aware that any bar in Atlanta had burned, though one would be consumed by fire just a few weeks after his conversation with Mama Dee. He also said that the Sting had a good crowd at the bar on the Friday night in question.

On a follow-up by the defense, Bill said that Mama Dee's threats seemed idle.

"And this conversation that you had with her at that time, it didn't alarm you, did it?"

"No, it didn't alarm me."

"And you've heard statements that would alarm you far more than that would?"

"Some of them would."

"Of course, as a newspaperman, you had the right to publish anything you wanted to, about any comments that anyone might make?"

"Yes."

Bill also noted that while Mama Dee had made her comments almost two years before, and that it was possible he had taken some out of context, he had told people about what she said shortly after they had spoken.

Bill had just one more question to answer to satisfy the prosecution. On redirect examination, prosecutors asked if he knew how many bars had burned since his encounter with DeBoard at the Sting. He said he knew of about four, including one that had burned completely, and another that had burned in part. A gay bar in Atlanta in the mid-1970s, by his estimate, stood a one-in-five chance of succumbing to fire, whether by accident or by arson.

///

As the trial proceeded, prosecutors discovered Llewellyn had repeated contact with the other defendants. Robert Larry Schneider told the jury that Llewellyn had offered more than once to make Schneider's family financially comfortable for the rest of their lives if he agreed to take responsibility for the murders.

"He said that I should say that Peter Winokur paid me for the fires at Mother's," Schneider testified.

Llewellyn had passed him evidence while both were confined to the Fulton County Jail, Schneider added. He said he had been told that if his confession got quashed, then he would walk away from the trial a free man.

///

The jury took fourteen hours to convict thirty-six-year-old Llewellyn guilty on all three counts of murder. Separate charges of arson for the fires at Mother's and for the fire at Cabaret After Dark were held for a later date.

At the sentencing hearing, the judge told jurors they were entitled to impose the death penalty. If they did, Llewellyn would be electrocuted at the state penitentiary at Reidsville, the same prison where Burt Reynolds had filmed *The Longest Yard*.

Robbie's sister Linda told the jury her brother's love for his family was strong and untouchable. She told them about his drunken visit on Mama Dee's birthday the previous year, when he'd brought a plant as a gift. "You couldn't touch [it]," she sobbed. "His love for his mother is just undefinable."

Mama Dee wept and pleaded against the death penalty. "[You] can't take his life for something like this," she sobbed uncontrollably. "Please don't take his life . . . I've got a worse temper than him. This whole thing is ridiculous."

Pauline Winokur, the mother of Peter Winokur, responded in barely suppressed rage: "HE took my son's life."

Llewellyn's three accomplices already had pleaded guilty. After Robbie's trial ended, Schneider drew two consecutive life sentences for murder, twenty years for first-degree arson, and ten years concurrent for second-degree arson. Millirons got life for robbery, and three consecutive life sentences for murder. Day got life for murder, and twenty years for first-degree arson.

After two hours of deliberation, the jury spared Robbie Llewellyn. He went directly to jail while he waited to be assigned to a prison, where he vowed he would appeal his life sentence.

Lavita Allen

The Sweet Gum Head

Spring 1977

Lavita's cheeks had grown rounded and full. She stood barely five and a half feet tall and was skinny, but by some miracle her face had swelled into a rounder, more feminine heart shape.

She kept pushing boundaries and refused to slow down her edgy performances when the audience couldn't keep up. During one show in early 1977, Lavita pulled her Streisand mirage out of the closet, after two years of doing classic songs and country tunes. She leaned backward into the classic *Funny Girl* pose, arm stretched out over her head, when a lesbian fan stuffed a dollar bill in her mouth. The crowd loved it, but Lavita threw a diva fit. She never performed as Streisand again.

Lavita wanted to be told she was beautiful. Instead they said she was funny. She thought the gay community still looked at drag queens as a joke.

"We are never taken seriously," she said. "We are considered a step above Anita Bryant in the gay world. It never ceases to amaze me how people will scream and holler and tip us money at the Gum Head, and then won't give us the time of day any other time. If you want to carry the analogy further, gay audiences can't be less annoyed with you ten minutes after you're offstage, but straight people will try their damnedest to get to go to bed with you!"

Lavita liked to make her fans uncomfortable. She fantasized about a beauty pageant where the most feminine drag queens killed themselves as they tried to prove who was the most beautiful.

"I like to watch people suffer," she said, "because I have."[5]

Rachel Wells

The Sweet Gum Head

April 5, 1977

Dollar bills traded hands. Flashbulbs popped. A transformation or three took place. Nearly every table in The Sweet Gum Head had been reserved even before the show began. People lined the walls, crammed in between the chairs and the bar. They always saw something new every week: The Sweet Gum Head didn't tolerate old acts. From the hit disco singles spun by the DJ to the drag acts that crossed its stage, the Gum Head show always was fresh and new, because fresh and new brought in tips. Anyone bored in a nightclub won't come back.

When the drag stopped, the audience got up and got down. They gyrated on the stage to the top-40 songs of 1977, a chain of irresistible earworms like the Emotions' "Best of My Love," Thelma Houston's "Don't Leave Me This Way," and Odyssey's "Native New Yorker." At the Sweet Gum Head, the disco fell somewhere between afterthought and prelude, intoxicating but ultimately a sideshow to the genuine three-ring circus of drag.

Nothing inside the Sweet Gum Head had changed since the day Rachel Wells walked into the club for the first time. Stars like Gloria Gaynor and Freda Payne belted hits onstage, others orbited in the audience, but the club itself still wore the blood-red carpet and dark paint it had acquired in the '60s. Rachel had matured; over time she had grown less bold and more professional, even as John developed more impersonations to add to his repertoire of old white ladies. They were lucrative but brought him less joy than the Amazon warriors of his past.

By 1977, Rachel performed a rote list of routine crowd-pleasers. As Streisand she mimed to "Wasn't Leaving Me the Best Thing You've Ever Done," "The Way We Were," and "Evergreen." The songs had a common thread: A big crescendo that reached an emotional peak, then recapitulated through a vulnerable, softly sung ending. In full drag, Rachel could reach out, thank the audience for listening to the drama of her life, drama both real and imagined. Songs by divas like Streisand proved to be timeless, and could be done time and time again on the circuit. When they petered out, a new character could break things up: Rachel knocked off Flo from TV's *Alice*, completed with Southern-style piled-high hair, a cigarette, a uniform, and an apron.

Rachel's image had mellowed; she'd become known as the Sweetheart of the South, and had inspired a slew of copycat drag queens. For John, the novelty had died. His best friend, Larry, told him the truth when he tried to shake things up with a semi-nude photo layout in *Cruise* magazine: "You look like a scarecrow." John didn't care. Tastefully captured from behind, the photos reminded his fans that Rachel Wells was a horny young man beneath her gowns.

Try as she might, Rachel's attempts to work on fast-paced numbers and soulful ballads were failures. As Hot Chocolate, Larry thrived on high-energy songs such as "Lovin' Is Really My Game," and John envied him. Larry could perform as Tina Turner, Patti LaBelle, or Diana Ross and pay the proper lip service to the reigning divas of the day. In the same role Rachel couldn't find the right place for her feet, or the right tone of impersonation. As a drag queen she could tear down her identity as a man and rebuild it as a beautiful woman, but she couldn't channel that same energy. Larry might not be the best choice for the swooping bleat of a Streisand ballad, but there was no way Rachel could do a Tina Turner number. She wouldn't be believed.

New performers would blanch at the chances they had to take to be noticed, but the Gum Head queens—and their high queen, Rachel—had polished their acts to perfection. They did it for themselves, but they also did it for John Austin. They trusted him, and he treated them with utter respect and honesty. As he began to open the club's doors to more political fundraisers and community events, they showed up and hustled for tips for the cause. They pushed the envelope of what a gay drag bar might do in the world, as John Austin did on April 5, 1977, when the Gum Head's door receipts went to a campaign to fight former beauty queen and Christian activist Anita Bryant's anti-gay vote in Miami.

///

Done up like Katharine Hepburn, Rachel took long drags off her usual Winston cigarette, backstage at the Miss Gay South pageant in Dallas in June, when a stranger approached her and told her something she hadn't thought of.

"Your name precedes your act," the stranger said.

Rachel had wanted to win a major pageant for years. Long ago she had won Miss Gay Atlanta, and though she'd competed for it, Miss Gay America had eluded her. "I'll just keep on performing as long as the face holds out," she sighed to reporters while she plotted a path through the 1977 pageant season, from Florida to Texas to Georgia, then finally to Miss Gay America.[6]

First, she returned to Miami for the Miss Florida contest in

May. No small affair, the pageant took up the 2,000-seat Grand Ballroom in the fabulous Fontainebleau Hotel, where Rachel had won the title of Miss David 1974. Hot Chocolate had won the year before, and Rachel dreamed that her friend would crown her in turn. Returning to Florida, Rachel performed as Katharine Hepburn in the talent competition. Huge pictures of Rachel's personae lit up behind her onstage: Raquel Welch, Carol Channing, Jesus, and one in boy drag, as John. In the swimsuit competition, a black 1950s-style suit set him off against a Coke-bottlecap background. In evening wear, Rachel shimmered in an off-the-shoulder black-and-silver gown. It was good enough for first runner-up, a slim loss by two points to Dana Manchester.

At the Miss Gay South pageant in Texas, she'd brought an old-school gown invested with high Hollywood glamour, and planned to pull out one of her regular winning characters for the talent competition. As she prepared backstage, the stranger had sent her down a different mental alley from the one she usually cruised before her performances.

Your name precedes your act.

She played it over and over again, even after she thanked him and moved on. What exactly had he meant by that? Was she now old news on the drag circuit, after just six years? Was she coasting on her past wins and padding out her act? She had only a moment to put it out of her mind before she went onstage.

Her talent-show act as Katharine Hepburn had been good; her evening gown looked fine. It wasn't Rachel Wells's worst effort, but it was far from her best. She took second place, her third second-place finish in a row, but it was enough to qualify for the Miss Gay America 1977 pageant that September in St. Louis.

Anita Bryant

Miami, Florida

June 7, 1977

A crowd cheered and praised their beauty queen on the evening of June 7, 1977, in a south Florida ballroom where Christian music piped into an assembly gathered in the name of hate. Anita Bryant had picked a fight with the gay-rights movement and a gay-rights ordinance in her hometown of Miami, and she had won.

The ordinance, passed on January 18, 1977, simply said that there "shall be no discrimination because of a person's affectional or sexual preference." The local rule would affect fewer than a quarter-million of the region's 1.5 million residents.

"This law will have the same effect for us that it had for blacks," Robert Basker, director of Dade Coalition for Human Rights said. "It's a matter of our feeling pride in ourselves, rather than feeling subjugated."[7]

The ordinance had passed on a 6-3 vote, and commissioners hadn't expected the blowback: fundraisers, rallies, demonstrations, even a fire bombing of a car belonging to a gay-rights advocate. Thirty-seven-year-old Bryant, a mother of four and second runner-up in the 1959 Miss America pageant, founded the group Save Our Children, which raised money to fight the measure.

"Gays cannot reproduce, so they have to recruit," she warned. Overnight, Bryant became the public face of the anti-equality movement.[8]

In her own Baptist circles, Bryant's unwavering stance drew stares and whispers. The concept of gayness being a disease had begun to dissipate, and fewer people believed gay people could be "cured." Conversion therapy by drugs or electric shock had begun to fall out of favor.[9] A firm minority of Baptists believed gay rights were civil rights.

The ordinance had strong backing outside Florida. Poet Rod McKuen called Bryant a "Ginny Orangeseed," spreading bigotry over the land, and said she was dangerous. Jane Fonda simply wore a T-shirt: ANITA BRYANT'S HUSBAND IS A HOMO SAPIEN! Churches in Atlanta raised $4,000 in the fight against Bryant. But Bryant and her followers quickly amassed more than 50,000 signatures against the measure, which commanded the county to either repeal it or to put it on a special June 7 referendum.

Almost half the county's voters had shown up to vote. Some 202,319 people voted against civil rights for gays and lesbians in Dade County, while 89,562 cast votes for equality. By a 2-1 margin, Dade County voters dumped the ordinance.

Bryant told a victory party that "with God's continued help we will prevail in our fight to repeal similar laws throughout the nation which attempt to legitimize a lifestyle that is both perverse and dangerous to the sanctity of the family, dangerous to our children, dangerous to our freedom of religion and freedom of choice, dangerous to our survival as 'one nation, under God.'"

A gathering of gay-rights allies heard former Air Force sergeant Leonard Matlovich voice their disappointment. "When you walk out of here tonight," he said, "you go out of here with your heads high and your shoulders back and you be proud you're gay and don't let anyone put you down." The crowd raised their hands and joined for yet another necessary chorus of "We Shall Overcome." Bryant had dared to use the anthem of freedom, in a perversion of its message of equality.

Bill Smith was not surprised by the outcome. He praised Bryant for identifying herself as a bigot. In a letter to the *Atlanta Constitution*, he noted that gay bar patrons were swearing off the orange juice that mixed in some of their favorite drinks. He professed to know of no national boycott of Bryant or her sponsor, the Florida Citrus Commission, but tried to lead others to the idea: "I personally can do without any Florida citrus products use," Bill wrote, "as long as the Florida Citrus Commission retains a person as its spokesperson who wishes to deny the basic rights to gay people that are enjoyed by non-gay citizens."

The backlash against Bryant had begun. Bryant skipped a summer appearance in Atlanta that would have honored her as "America's Greatest American." Protesters turned out anyway in the hundreds, and picketed her in absentia with posters that asked, without irony, "Is Anita Hitler in Drag?"[10]

Mayor Maynard Jackson

Gay Pride, Atlanta

June 1977

"*Democracy not theocracy!*" the crowd chanted as they were led by a flag-waving Abraham Lincoln wearing an avuncular sweater over his clownish garb, despite the extreme heat.

Each summer, Atlanta's Pride organizers poured months of work into the annual protest. Each year, Pride drew its usual few hundred protesters. The movement inched forward, in fits and starts, but in 1977 organizers hoped for much more.

Maynard Jackson had fanned the flames of revolution when he proclaimed Gay Pride Day in 1976. The Pride protest of 1977 would test his ability to overcome hostility to his stance.

Pride organizers Vic Host and Linda Regnier had written to Jackson on May 5, 1977, to ask that he proclaim June 25 as Gay Pride Day, as he had done the year before. Other "Days" on the calendar, they noted, included nationally important events such as Atlanta Braves Day, Phil Donahue Day, Foot Health Day, Ramblin' Raft Day, Dixie Dregs Day, and Respect for Law Week.

But Jackson had already suffered a year of grinding blowback from every direction, including pastors and politicians. He had dared to put gay equality on the same shelf as civil rights, and he paid for it in hundreds of letters of protest and public calls for his resignation. While police and gay leaders met to talk about increased violence around gay bars and haunts, groups such as the Citizens for a Decent Atlanta said gays had no right to destroy the heterosexual family.

The group published full-page screeds in the local paper, and a research scientist from Dunwoody, forty-three-year-old Jerry Nims, spoke out on behalf of the anti-gay group. Nims had two young children and a home in the suburbs, and watched the rise of gay life in the city with alarm. He believed in God and the devil and the Bible, in morality and immorality, right and wrong. Nims said he didn't oppose anyone's right to speak out, but he believed the gay activists were bent on destroying the most basic unit of society, that of the family. Nims's position was identical to that of Anita Bryant.

When it came time to craft his 1977 proclamation for Pride, Mayor Jackson blinked, and sought out some alternative to "Gay Pride Day" that the gay civil-rights community could accept. Memos flew around city hall, insisting that the Community Relations Commission needed to be a part of any 1977 Pride declaration, so that the newly finessed designation "Civil Liberties Days" wouldn't leave a sour taste. The final proclamation did not mention Pride specifically, but included sexual orientation on its list of the protected rights.

The Citizens for a Decent Atlanta said in a statement that Jackson had taken a "statesmanlike position" and had resisted the pressure applied by a "small group of militant moral anarchists."

"That's better than calling it Gay Pride Day," said Robert C.

Beard, a fifty-seven-year-old taxi driver in the city. "If he'd called it that again it would have shown that he condoned being gay and also being proud to be gay. The Mayor is a smart politician."

Gay leaders said Jackson had bowed to pressure from the anti-gay crusaders. "What's militant about fighting for every-day human rights?" Vic Host of the Gay Rights Alliance asked. However, he let Jackson off the hook and said gay groups hadn't pressed the mayor on the declaration, and played off the change in wording as a minor adjustment to the course of progress. "Gay Pride Day and Gay Pride Week don't depend on one man's proc-lamation. We've got a gay community to build and we don't have time to nitpick."

"The mayor is facing an election year and I think he's avoiding controversy," said Linda Regnier, a co-founder of the Gay Rights Alliance and one of the most politically active women in Atlanta. "But there's no way he can put his foot half in and half out on the issue of civil rights."

Perhaps as a concession, and not without more risk to his reelection campaign, Mayor Maynard Jackson shook the hands of gay civil-rights protesters along Peachtree Street. As crowds swelled and pulsed on Atlanta's main drag, Jackson saw firsthand how the Bryant controversy had shifted the discussion. Bryant and Dade had done what organizers couldn't do by word of mouth or flyers: More than 1,200 people lifted their hands and held post-ers scrawled with poignant biblical allusions: "Jesus died for my sins, not my sexuality!"

Some marchers grew upset and yelled at TV cameras when they focused on the few drag queens interspersed among the con-ventional protesters. "That's a stereotype," they said. "We're not all like that."

The parade passed peacefully and ended in Piedmont Park with more than the usual swell of pride. Lesbians rallied. Gay Christians and Socialists marched next to each other. To anyone who had never left the closet, outside the furtive dark world of the gay clubs, the Pride march showed the community as expansive and diverse.

Jackson evaded the tougher questions about an antidiscrimination ordinance of Atlanta's own, at least for the moment. He gave protesters some continued faith in him, though many were already disgruntled by the slow pace of progress. His presence alone felt like victory, no matter how slight. And there would be no going back.

"Once you've tasted freedom," one marcher said, "a diet of oppression will make you vomit."[11]

Bill Smith

Atlanta

Summer 1977

The phone clanged to life one summer evening in 1977, as Bill lay in bed, confined there for two weeks of "doctor-ordered exile," a salve for his increasingly profound bouts of anxiety and depression. After he had taken over control of the *Barb*, Bill battled the paper's beleaguered balance sheet. It kept eating more and more money, and the stress led Bill to seek medical help in the form of a trio of drugs: a sleeping pill, a tranquilizer, and Preludin, a synthetic methamphetamine used to quell anxiety, and abused for its euphoric and pro-sexual effects.

He had hired Gary Poe, a reporter from Memphis, to come to Atlanta and take over the *Barb*'s daily operations. Poe arrived and moved into the house on Peachtree Place in time to edit the June issue. Bill would give him uppers so they could stay up all night to finish the paper, then offered him free passes to the Club South baths, where they could relax for a few hours until coming back home to sleep. Bill and Gary had sex a few times, but they never developed a deeper relationship. Still, Bill was fun, and had a bawdy sense of humor Gary loved.

Gary assumed Bill had the formula that would allow a gay newspaper to survive, but realized soon enough that Bill didn't. He had not told Gary about the escort agency before Gary moved to Atlanta. Gary realized he had been naïve when he questioned him, and believed Bill when he told him a pack of lies: "If we do this," Bill told him, "we'll be able to keep publishing the paper. If we don't, we won't."

Gary took note of the slew of people who were constantly coming and going from the house and worried. If Bill had been dealing drugs, it wouldn't have surprised Gary.

Bill had several boyfriends—all escorts. But Gary saw him as physically weak and emotionally distant, and thought he couldn't handle all of his ambitions or appetites. Bill was in bad health; Gary never saw him use needle drugs, but he assumed Bill had hepatitis. Bill drank a lot too. He never talked about what his condition was or about his hospital stays. Gary watched Bill deteriorate quickly in the short time they knew each other.[12]

Bill's anxiety had sentenced him to bedrest. When Robbie Llewellyn called, he woke Bill from already irregular sleep. Bill hadn't spoken to him since before the arrest, but Robbie sounded hopeful that he would be freed on appeal.

Bill didn't share his optimism. He listened to Llewellyn talk as if nothing had happened. He worried that, maybe, the jury had been wrong. Imprisoned in his own room, under a doctor's order, he imagined how Robbie's confinement felt, how much it felt like his own. Cruel.

Bill fell back asleep finally at dawn, no longer tired but still overcome with emotion.

Rachel Wells

The Sweet Gum Head

August 1977

The sound system at the Sweet Gum Head blared before the pageant began with the pomp du jour, Meco's disco-vamped overture to *Star Wars,* a silly note of pure camp that ran up the Billboard charts in the summer of 1977 in tandem with the epic that had inspired it. From the moment it opened on thousands of movie screens in May of 1977, the film—an entertaining yarn about an underground band of freaks and rebels trying to break through in the name of justice—had infiltrated every extension of pop culture, from lunchboxes to network-TV comedy specials.

"*Star Wars* may not be the best movie of the season, but it's outgrossing everything since *Jaws,*" read the *Barb's* review. "It's just for fun, comic-book science fiction with some of the best special effects ever. Gay men can choose between boyish Mark Hamill and manly Harrison Ford—they're both hunks. And if you're of a scientific bent, you can try to figure out how the robots, Artoo-Detoo and See-Threepio, do it—they're obviously lovers."[13]

///

In Greek mythology, Zeus held a banquet to celebrate the marriage of Thetis and Peleus, who would become the parents of Achilles. Zeus didn't invite Eris, the goddess of discord. She showed up anyway, and brought a golden apple inscribed with a short message: "for the fairest one." Three goddesses laid claim to the fruit—Athena, Aphrodite, and Zeus's wife, Hera—and clamored for Zeus to choose which of them should win it.

A smart god, Zeus skirted the decision of who was most beautiful, and left it to a prince, Paris, to decide. Athena promised Paris wisdom in peace and in battle; Hera offered him Asia and Europe. Aphrodite promised him the hand of Helen—the most beautiful woman alive—in marriage, although she already was married to Menelaus, the king of Sparta. When Paris chose Aphrodite and eloped with Helen, Menelaus gathered other Greek city-states together to fight for her return, which launched the Trojan War.

In the Gum Head, the Miss Gay Georgia pageant would borrow heavily from the ancients, only it would give the gods more female faces from which to choose: Rachel Wells, Hot Chocolate, even other performers from around the state, like Savannah's Lady Chablis.

Dressed as Zeus, Frank Powell was carried by six athletic young men in a sedan chair to the judges' table. The *Star Wars* soundtrack that thumped from the speakers collided with the Greek mythology theme in nearly incomprehensible fashion, but when it all was infused with alcohol it just barely made sense.

The Gum Head gods marched in procession, to award a golden apple from their made-up Olympus to the most beautiful drag queen of all. They took their rightful place in the heavens, which at the seedy Cheshire Bridge club meant a seat somewhere within easy reach of the bar. Frank, Billy Jones, and the rest of the judges carried themselves like a bunch of drunken idiots. It was a true bacchanal.

Lily White made the trip over from the Locker Room, on the shoulders of handsome male dancer R. C. Cola, who wore clusters of grapes and not much more. A veteran of hundreds of trips on acid, Lily refused to live up to her stage name—she excoriated everything the world sanitized for its own consumption. She wore rags and soiled hand-me-downs, pulled fake clumps of hair from her head when she performed Patsy Cline's "Crazy," and dove deep into the eccentric, proto-horror aspect of drag, keen to explore the irony that surrounded her in the form of pageant queens and femininity. Other drag performers laughed at her, considered her a joke, and thought her drag lampooned theirs. She called bullshit and decided her own style of drag was more important than being loved.

Twenty-three contestants in all paraded before the judges and the 1976 winner, Vicki Lawrence. Rachel worked on her evening gown until the minute the movie's theme trumpeted the room to attention. She shook out a frosted shag Farrah Fawcett wig one more time and preened her blizzard of chiffon, in orange and black.

For sportswear, Rachel wore a mid-leg fur coat that covered a stunning red-and-white swimsuit, a shock even to a crowd that had seen her perfected feminine figure hundreds of times. Lily White emerged in bondage ropes and chains, the closest thing to a sport she enjoyed. Hot Chocolate walked the runway in a safari suit, escorted by a male companion. A New Orleans queen, Zette, confused everyone with a black bag on her head and a space suit on her body.

Contestants brought their best acts to the talent competition. One vamped to a medley of "Purlie," "Sweet Georgia Brown," and "Hello, Dolly." Three queens danced to songs from *A Chorus Line*. Heather Fontaine performed her famously on-point impression of Marilyn Monroe. Tina Devore brought out "This Is My Life" in full Shirley Bassey drag. Hot Chocolate brought out four backup dancers dressed as stereotyped African natives; they chained her to a tree and King Kong appeared behind her. The dancers came back to join her in "Lovin' Is Really My Game," then left her to Kong's grasp as he carried her off. Others played marionettes and most hogged stage time, except for Lily, who performed a one-minute-long number called "Drop Dead."

Rachel appeared onstage as a voice-of-God narrator told the crowd her real name, John Greenwell. She performed for the talent competition as Miss Hepburn. The spotlights went up as they had before, when Rachel had played Raquel, Carol, and Jesus, on the very same stage.

Mythology cast Aphrodite as the winner of her beauty pageant. At the Sweet Gum Head, Lily White had been disqualified when she stepped on the stage in a bloodstained dress. Hot Chocolate went home with first runner-up. Rachel Wells, the goddess whose beauty had stunned all of Atlanta from the moment she emerged from John Greenwell, took home the golden apple.

Bill Smith

Somewhere on I-85

August 1977

"I don't think the bedroom will work out," Bill confided to Diane about his latest lover, on parchment paper embossed with his name in fat brown lowercase type. "He is quite dominate [*sic*] in bed and I like versatility, trying to get him to flip over is a flop and me flipping other people seems to be a flop too."[14]

Bill needed a break in the summer of 1977. He traveled more and enjoyed it less, but the *Barb* needed more advertisers, though none had abandoned him since he had testified in the Robbie Llewellyn trial in March. He still had the escorts who sold their bodies through his Youngman agency, but his needs were more than just sexual.

In June, Bill had been dismissed from the National Gay Task Force when he missed two directors' meetings in New York City. He had replaced his role on the NGTF with a spot on the board of the ACLU of Georgia, at the head of its Equality Committee— but the ACLU's finances were as dire as those of the *Barb*. He still sat on the failing Community Relations Commission, which one councilman called a $100,000 waste before he demanded it be abolished. The city was headed for financial ruin, Councilman

George Cotsakis said, and it couldn't afford a do-nothing commission's expenses.

So while the latest issue of the *Barb* warned readers about the fake Quaaludes making their way through the city and their fatal potential if the counterfeit pills were mixed with alcohol, and while Bill promised his readers that the newspaper soon would be available twice a month, he ran away from home.

He took off on a road trip with a friend to Knoxville, to Greenville, to Columbia and Nashville. They took pictures of drag queens at Ye Olde Playhouse, and sat around drinking and singing dirty songs. In Montgomery, they recruited handsome young men as potential cover models for the newspaper but got nowhere, and spent the night shooting the shit with the owner of the gay-friendly Forum adult bookstore, which carried the *Advocate* and *Blue Boy* and the *Barb*. They ate 89-cent microwaved sub sandwiches from a 7-Eleven for dinner, and stopped en route to cruise a Union 76 truck stop near the Montgomery end of Interstate 85, trading smiles with a blond busboy who showed off his muscles and a large bulge in his pants. It was wholesome fun for Bill to flirt with the young man behind the counter at a gas station in rural Alabama. It let the young man know he was not alone.

On the second leg of his trip, Bill traveled south to Florida, to the Parliament House motel in Orlando, where men circulated for sex throughout the night; to Pensacola, where the Red Garter Lounge had a game room upstairs and a show bar on the main level—and where Gene, a twenty-four-year-old waiter, agreed to pose on the *Barb*'s cover; on to Biloxi and New Orleans, where a charming Creole cottage in the Bywater had been converted to the Country Club, where the pool was less popular than the anything-goes cabanas tucked discreetly among the elephant ears and banana palms; then on a whirlwind through Memphis to Nashville, where Charlie Brown headlined the Cabaret's shows, and finally to Chattanooga. The fast-paced tour that took his car from oasis to oasis, Bill confessed, left him flat on his back.

He had reversed the migration that so many young gays and lesbians had undertaken when they left the rural South for Atlanta. Bill held out hope that one day they wouldn't have to leave home—he wanted the rural world outside of places like Atlanta to see the benefit of equality, but admitted it still felt strange and unsafe to leave his bubble. "When you're here in town and running around in your Anita Bryant T-shirt, no one looks and points a finger at you," he told the *New York Times*. "But just go 10 miles outside the city limit to some of those smaller towns and you are treated like a freak."[15]

He wanted those young gays and lesbians to feel the same freedom he had felt almost a decade before when he came out. "I remember working as a teenager in an office where the girls would invite me to parties. They'd ask me what I did over the weekend and I'd lie. I had to make up stories about going to straight night clubs instead of telling them that I went to the Miss Gay Atlanta pageant the night before," he recalled. "It was . . . a relief when I discovered the gay nightclub scene and saw that, my God, I'm not alone. There are thousands of us."[16]

He had traded his usual suit and tie for jeans and a T-shirt, but Atlanta followed him around the South. The *Barb* had given him license to go outside and preach the gospel of freedom to a world that mostly would not have it. He would still have to return and face dire decisions about his business and his life, when what he wanted to do was have more sex and take more speed. The specter of Atlanta cut through his mind while he caroused from bar to bar, while he connected the friendly waypoints on the map, while he tried to plot a way out of the myriad predicaments that darkened his inevitable return.

Rachel Wells

Machinists' Hall, St. Louis, Missouri

September 3, 1977

The Machinists' Hall near St. Louis repelled beauty, and it was loud. The anonymous redbrick two-story building sat in the acoustic shadow of the St. Louis airport, far from the graceful Gateway Arch near the river or the charming horse-drawn carriages at Laclede's Landing. It housed union offices for machinists and aerospace workers, and made money on banquets and conventions on the side.

In September 1977, the hall hosted the biggest drag pageant in America to date. Drag still was illegal in the city of St. Louis, so the pageant had to find the best venue it could outside city limits. Organizers strung blue crepe paper as a backdrop, went without stage lights, and fashioned a short runway leading to the small stage. The low-budget surroundings bucked the trend of more expensively produced and more lavish drag pageants that had become the norm. In the early days most pageants ran for one night, with evening gown, talent, and interview segments that led to a finale. Miss Gay America required contestants to have a win or second-place finish in a preliminary contest to even compete, and the pageant itself could sprawl over a few days between rounds of interviews, in and out of drag, and the inevitable pearl-clutching finale.

The 1977 Miss Gay America pageant had several stages, with preliminaries that winnowed the field of thirty-three to ten. Rachel had her reputation to precede her, but the Miss Gay America pageant built itself around overachievers. Rachel represented the Sweet Gum Head. Lisa King, another Gum Head regular, had entered. Hot Chocolate had been sponsored by the Potpourri, a local club in St. Louis, and she brought her best pageant game with a talent act built around her favorite disco song of the day, "Lovin' Is Really My Game."

"Lovin'" is one of the underrated gems of the disco era. Released in 1977 by Detroit-based Brainstorm, the song had been written by lead singer Belita Woods and coauthor Trenita Womack. *Billboard* called it the best heavy disco song of 1977; it reached number 14 on the charts and would be covered half a dozen times, including versions by Parliament's Betty Wright and disco queen Sylvester.

Powered by a thumping beat, "Lovin'" sounds like an answer to Marvin Gaye's "Got to Give It Up, Pt. 1." Both are songs about wallflowers who profess their inner discomfort. Gaye sings about his shyness, and about overcoming it. In "Lovin'," Woods takes a similar route to satisfaction: *I got my way of groovin'/ Sittin' down right in my seat,* she sings, and promises there's better fun if her crush follows her home. The song ends in an optimistic refrain and keyboard notes that wash over it like gentle rain. Woods famously delivered the song on Don Cornelius's *Soul Train* in a satin halter and harem pants.

Hot Chocolate first heard the track in San Francisco night-clubs, where she wandered with her sometimes roommate and romantic companion Sylvester. She jerked the St. Louis pageant crowd to life when she appeared onstage for the first few bars of the song dressed as a gorilla. She towered over the crowd in furry regalia, accompanied by four backup dancers dressed as African tribesmen. She pantomimed to the song, then stood while they ripped the suit off her to reveal a breathlessly skimpy costume. "Lovin'" had become her pageant staple, and it was a proven winner, much like Rachel's Katharine Hepburn.

Rachel had repurposed her fur coat and bathing suit from Miss Gay Georgia, and won $250 for her Hepburn in the talent competition, but during the evening-wear competition her dress caught on her shoe and awkwardly pulled it lower with each step down the runway. Hot Chocolate wore a beige Yves St. Laurent ensemble to a standing ovation, though judges gave the evening-wear nod to another performer with a less "New York" look. Together with Lisa King, all of the Gum Head girls made it through to the finals.

None of them won. Hot Chocolate took home $2,000 in runner-up prizes, but Jimi Dee, a crowd favorite who had performed at the Gum Head, turned in a flawless Diana Ross medley of "Smile" and "Send in the Clowns" to win the title of Miss Gay America 1977. Rachel watched and admired Jimi's act and realized what it would take to become Miss Gay America: perfection, something she had always demanded of herself, something in which John Greenwell always felt he had fallen short.

John Greenwell

The Sweet Gum Head

September 15, 1977

Where is she? She's supposed to be here by now, John thought as he looked out on the crowd for a familiar face. His own face had been painted to resemble Carol Channing, a character he loved to perform. The impersonation came easy, with his tall and lanky frame and with his wild characterization. John had no problem changing from one character to the next once he inhabited the character of Rachel Wells herself. Once John was over the central conflict of being gay—telling the people closest to you, "I'm not who you think I am"—changing his identity was simple.

His Carol Channing impression would be one of a half dozen

he staged during his first special at the Sweet Gum Head. John had been experimenting with how long he could be onstage before people got bored. He found he was one of the few who could tackle an entire show alone, as he rotated through all his crowd-pleasing impersonations. As he pulled together the series of looks and songs for the special in September 1977, dubbed *Faces,* he decided to invite his mother, who flew to Atlanta to see her son in drag for the first time.

///

John's mother had responded calmly when he called her in late 1972, and came out from two hundred miles away. She had told John just to make her proud of him. She didn't always understand what he did or why, but when John needed help, his mother knew it. She never preached to him, even when his father would smirk at him or cut him to the quick with insults.

John decided that if his family and friends couldn't accept that he was the most famous female impersonator in Atlanta, or a gay man, or just a persnickety man who lived with two other men in an impromptu nest in a gay neighborhood, well, then that would be on them. He didn't have to hide anything, now that his father had passed, or even when he was alive. Now he had his mother on his side once again, completely. He had set it all in motion when he left Alabama in 1971, and it had turned out all right, mostly.

At some point his mother began to sew for him. She'd call from home and let him know his dresses were ready.

"Costumes," he chided her lightly. "They're costumes, Mother."

///

But his mother wasn't there yet. Her flight had been delayed, and it was ten p.m., time for the show to start. Rachel dragged out the intros as long as she could, and the crowd played along for a bit. The club's lower level was full, and for a weeknight that was good, but she didn't look upstairs to see if it was packed. The show would already be long, and one thing she'd learned was to leave the audience wanting more.

Oh well, she thought. The show must go on.

The opening notes of "Hello, Dolly" came from the speakers. Rachel looked up—and his mother, Dolly, had taken her seat at a table, up in front, stage right. His throat tightened at the bizarre note of happiness that washed over him. He tried to get a look at his mother and her reaction while staying in character. John just wanted her to see that he was a performer, that he was portraying characters, that he wasn't just putting on a dress.

John's mother was in her late forties, and not a social butterfly. She was stoic. She had her opinions, but in public she could keep them to herself, and keep mostly to herself.

As Rachel was introduced to the audience, the cheers lit up her mother's face. She smiled. Then Dolly joined the crowd in applause. Rachel's friends gave her a dollar and ushered her up to tip Rachel. When she did, they embraced, and she laughed and clapped through the entire show.

It was almost midnight when they got back to the apartment across the street, and Dolly was tired from flying. First John put her to bed, then he put Carol Channing to bed, then finally, exhausted from putting the two halves of his life back together, he put Rachel Wells to bed for yet another night.

Mayor Maynard Jackson

40 Peachtree Place, Atlanta

October 5, 1977

During the mayoral election year of 1977, the *Barb* filled its pages with election coverage that contrasted less sharply than it might have with stories from local drag contests. Elections were a kind of beauty pageant anyway, a way to try to judge the inner beauty of a person, their soul, and their intentions, from beneath their veneer of looks and words.

Bill had taken issue with Mayor Jackson since the Civil Liberties Day proclamation. As the mayor prepared his reelection fight, Bill decided that Jackson hadn't come through with his promises. He toned down his support for Jackson. He began to rebel.

All acts of rebellion are personal. So are all acts of politics.

Maynard Jackson had eased into his role as Atlanta's chief booster. His comfort in acting in his new role took dramatic form: He proudly took membership in the Screen Actors Guild, and played a preacher in *Greased Lightning*, with Richard Pryor and Julian Bond. He married a second time, to Valerie Richardson. He lost a tremendous amount of weight, some 122 pounds in the course of little over a year, by fasting on alternate days and by cutting out sweets and starches. At 193 pounds as 1977's Election Night approached, the six-foot-two Jackson looked lean and ready to power through another term, versus the 315-pound man who had taken office as mayor in 1973. "It's been painful, rewarding and joyful," he noted, "in that order."[17]

In the weeks that led up to the election, Jackson had begun to backtrack on what the gay community considered a promise. As vice mayor in 1973, Jackson had told crowds in a rally in Winn Park that he supported gay rights to their fullest, that he would back gay-rights legislation. By the year of his mayoral reelection campaign, the legislation still had not been passed. Would he support gay rights in his second term? "I'd certainly consider the idea," he hedged, "then it would depend on what I decided after considering it."[18]

Bill was at a loss to explain the mayor's actions. "It seems peculiar that a man who refused to withdraw a Gay Pride Day proclamation in the face of strong opposition would not be willing to say publicly that he would support a gay rights ordinance at this point in time."[19]

Jackson didn't need the endorsement of Bill, the *Barb*, or even the gay community as a whole. Polls showed he would be unbeatable at the ballot box, that he had a strong enough majority to avoid even a run-off election, despite a crowded field of hopefuls. Jackson never showed up to a candidate forum held at the Sweet Gum Head on September 12, where First Tuesday organizer Gil Robison was sprayed with a fire extinguisher in the parking lot by a group of anti-gay hecklers. Robison reported the incident to the police and was greeted with a shrug and told nothing would happen, even though he'd taken down license-plate numbers as the thugs ran away. He had to pressure the police to even take a report, since attacks such as those happened to gay people on Cheshire Bridge Road all the time.

Robison's First Tuesday group had begun to take the steps that Bill hadn't, as he lost interest in the fundamentals of politics. They held voter-registration drives and held public forums for candidates. Bill had talked about working with First Tuesday on election strategies and organization but never followed through with any of it.

He did the only thing he felt he could do as a commissioner and as the publisher of the city's gay newspaper: He endorsed candidate Emma Darnell. She had worked for Jackson until the mayor fired her. She appeared at the Sweet Gum Head and received several rounds of applause from the crowd that greeted Jackson's name with scattered hisses and no applause. Darnell made a promise to enact a gay-rights ordinance in the city of Atlanta.

Jackson would not be denied a second term. On October 5, 1977, he won reelection by a resounding margin, taking 63.6 percent of the vote. Emma Darnell got 4.1 percent. Almost immediately the whispers began: Jackson, they said, would not serve out his term. He might run for Senate.

"The world's next great city has come of age," Jackson said in his victory speech, as he promised to continue to "rock the boat" for social justice.[20]

Bill Smith

40 Peachtree Place, Atlanta

Fall 1977

"Sometimes I wonder what I'm doing in this business," Gary Poe had written in the September 15, 1977, edition of the *Barb*. "What with long hours, low pay, and responsibilities that you just can't ever seem to get away from . . . it's enough to drive you to drink . . . and often does."

The gay-rights movement had hit a nadir after Anita Bryant's victory in Florida. It was an age of apathy, one in which pot and poppers and booze and discos were fulfilling enough for some. "Concerns about acceptance and discrimination seem like tired old concepts from the Sixties," Poe wrote, heavy with irony. "The days of entrapment and outright harassment seem as distant as the concentration camps of Hitler. Those things couldn't happen today!"

The victories of the gay community seemed to be unraveling, and so was the newspaper. The *Barb*'s expenses continued to rise more quickly than its ad sales. Even Youngman couldn't generate enough to overcome the drain. Bill portrayed himself as the successful publisher and city advocate wherever and whenever he could; he spoke to the *Washington Post* about Supreme Court decisions and offered his thoughts to Atlanta's city leaders. He wanted others to believe what he wanted to believe about himself. Friends never knew the extent of his difficulties, or where he made the money to cover the rent, or exactly where the money from the escort agency went. Bill barely let on that the paper had failed.

In the fall of 1977, Bill came back from his trip across the South without having raised enough ad revenue, and printed the final issue of the paper. It featured two naked men walking away from the camera. The final masthead read, "Published over the past four years by a dedicated staff of volunteers. We take full responsibility for its successes and its failures." He even thanked those long gone from the masthead, including Richard Evans Lee.

"Things lost, like things broken," Bill had written to Diane years before, "are never the same."[21] In late 1977, Bill shut down the *Barb*.

1978

///

FUCK ANITA BRYANT

John Greenwell

Sweet Gum Head

February 1978

John had to be lured to the dance floor, when Larry could even get him out of the Sweet Gum Head's dressing rooms, that is—except, of course, for performances. John kept to the small room he and Satyn had crammed with their elegant gowns and their boxes of blush and eyeliner and their curled, twirled, frizzed, braided, waved, weaved, and teased wigs. He'd never dance in drag; Rachel's explosive hair would never survive a dance-floor crowd. People might try to offer tips. Or worse, they wouldn't.

When he did emerge from the dressing room completely out of costume, John usually left quietly and went straight home across the street. That night, Larry nudged him to dance, to have fun, while he visited. Larry had come to Atlanta from Texas, where he'd moved in 1977 for a permanent gig at a gay club called the Old Plantation. When he landed, he promptly took over the third bedroom in John's apartment. Whenever he visited, it was as if a tornado touched down and swept everyone up in a thrilling drama of his own creation. It didn't happen often enough.

John relented, and when he was finished with Rachel for the evening, he and Larry went out in their boy drag, washed clean of the layers of makeup that took hours to apply, in tight jeans and shirts, with the excited sighs that switched the workday off and turned on the night. They blended in discreetly with the stream of disco pouring from expensive turntables and speakers, a constant mix of "Night Fever" and "If I Can't Have You" and "More Than a Woman." For a moment the latest number-one disco hit brought close friends even closer together. Then Larry began to jerk.

///

In nearly every nightclub in Atlanta, speakers throbbed with a steady 4/4 beat, the sizzle of a high hat, the burble of a bass and the mutter of a Moog, with breathy staccato male voices vaulted into female registers, balanced precipitously on the edge of femininity. *Stayin' alive, stayin' alive.* The words poured out everywhere in the spring of 1978, from hair-salon speakers, FM car stereos, portable beach radios, from the DJ booth at the Sweet Gum Head.

Disco had percolated to the surface of pop from the underground dance clubs of the early 1970s. The movie *Saturday Night Fever* cemented it as the common party language of the decade. Disco had already become an antidote for the malaise of the '70s when the made-up Brooklyn nightclub fantasy of British journalist Nik Cohn, "Tribal Rites of the New Saturday Night," appeared in *New York Magazine* in 1976. The story translated neatly into a gritty take on the phenomenon and on a culture where struggle was second nature when the movie debuted in December of 1977. John Travolta danced in a searing portrayal of a vibrant life while he mourned the death of his partner, the actress Diana Hyland, twisting his body and contorting it into classical and avant-garde poses during the grueling shoots of ruthlessly rehearsed routines backed by Boz Scaggs and Stevie Wonder songs, since the film's soundtrack wasn't yet finished.

The soundtrack, so inextricably wedded with the film's narrative arc, was conceived in a whole other world—in a suburb of Paris, where the Bee Gees had begun to flesh out what was to have been their next album. When they agreed to tackle the movie soundtrack, they meshed a batch of songs already in progress with a haphazardly brief outline of the movie, and recorded much of it in a single weekend in a French chateau. The brothers

Gibb swamped their melodies in glossy chords and synthesizers and sank it in gilded falsetto amber, preserving their version of disco as one of the art form's reference samples for all time.

Saturday Night Fever became a blockbuster in theaters, and the soundtrack exploded as well. By 1978 more than 40,000 discos kept turntables spinning with the Bee Gees, Donna Summer, Tavares, and Andy Gibb: straight discos, gay discos, elegant discos, Holiday Inn discos and ones in abandoned churches. Disco had revived a flagging music industry, selling more than 150 million tapes and records that year. It spawned a $6 billion industry that sold everything from disco-themed travel to dog clothes.

Disco proved an irresistible temptation for anyone who could learn a few dance steps. For a few moments, they could become a star, backed by the pulsing beat of a 12-inch remix of the latest hit. They could create a new identity while a combustible, short-lived version of fame washed over them along with beads of sweat and an easily scored Quaalude. A dance that had emerged from the underground for partners had become a showcase for solo dancers; disco turned the participants into the show. The fame of Travolta had turned the dance floor into a free-for-all for attention.

In any big city like Atlanta, disco clubs could be phenomenally lucrative, if equally expensive to open. A club might cost a few million to build, and the money had to come from somewhere. Banks wouldn't call a mirror ball and a stack of extended-remix dance tracks a business plan, so the clubs were an irresistible lure for untraceable cash. Once open, a disco that could hold three to five hundred people could pull in nearly $2 million a year in cover charges and drinks. Owners could net more than a half a million dollars a year, especially if they held one of the twenty-four-hour licenses that let them blare music and sell drinks nonstop.

The Gum Head dove headlong into disco years before. By 1978, Diamond Lil greeted patrons with her high-pitched warble when she emceed on weekends: "Let's disco, children!" DJs spun as many disco hits as rivals like the Magic Garden and Backstreet. In turn, those clubs hosted drag shows when they didn't interfere with the Sweet Gum Head's big-money weekend nights. The clubs had begun to wobble around the same axis. Drag had welcomed the straight-but-curious world into gay subculture a few gawkers at a time, but discos reversed the formula. Straight couples writhed on the dance floor next to gay couples and singles who cruised other open-minded patrons of any gender. Disco pushed gay culture into the mainstream, and gay culture didn't push back; it ran to the light.

Discos had cost the Gum Head some business, especially Backstreet, especially on Friday nights when patrons would come into the Gum Head early and then leave to dance elsewhere. The Gum Head made Friday shows free, and for a brief time the club could stay open until four in the morning. Gum Head patrons mingled and got to know one another in the closer confines of their club's smaller disco floor—where Larry and John were when Larry started to jerk.

Then he started to twist, and pony, and do others in a series of ancient dances, just to embarrass John. Neither of them had trained as dancers, not like the Gum Head's new choreographer, Marc Jones. John tried to shame Hot Chocolate with other old moves, long since defunct and deformed by time. Even at its peak, when the straight world explored gay culture inside its anonymous walls, the Gum Head remained that kind of friendly clubhouse for its regulars and its entertainers, a clubhouse fueled by an undercurrent of hedonism.

Hedonism was high fashion in 1978, when the Sweet Gum Head peaked as the drag tabernacle of the South, when disco drove through speakers into the ears and the hips of its worshippers, when Quaaludes and cocaine fueled revelers into the night, when Bill Smith staked a new claim to his pulpit as the high priest of gay rights in Atlanta, when John Greenwell set his sights on a shiny new treasure. When the lives of both became spectacle, the likes of which they never had dreamed.

Rachel Wells

The Sweet Gum Head

March 24, 1978

John's blue top had wrinkled, his tight black pants felt too tight, and his makeup already had lost the luster from when he'd put it on half a day before. He was tired, and his feet hurt. He wasn't in any mood when Nancy Scott leaned in toward him and asked the gotcha question.

"Are you a homosexual?"

The Sweet Gum Head had opened its doors to the outside world in a very visible way: on morning television. The club's manager saw the opportunity to be treated with respect—but the morning show had left plenty of room for the Gum Head's star performers to be mocked, to be treated as spectacle.

Oh, OK, it's going to be like that, John thought. On televisions across Atlanta, a few still in black and white, viewers saw John pause briefly, taken aback by Scott's question.

Phil Donahue's punchy and provocative show had melded seamlessly into Scott's *Today in Georgia.* A former Miss Florida and Orange Bowl queen, Scott dismissed beauty pageants and had slashed her sash-winning hair into a fashionable pixie cut by the time she took over the morning show in 1975. She had dropped the dry format of her predecessor, who quoted Bible verses and shared recipes and advised viewers on how to wrap Christmas presents so airport security wouldn't tear them apart. Scott reported stories about cheating husbands and breast recon-

struction and psychic healing and lesbianism. While her viewers reached for a second cup of coffee on a Monday morning that
March, a half hour before the usual morning drama began with
NBC's soap-opera parade, Nancy brought them a live program
straight from the Sweet Gum Head, one of Atlanta's more notorious nightclubs, one where female impersonators performed
three shows a night, six nights a week, on one of Atlanta's more
notorious roads.

John had stayed up all night, and as Rachel he was a little
bit of a mess; his signature explosive hair had flattened in the
unflattering early hours. He and Lisa King and Tina Devore had
made it through to seven in the morning before they began to flag.
John still had on Vicki Lawrence's shoes, very high heels with an
uncomfortable strap around the back. He had to pinch his toes
into them and it hurt to walk even after a few minutes. His calves
cramped, and he felt like a wreck, but to the television cameras
that panned around him, he gave off the extravagant caricature
of feminine beauty known as Rachel Wells.

The conversation had gone smoothly at first. Nancy had peppered John and another performer, Lisa King, with all sorts of
polite questions: "What do you do? How do you do it?" John Austin had told her that any questions about being gay were off the
table—but still, when the glow of camera lights and live camera
lenses panned to John, she queried him.

Really? We're going to talk about this? John thought, and stared
back at the petite anchor. *That's not what this was supposed to
be about.*

Lisa piped in, with her hair still drawn tightly and beautifully
away from her face. She was always quick with a retort.

"No, he's try-sexual."

"What does that mean?" Scott asked.

"He'll try anything sexual."

John couldn't look at Nancy—he looked at Lisa and laughed,
thankful to her for coming to his rescue. The gotcha question

snared the TV host instead. Embarrassed, she quickly moved the performers along to what was supposed to be a showstopping number, Barbra Streisand's "One Less Bell to Answer." Lisa began to lip-sync the words to the Burt Bacharach song about loss after love, and Rachel would take over for the second half. John stood in the background waiting, and his feet started to throb again— and then he heard the crew sign them off. The cameras bowed, the lights dimmed. The show had run out of air time before John could perform his part.

Nancy Scott's probe pulled in so many viewers, she asked if *Today in Georgia* could come back and do it all a second time, on May 24. Lisa and Rachel refused. Scott had lied to them. It had been a lot to do for a television show anyway, staying up all night. It was good exposure to reach out to the straight audience that came to the club's shows in increasing numbers, but the Sweet Gum Head really didn't need it, or so Rachel thought.

John Austin had readily agreed to do the show when they called his office, eager for the free publicity. He did anything he could to shift attention from the obvious. The Sweet Gum Head hadn't been updated in years, and people had begun to notice. The gay-bar magazines said the Gum Head was in the worst shape of any gay bar in Atlanta, with its filthy and sticky carpeting, its dirty curtains, its old paint. The owners hadn't put anything back into it in a while, even though crowds had never been thicker on Saturdays. The rumor mill offered an explanation: Several Atlanta gay bars were said to be for sale in early 1978, among them the Sweet Gum Head, for the low price of $60,000.

Bill Smith

Atlanta

Spring 1978

I n a doctor's office, or in a home with the curtains drawn, a young
man would be told to unbuckle his pants. Gripped by fear, he
would lower them in obedience. Electrodes would be affixed to his
genitals, then he would sit as he was told, with a view of a screen
in a darkened room.

A slide projector would be coupled to another machine that
snaked wires to the young man's privates. The slides would be
interspersed with special ones that contained lewd images of male
arousal, male homosexual acts, or male nudity. The special slides
would trigger shocks that shivered through the cord. The patient
might yelp in terror for a moment until they could press a button
to reject the slide, and move on to one with acceptable images,
perhaps a pretty girl posed fully clothed.

The torture machine proved cheaper than lobotomies or psychi-
atric cures, its makers claimed. It could treat alcoholism, trans-
vestitism, addiction, even sexual preference.

The only other cure offered for homosexuality was prayer—not
the prayers offered by gay-friendly churches that had come out
of the faithful closet, but the true-believer prayers of people like
Anita Bryant, who believed that gay people could change their
behaviors and beliefs if only they gave themselves to God.

Coverage of Bryant took up page one of the first issue of the *Gay
News: Atlanta and the South*, a new publication that appeared in
gay bars, gay bookstores, and gay-friendly businesses in Atlanta
in the spring of 1978. Readers who paid 50 cents for the inaugural

issue were greeted by the twin specters of religion and venereal disease on the cover, juxtaposed with the image of two handsome, shirtless men, boxed in a red-tinted frame, and the big news story of the issue, about a demonstration planned for June 11 to protest Anita Bryant's speech at the annual Southern Baptist Convention's Pastors Conference.

Bill Smith had closed the *Barb*, but early in 1978 he called an acquaintance with an idea. Mark Segal published the *Philadelphia Gay News*, and had spun off regional editions. Bill proposed an Atlanta version, and Segal flew to the South to gauge the reception. He and Bill drove around Atlanta and visited its gay businesses by day, its bars by night. Drag clubs like the Sweet Gum Head astounded Segal; this wasn't New York, or even Philadelphia. The newspaper would have to cover the drag clubs if it wanted to succeed in Atlanta, but it could work. Bill would bring in the advertisers; he would bring the *Barb*'s editor, Gary Poe, as well as news writer Marti Elliott, to the masthead. The paper would carry ads for the Youngman escort agency too.

The first issue of the *Gay News* pushed back in print against Bryant, while Bill told the *New York Times* about Atlanta's own push for gay civil rights. Inspired by Harvey Milk, who had championed a gay-rights ordinance in San Francisco in the spring of 1978, Bill demanded in April of 1978 that, even though he had endorsed another candidate for mayor, politicians like Maynard Jackson should help Atlanta get its own gay-rights ordinance enacted: "They received our help during the election, now it's time we got theirs."[1]

Anita Bryant had provoked Bill in a way no politician had. He was stunned that she and so many others could believe that gay people could simply convert children into homosexuals. He tackled her political positions while he defended religion itself: "My prayers have always been that if I'm wrong, then I'll be forgiven," he said, "and if I'm right then God will give me the strength to carry on."[2]

While he professed a clear conscience, he struggled to balance his life on the fulcrum of religion, where his Baptist upbringing ran into raw conflict with his physical desires. When friends asked, he said his family had made peace with his homosexuality since he left home at seventeen, but that was a lie. Bill's parents still prayed he would eventually revert to heterosexuality and prayed that he would marry his on-and-off girlfriend Diane, whom he brought to family reunions, gritting his teeth, tense as relatives asked about her and about their plans.

His family did not understand the chaos in his life. Not long after he moved to Atlanta, Bill's devout sister had stumbled into his apartment only to find Bill in bed with Diane. A few hours later, his father's voice crackled over the phone stern with judgment. The lifelong member of the First Baptist Church of Conyers reprimanded him briskly and pleaded with him all at once.

"Son, you're going to have to choose between the little boys and the little girls," Bill Sr. said. "It's confusing for your mother."

Bill's homosexuality had been a family demon that could not be slain since he was a young man. When his parents realized their young son was gay, they forced him to submit to the horrific treatment intended to reverse his homosexuality. Doctors attached electrodes to teenage Bill's genitals and showed him photos of nude men and nude women. When he became aroused at the pictures of men, agonizing electric shocks coursed through his testicles and penis, until he lost all faith and had begged for mercy, until they deemed he had been cured.

Lavita Allen

The Sweet Gum Head

June 1978

While a beauty queen spun onto the Sweet Gum Head dance floor, a handsome male dancer in tow, John Greenwell sat in the balcony with friends for a change. He smoked a cigarette and sipped from his usual Bud Light at one of the small oak tables that looked over the bar to the stage. A few hundred people had packed the club for the 1978 Miss Gay Atlanta pageant. On a night like tonight, performers in the upstairs dressing room had to rely on a jab and a shove just to get to the stage. As they walked down the stairs, drag queens would stick guests with needles to get them out of the way: *Ow!* They'd wince, then relent.

Hot Chocolate had entered—and so had Lavita. She was no Rachel Wells, despite adding a touch of glamour to her wardrobe and softening her look. She'd never won a pageant.

Before Christmas, Lavita had taken one more chance at acting, in the basement of the dingy Our Place gay bar, as the lead in Michel Tremblay's *Hosanna*. Set in Montreal, the play observes the relationship between Cuirette, a gay biker, and Hosanna, a drag queen who favors Elizabeth Taylor's Cleopatra guise.

Onstage, Lavita played Hosanna while her lover Raymond Gideon Fletcher played Cuirette. Reviews likened the play to *Who's Afraid of Virginia Woolf?* and noted its coarse language and acrid wit. In the arc of the drama, both characters delve into the gay male identity at their core. The play ends with both characters nude, in an embrace.

Previously lauded for her comedy, Lavita won kudos for her

compelling character. Her second-act monologue was deemed particularly gripping. Reviewers were impressed by her reflection of contemporary gay life. One wrote, tellingly: "Theatre is the basic metaphor of our lives. Gays must invent—write—themselves, drastically in order to hold jobs, rent apartments, be noticed in bars, etc. . . . Gay life is so theatricalized that we can do nothing but act out scenes, day and night."[3]

Lavita found the performances draining. The show didn't make money. It stranded her on a dramatic island, and she struggled to return to comedy at the Gum Head when it was over.

"*Hosanna* was a big mistake for me," she said. "It showed me something I could do that I would never get the chance to do. Suddenly, I saw a whole world behind a plate glass window—legitimate theatre was right over there—and I could do it but I can't do it."[4]

John rooted silently for Lavita to win the pageant. There would always be another chance for Hot Chocolate. For a moment, it seemed as if Lavita might triumph, just this once.

Taisha Wallace and Ron Ellis swept across the dance floor, then offstage when the pageant began, jammed with guest stars from Miss Florida (Tiffany Areagus) to Miss Gay Universe (Roxanne Russell), from former Miss Gay Georgia Vicki Lawrence to Rachel Wells, former Miss Gay Atlanta and reigning Miss Gay Georgia, up in the balcony, clapping and sipping on her beer behind a half-full ashtray.

The queens painted and posed through the first rounds. Each category awarded 25 points, and a win in any category could land a performer in the top five. Lakesha Lucky stunned the judges with her usual poise and femininity. Vonda Delaine draped herself in a Cher-style gown to take the evening-wear nod, while Tissy Malone broke out with a showstopping medley of Donna Summer songs.

Lavita's appeal lay in her talent for comedy, not in pristine pageant-girl beauty, but she had a flair for the dramatic. She emerged for the sportswear competition on a platform framed by two mannequins, stood perfectly still, then sprang to life—but still fell behind Lene Hayes in that category. She won the judges over in talent with a backdrop she'd built herself—her name written in cursive in neon paint like the cover of Dolly Parton's latest album. She swung on a swing while she performed "Here You Come Again" to start a medley of Dolly Parton songs that concluded with Parton's plaintive ballad "I Will Always Love You"— and edged out Hayes into the top five.

Lavita had been a kind of sideshow at the Sweet Gum Head, comical and always good for a laugh, but she took the Miss Gay Atlanta pageant quite seriously. So did her rival in that pageant, Hot Chocolate, who earned the fifth spot in the finals, just a few months after she had posted a runner-up finish in the Miss Gay America contest. Perfectly coiffed in an upswept Gibson Girl hairdo, Chocolate had taken the hair and makeup award before judges saw her talent act, complete with a costume change and two backup dancers. She had become a star, and could afford them.

She could perform old classics and new songs, as she did in the talent competition with "If My Friends Could See Me Now," with a segue from Shirley MacLaine to Linda Clifford. Clifford had just performed down the street at the Magic Garden when it reopened in a blaze of klieg lights and a fusillade of popping Champagne corks, dressed to the hilt in white lattice and neon lightning bolts that masked the damage from its recent fire. Clifford loved gay audiences, and drove all night from Chicago to perform her massive disco hit.

The translation of "If My Friends Could See Me Now" from Broadway to disco fairly flew off the turntable. The original bowed onstage in *Sweet Charity* in 1966, and made its way to film in 1969. Gwen Verdon sang the Cy Coleman song on Broadway, while Shirley MacLaine gave her rendition in the movie. Both actresses deliver the song in a Kewpie-doll tone, which suited the intentionally anachronistic lyrics:

All I can say is, wow, hey look at where I am
I've landed, pow, right in a pot of jam

Released in 1978, the Linda Clifford version rips the song free of context and slaps it over a sultry longform beat. Clifford, a former beauty queen and an experienced jazz and Broadway singer, had in fact been an extra in the *Sweet Charity* movie. A secretary at her record label thought a revved-up version of the song would play naturally off disco's inclination toward drama and theatricality—but Clifford thought it would be a bad idea. Blasphemous, even.

Producers recorded a backing track full of energy and she changed her mind. The song cues with an angry buzzing hive of violins and a percolating disco backbeat, peppered with plucked bass and interjections from the backup singers, then widens into cinematic melodrama, all orchestral sweeps of pianos and swirls of strings and forceful, fervent vocal attacks by Clifford through all its distinct movements. Her voice washes above the propulsive beat and reaches a climax at a whirling-dervish moment at the middle of the action, where tootling woodwinds allude to the song's vaudevillian origins. The disco version cleverly reformats the song from narrative embellishment into a thumping clarion call for independence. It threatens for seven minutes and fifty-six seconds to descend into self-parody and teeters on the brink, measure after measure, but never falls.

Critics called it camp and a disco tour de force. Clifford loved how full the song sounded, how it pulsed with real musicians who played real instruments and fused the song's classical elements with huge pop appeal. Clifford could relate to people who had been through dark and negative times in their life, and had pulled themselves out by the force of will. She sang the lyrics as a form of protest.

Hot Chocolate veered slightly away from the defiant interpretation. She only saw the love in the track, and performed it as an homage to her mentors. Larry Edwards had taken his family's support to Atlanta. He counted on John for friendship and for inspiration. He nurtured his own obvious gift for lip-sync and for transformation: He could channel the voices of Black disco queens onstage with uncanny energy, something John envied as he poured out his heart in white-girl ballads and midtempo pop songs. Drag distilled the emotion of music, and in Larry's songs, that essence was one of pure joy.

"If My Friends Could See Me Now" hit number 1 on the disco chart in late April 1978. Clifford was at home washing the floors when she found out. She hung up the phone when her label called with the news, convinced it was a joke. The song would stay at number 1 on the disco chart through the whole month of May. At the Sweet Gum Head, it would propel Hot Chocolate to victory when he became Miss Gay Atlanta 1978.

Lavita took home second place. It had been her best finish yet, but it broke her heart, and she wept bitterly when it was over. John comforted her with soothing words and a warm embrace, even while he had begun to think ahead to the biggest pageant of the year, to the one title he coveted most of all.

Anita Bryant

Georgia World Congress Center

June 12, 1978

Some waved handwritten protest signs, some cupped their hands around their mouths to make their voices project louder and farther so that the audience inside could hear them. The crowd strained behind police lines set up outside the Georgia

World Congress Center as their chants floated above them and alighted into the warm evening sky.

"Hey-hey, ho-ho, Anita Bryant's got to go!"

In a strong year, Atlanta's Gay Pride celebration might count four or five hundred people. Small cliques would stitch themselves together and march the streets from downtown to Piedmont Park. When the sun went down and the park reverted to a more clandestine meeting place, the marchers would go their separate ways. Turnover was the rule: politically active gay and lesbian people in Atlanta would be very active, then many would burn out. The growing crowds outside the World Congress Center demonstrated something new, something that had taken root, something beyond gays and lesbians marching alone in the name of dignity.

"Out of the closet and into the streets!"

By the time John got downtown, the crowd had swelled and marshals were stationed around it to maintain peace. Some lifted fruits high above their heads, in a parody of Bryant's Florida orange-juice endorsements and commercials: "Man cannot live by oranges alone!" They hoisted signs that countered Bryant's biblical pronouncements: "Anita, judge not that ye be judged!" They nominated Bryant for "Bigot of the year!" They surged forward when a few protesters thought they saw the former Miss Oklahoma ushered into the building. The marshals held their positions. They steeled themselves for a riot.

///

Anita Bryant glided into the auditorium, microphone in hand, gown frilled at the wrists of its full sleeves and at its tightly covered throat and down its bodice in high Victorian fashion, under a wave of suburban auburn hair. She gripped a red-leather New Testament and crusaded through 20,000 Baptists in the vast central hall while Atlanta police followed closely and protected her, in case a Judas sprang up from among them. "Lord, bless you" and "God bless you," she told them as she sang bits and pieces of "I Want to Be a Friend" with the savvy audience worship of a lounge singer, praying for the sin of homosexuality to be washed away between choruses and verses amplified to make it impossible to hear the clamor outside.

Bryant was one of the first speakers at the Pastors Conference, a two-day set of sermons and prayers that preceded the actual convention, where President Jimmy Carter would be the featured speaker, where Bryant hoped she would win the vice presidency of a denomination some 13 million worshippers strong. When polled, most of the sect's faithful thought Bryant held the moral high ground with her vehement anti-homosexual speeches; she'd spoken out and suffered the consequences. The rest thought gay rights were also civil rights. Organizers had put Bryant on the schedule earlier in the year, but when they found out Atlanta's gays and lesbians would protest, they wavered, and nearly called to cancel. Then they reconsidered: if her own people would not stand up for Bryant, who would?

Vibraphones washed over a backing track while Bryant flipped from preaching to singing about how she could trust her life to Jesus, and would give him all she could give. "Now don't step on my cord!" she said with a laugh as she made her way to the stage.

Her sermon began with a nod to her day job, as an official spokeswoman. "Jesus Christ is my very best friend. He's even better than Florida orange juice, because if you taste Jesus Christ, you'll never thirst again. And in this dry old land of ours, that's really good news."[5]

Bryant had refused to directly challenge the protesters gathered outside. The Southern Baptist Convention knew that would be disaster for the evening news. Instead she quietly moved in the opposite direction of the crowds when her car arrived downtown. She went in through the back door.

///

Anita Bryant had shown up in effigy in drag clubs across America in the fall of 1977. Pageant after pageant hosted rafts of Bryants, dressed in ghastly formal clothing and lip-syncing to turgid religious and patriotic tunes. Like Santa Claus, it wasn't possible for all of them to be the real thing—but some of the drag queens who parodied Bryant that year were *so* convincing.

Anita Bryant look-alike pageants dealt with Bryant's existential threats to gay life in a humorous way, but her campaign against gay civil rights continued to spread. Bryant's Save Our Children had put together a list of targets in other cities, from Wichita, Kansas, to St. Paul, Minnesota, where a state initiative to ban discrimination had failed, where an activist had thrown a pie in the face of a local archbishop blamed for the failure of the statewide rejection of an equal-rights law.

On October 14, 1977, gay activist and nurse Thom Higgins left St. Paul with three other "self-proclaimed homosexuals" to repeat the stunt, but this time, he chose Bryant as the target. He drove nearly five hours to deliver a strawberry-rhubarb pie to Bryant at an event in Des Moines. Reporters blitzed her about her campaign against gay men and lesbians, and during her brief remarks, Higgins leapt forward and smashed the pie in Bryant's face.

Covered in cream, Bryant recovered and stayed on message: "At least it was a fruit pie," she said.

"Let's pray for him right now, Anita," her husband, former disc jockey Bob Green, said before Bryant lapsed into tears. "Let's pray."

While Bryant would have been ignored, or pelted with fruit pies in New York or San Francisco, Atlanta gave her safer harbor. A sea of hardline conservatives surrounded its progressive oasis. Atlanta had also given shelter to the resurgent Klan when it had been reborn in the 1920s and had never really gone away, but the city also had what was reputed to be the third largest community of homosexuals in the nation.

Atlanta's Gay Pride celebration had always taken place in rough conjunction with the anniversary of the Stonewall uprising. Bryant's speech gave the gay community the perfect opportunity to move up Pride, to confront Bryant. Organizers decided to shift the annual Pride march up by two weeks and to stage it instead as a protest outside the Baptist meeting. They papered gay bars and businesses with flyers to drum up support and donations. The flyers warned the gay community that a quarter million homosexuals had gone to the Nazi death camps. In a triangle formed from words, against a black backdrop, the flyer read: "The Jews wore yellow stars of David, the homosexuals wore pink triangles." It urged gays and lesbians to protest on June 11, at 6 p.m., while Bryant spoke.

The Sweet Gum Head held its anti-Bryant benefit the Thursday before the speech. Outside, in the parking lot next to the Varsity Jr. hamburger stand, aging punks lit cherry bombs that spit their disgust into the sky while they slashed the tires on a few cars. Inside the club, drag queens mocked the Florida orange-juice spokeswoman while they passed the collection plate in protest and raised hundreds of dollars to fund the protest.

///

A piano tinkled in the background while waves of applause greeted Bryant's engineered pauses. At eight years old in Oklahoma, she told family that she would be a star. In the same year, she testified, she had met the creator of stars, Lord Jesus Christ.

She acknowledged that it had been a tempestuous year, and said she appreciated the strong support she had received and the prayers too. Standing ovations and light piano subsided, and Bryant confided her fears to the swarm of faithful: "I do believe that we're living in a serious hour." God had removed His hand from America, she said, and it could be destroyed, the same as Sodom and Gomorrah. The problem, she explained, was that too many people were demanding their rights.

She persevered not because she wanted to, but because she was called upon. "Why me, Lord, why me?" she asked. "I don't have the qualifications, I don't have the education, I don't have the intellect, I don't know how to express myself that well. I'm not a minister. I'm just a woman. I'm a mother who has a mother's heart," she said as her voice broke.

To one of many standing ovations, she said, "I believe in all my heart that the picketers out in front tonight shouldn't be picketing Anita Bryant. They should be picketing the ministers of this nation for telling it like it is."

A bluesy piano struggled against the crowd's approval, then Bryant sang in an exaggerated formal voice spiked with a country inflection: *One day at a time, sweet Jesus! That's all I'm asking from you.*

///

At 6 p.m. marchers began at assemble at the city park for a planned route that would take them down Forsyth and Marietta Streets to the front of the World Congress Center. The staff of *Cruise* magazine, a gay community publication, stood with the First Tuesday Democratic Association. Members of the Workers of the World Party lined up next to the Youth Against War & Fascism, directors of the ACLU of Georgia and of the Young Socialist Alliance. Ministers from Unitarian churches stood their ground with rabbis from nearby temples, doctors, attorneys, and with the editors of local weekly newspapers. They streamed through downtown, led by volunteer marshals trained to keep the protest as orderly as possible, but even led by police motorcycles, the blocks-long march stopped traffic dead for fifteen minutes in a din of chants of *"Gay rights now!"*

Southern Baptists worried that the protest would reach a flash point. Leaders said their own zealous defenders of the Baptist faith worried them more than the homosexuals. They called to ask the HRC about the protest, but they also implored their followers to behave. They didn't want violence, or for anyone even to be unkind. They wanted to win the homosexuals and their allies to Christ with love, they said.

Gay leaders returned in kind: they didn't object to Bryant's right to speak or to the convention itself; they objected to the content of her words. But they still feared violence. Some had been so scared that snipers would shoot at them, they looked into bulletproof vests.

Rumors suggested eight busloads of pro-Bryant fans would pull up to the convention center. All were ready for a fight—but as both sides lined up in opposition, only about fifteen Baptists chanted *"Praise the Lord!"* and held up placards with messages such as PRAISE GOD FOR ANITA and STOP ERA AND GAY RIGHTS—NORMAL PEOPLE FOR ANITA. One well-dressed counterrevolutionary wore a green summer suit and flipped off protesters with his middle finger.

Another of Bryant's supporters, Bill James of Stone Mountain, carried a twelve-foot wooden cross through the crowd on a wheel mounted to its base, while protesters booed. "It doesn't bother me," he said. "Jesus came for a purpose, and they hissed and booed him with his cross."

"I didn't know there were this many queers in the world," said Sam Creel, a pastor from Jackson, Mississippi.[6]

The melee had failed to materialize. Marshals even insisted protesters sit down when they engaged in heated debates with the meager handful of Bryant defenders who stood outside. More people rose to defend the marchers; a blond woman leaned from her car and shouted in support, "Give her hell!" while another woman waved sheepishly from a passing car.

The protest resounded widely across the country, on national television news, when a young lesbian named Maria Helena Dolan took the mic and electrified the crowd as she came out with a shout: "I come here tonight as a defiant dyke! No longer will fear or shame or passivity drive us to cower on our knees, hoping the shadow of death passes over someone else's head, because all our heads are at stake!"

Back at Dolan's home, Maria's mother heard the phone ring. It was her sister from Connecticut, who had been watching the morning news.

"What's Maria doing on TV?"

/ / /

Bryant cruised through treacly patter. She told the crowd God's grace had given her a love, even for the homosexuals teeming outside the auditorium, whom she judged could not possibly be Christian. "Because God first loved us, we can love each other. Not only as Christian brothers regardless of our differences, but to love someone outside of the Christian family, to love them enough to tell them the truth."

In prayer, she offered 1 Corinthians 6 as she told the audience that thousands of ex-homosexuals had thanked her for her stand: *Do not be deceived: neither the sexually immoral, nor idolaters, nor adulterers, nor men who practice homosexuality, nor thieves, nor the greedy, nor drunkards, nor revilers, nor swindlers will inherit the kingdom of God.*

She urged the audience that time was short, and that all would have to answer, that they should say no to immorality. She offered a scripture when the piano awoke again faintly in the background. Bryant chose Hosea 4:6 to finish her sermon, in prophetic fashion: *My people are destroyed for lack of knowledge. Because thou has rejected knowledge, I will reject thee. Thou will be no priest to me.*

For her finale, Bryant dropped her voice into its lowest register, lower than the vibraphone that rang out in solemn notes, and drew out the opening measures of "The Battle Hymn of the Republic" for nearly a minute. Snare drums filled in quietly at the first chorus, and were joined reverently by piano. The crowd held silent, from pastors who would lead the Baptist nation to the police that scanned the crowd for any signs of trouble to the warriors against sin who had spent everything they had to travel to hear Bryant speak in Atlanta. After a tempo change and a key modulation worthy of a middle-school band instructor, Bryant blessed the end of her half-hour stump speech by skipping ahead to the anthem's fifth verse, in a final call to action:

> *In the beauty of the lilies Christ was born across the sea,*
> *With a glory in His bosom that transfigures you and me.*
> *As He died to make men holy, let us die to make men free,*
> *While God is marching on.*[7]

///

The evening sky had shifted from amber to violet as the marchers began to break up. They had their own anthem, one written by country singer and songwriter David Allan Coe, who'd penned the massive hit "Take This Job and Shove It" just the year before. In 1978 he told the music world to shove his celebrity with a pro-gay song that took down Bryant's hypocrisy in a few jangly choruses and verses. Coe had spent decades in correctional facilities from the time he was nine; his contact with gay men there was made obvious by the lyrics that defended homosexuals by comparing them with the would-be vice president of the Southern Baptist Convention: *Some are killers, some are thiefs* [sic]*, Some are singers too / In fact, Anita Bryant, some act just like you.*

The song's title: *Fuck Aneta Bryant.*[8]

Bryant had unwittingly given the gay-rights movement a new reason for being. Many gays and lesbians just wanted to be left alone, but now they saw how bigotry could reverse everything that had been won. She drew the focus of the movement when it threatened to drift apart. She gave the movement open, unfettered access to national television and newspapers. It was Anita Bryant—and not the gay rights movement—that made "homosexual" a household word, and it was Bryant who threw new fuel on the debate over the nature of human sexuality.

Among the marchers who began to disperse were some of the drag performers who were often dismissed or sidelined, even by gays and lesbians who thought drag queens did not represent real gay people. Nothing could draw a television camera or a reporter so easily as a drag queen; they were used as shorthand for an entire movement, and they were often used as a face of perversion—as something to hate.

John could have marched along with the drag queens as Rachel, defiant in his bombshell auburn hair and high heels, but he still didn't believe what he did onstage every night was revolutionary in its own way. Instead, he marched as John, as a man who had now outlived many of his fears. John lingered as the sweet first breaths of summer air started to cool, after the sun finally dropped below the horizon nearly three hours after the march had first stepped out of Central City Park, exhilarated just to have chanted with a big crowd for the first time. Bill Smith and Gil Robison and other activists had nursed gay rights out of its infancy. They stirred the pot constantly when, most days, all John worried about was getting ready for a show. Now, John understood, they had to join together.

Bill Smith

Atlanta City Hall

August 1978

The most vocal protest for gay rights in Atlanta history had brought thousands to the Georgia World Congress Center. The next step would be to press for an equal-rights ordinance in the city, which Bill Smith would have been in a perfect position to do.

But Bill had gone absent from many events. Friends didn't even recall if he'd shown up to the Bryant protest. At a historic moment where Atlanta's gay civil-rights movement appeared to be on the brink of a major victory, he had all but disappeared.

At one gathering, activist Dave Hayward realized, yet again, that Bill wasn't there. He looked around and asked others: "What's going on with Bill?"

///

In a more ordinary set of circumstances, Bill would have rolled a sheet of clean paper into a typewriter and composed a letter to the Mayor's Office. The click of the keys, the hammer of metal against platen, the scent of the ink on the ribbon were more than familiar, they were a form of lifeblood. Bill wrote his friends when they lived in nearby states; he sent them thank-you cards when they lived just a couple of miles away. He believed in the formal but personal touch of a letter. He would have spun the paper out of the typewriter, signed it, and sealed it in an envelope when he was finished. He might have exhaled, but not in relief.

He would have driven downtown to deliver the letter himself, dressed in a suit, because he wore a suit when he appeared on television, when he attended meetings for various commissions, when he appeared before the mayor, sometimes when he went out to nightclubs in an official role as newspaper publisher. Bill would have climbed some thirteen steps and walked through tall oak doors, under gilt script and friezes of marble and terra cotta carved like those on a Gothic cathedral, into Atlanta City Hall, the handsome Art Deco tower raised during the Great Depression. He would have walked to the desk of the secretary who helped the Mayor's Office keep a schedule, to hand-deliver his resignation letter from the Community Relations Commission.

But nothing about the circumstances of the summer of 1978

would be normal for Bill, when he quietly removed himself from all his positions of influence.[9]

Bill had been present for a May 5, 1978, meeting of the ACLU of Georgia, in which directors discussed the poor state of its finances, death-penalty cases in Texas and Georgia, and over-crowding at the state prison in Reidsville. Bill would not be mentioned in official ACLU of Georgia communications for nearly two years after that meeting.

His name appeared on at least one CRC memo that summer, dated July 13, 1978. It listed him as a commissioner when it detailed work on a committee that assessed the status of women in Atlanta, as the national equal-rights amendment plodded slowly through state legislatures. The CRC's influence had waned, but it remained an official organization with a direct line to city hall. Bill had abandoned it.

Bill's name did not appear in the August 1978 issue of the *Gay News of Atlanta*, which reported that high schoolers had told the *Ladies' Home Journal* that Anita Bryant had done the most damage to the world, along with Nixon and Hitler; that so much money had been raised for the Anita Bryant protest, the newly formed Human Rights Coalition could fund an ongoing presence; that Gil Robison was running for a seat on the Fulton County Democratic Party; that Robbie Llewellyn had reported to prison.

Bill's name never appeared on a single issue. In the *Gay News*'s accounting ledger, there would be only a single cryptic note about proceeds from newspaper sales: "June 1978 Tally Atlanta Ad Rev 244.75 print run 1100 copies sold 401/$40.10. Gary + Marty/ Smith Control."[10]

///

In the early 1970s, dropping out and turning on was nothing new. But Bill Smith had left his rebellious hippie years behind. He had a city job, a seat on a city commission, had been in the national media and had run two newspapers, until that fateful summer.

Bill may have grown tired of living two or three different lives in parallel. The stress of his activism may have caused too much strain on his relationship with his family. He may have gotten tired of working with a lot of agencies that weren't getting anything done, because he wanted to do things, not talk about them. He may have grown tired of the lack of real activity from any of his political activities.

He may have been anxious that someone would call city hall and tip off the Mayor's Office about Youngman at a time when prostitution, male and female, had turned some downtown Atlanta streets into open-air sex markets. A single anonymous phone call could out him and oust him from any role in politics.

He may have felt threatened by people who had hired one of his escorts, and themselves felt threatened that their secret would be disclosed. He may have been ordered to more bedrest, as he had been after he testified in the murder trial of Robbie Llewellyn. He may simply have decided that prescriptions and isolation offered him all the solace he needed.

Bill's friends and acquaintances couldn't be sure, because Bill would not speak to them about his emotional and financial problems, and soon stopped speaking to them almost entirely. They suspected something was wrong, and that he was suffering the consequences alone.

In another time, perhaps a few years before, he would have simply shown up for meetings the next day, amused by the blank stares and at the very public way his personal life had been disclosed as he'd done the day after he faced TV cameras at his first Pride march. Instead, he began to erase himself from public memory. He put away the notion of a life at city hall forever. The ads for Youngman disappeared. Bill distanced himself from old friends. He began a new life, one without purpose, and began to slowly fall apart.

Rachel Wells

Fox Theatre

September 21, 1978

The walls of the grand temple of Karnak rose twenty-five feet in the air, inscribed with hieroglyphics that spelled out mystic messages as-yet-undeciphered. Massive pillars, fluted with gold and winged in silver, held the sky aloft above an ornate altar to Ramesses II that elevated the most powerful pharaoh of the empire into the heavens, above the queen who had entered the room.

Hot Chocolate reigned over the Egyptian Ballroom, and fired a competitive warning shot when she slid out of a cannon and landed on the shallow stage into the arms of four very attractive, muscular dancers, then peeled off a medley of three of her favorite songs, a mix of the disco smashes "Hot Shot," "Lovin' Is Really My Game," and "If My Friends Could See Me Now."

The Egyptian Ballroom seated some 800 people in Atlanta's Fox Theatre, a dolled-up Depression-era movie palace built as a banquet hall for the Shriners, with a 3,622-pipe organ, a red-carpet entrance, a replica of King Tut's throne in the Ladies' Lounge, handmade stained glass, and a cobalt-blue sky with thousands of hand-painted stars. Even during construction, it became clear the Fox was a white elephant, as its construction costs ballooned into the millions of dollars. The Shriners quickly leased it to a movie chain, which opened it on Christmas Day in 1929 then lost it in bankruptcy three years later, when it was sold at auction to a private company. As a movie theater the Fox thrived until the 1960s, when it fell into disrepair and barely avoided the wrecking ball.

A rush of activists and a slew of concerts given by glitterati from Liberace to Lynyrd Skynyrd spared the grand old dame, and after a renovation, the Fox reopened in 1975. It had survived, while all its rival theaters were buried by time.

Nothing was as it appeared in the Fox, despite its aching attention to detail. Plaster beams were painted to resemble wood; gold paint stood in for gold leaf; fireplaces had no chimneys; plaster and steel comprised the clever tentlike canopy in the main auditorium that reflected sound into the upper reaches of the balconies. Even the hieroglyphics on the walls of the 7,000-square-foot Egyptian Ballroom were false: The characters were authentic, but they had been painted out of any recognizable order, gibberish that television cameras could not read with their cyclops eyes during a promised airing of the finale of the Miss Gay America 1979 pageant, which felt like a homecoming for queens past and present from the Sweet Gum Head, including two best friends: Hot Chocolate and Rachel Wells.

///

John adjusted his Jesus costume and patted down his scraggly Jesus beard while he waited backstage. The cross had gotten heavy, and the layers of his costume made him hot. He worried that his talent competition would go poorly, as it had during the week at the Sweet Gum Head preliminaries. He didn't know how he'd even made it that far, with the rare miscues and misunderstandings that had marred the week. He just wanted to be Miss Gay America, and there were lots of talented queens to get past, not to mention Hot Chocolate with her showstopping disco lip-syncs.

He had labored for months over his costume and his performances. Sweet tap-dancing Jesus? Or maybe Mary Magdalene as a Rockette? Just what would it take for Rachel Wells to become Miss Gay America, after all his tries? He approached it methodically, with purpose. He riffled through Rachel's wardrobe to find a winning look, and cycled through the mental index of characters to find the one that would give him the crown. He let the technical thoughts occupy his hands while he preoccupied his mind with the words of the fan in Dallas who told Rachel that her reputation preceded her. She still couldn't decide if it was a compliment or a warning that she'd leaned on her name too long while it carried her on profitable tours across the South.

The costumes fell into place first. Hot Chocolate had shipped a red gown to Atlanta for the pageant, a pricey hand-me-down from a former Miss Florida, but it wouldn't close around her substantial neck. It fit Rachel perfectly around her slim waist and throat. She wouldn't leave the talent competition to chance. Rachel had always turned to Jesus when inspiration lacked; Jesus had paid her back half a dozen times in hundreds of dollars in tips and prize money. In the end she decided Jesus would save her again.

The savior had let her down—or she let him down—at the Sweet Gum Head, during the pageant preliminaries on Tuesday. Even the friendly Sweet Gum Head crowd couldn't overlook Rachel's unforced errors. She'd hired her dressing-room confidante Satyn to press her costumes, to help with hair and makeup, to watch every detail like a mother sending her daughter out to prom. Rachel had staged her Jesus Christ just as she'd done it in productions for years, with a pair of Roman centurions flanking her at her entrance, but had changed her costuming—and flubbed her choreography. The judges sniffed, and gave tap-dancing Vicki Lawrence the talent points. But in the sportswear category, Rachel borrowed an animal pelt from another performer and paired it with a simple swimsuit, and outfoxed rivals in full fur coats and thousand-dollar Calvin Klein runway looks to make the finals.

///

The pageant climaxed on Thursday night in the Egyptian Ballroom, consuming every inch of the low stage. John Austin had built an elaborate backdrop in the shape of a tiara, made out of dozens of tiny lights and mirrors that increased the glamour of the room.

The field of forty-one contestants had been narrowed in the previous days to ten finalists. They paraded for the crowd, dressed in pure white gowns that mirrored and mocked the one worn by Anita Bryant in Atlanta just a few months before. They then ran through the sportswear, evening wear, and the all-important talent heat one more time. Hot Chocolate pitched herself into the thick of the battle with the help of the cannon, and her trio of disco hits. Lisa King went with her usual closing numbers, Donna Summer's "Last Dance" and Natalie Cole's "Party Lights." Fabulous Florida queen Roxanne Russell tap-danced as Marilyn Monroe to "Diamonds Are a Girl's Best Friend," while Gum Head alumna Lady Shawn drew thundering applause for her rendition of Patti LaBelle's "You Are My Friend."

Barefoot and penitent, with a cross slung over her shoulder, Rachel made her way to the door, fidgeted in her Jesus garb one more time, then began the slow march through the ballroom, flanked by the centurions. She had gooped on the rubber cement one more time, and fixed a flowing beard to her lip and chin. She had focused on herself in a mirror, trying to get into the right frame of mind as she first put on her Mary Magdalene robes, then covered them with a flowing white tunic.

Her act went perfectly, but she could hardly see the audience or their response, much less the lavish details applied to the Egyptian Ballroom. The lights shone on her so brightly, the crowd turned into a mass of faces, and she tuned them out. She paced in her flowing garment, and dragged her cross on the stage to reenact one more time the Gethsemane prayer from *Jesus Christ Superstar*. Thunder rumbled over the Fox's sound system while cracks and flashes of light outlined her figure, then cast it into darkness. She crouched and hid herself in her robes and hair, no longer the ingenue who had stumbled through her first night in drag, or even the newly christened queen of Atlanta drag. She was John Greenwell and Rachel Wells—and she was Jesus Christ and then Mary, reaching toward the audience as the words finally made sense coming from her mouth: *In these past few days, when I see myself, I seem like someone else.*

Rachel could barely hear the music over the applause that rose and reverberated throughout the temple at the end of the plaintive song. The judges gave her a spot in the final five, along with Miss Gay Midwest, Donna Drag; a Michigan queen, Jennifer Fox; the reigning Miss Gay South, Lady Shawn; and for the second year in a row, Hot Chocolate, with the dual titles of current Miss Gay Atlanta and Miss Gay Texas.

The only hurdles to the crown were three interviews held offstage with the judges, and a final interview of a single question, posed in front of the rowdy and sometimes rude Egyptian Ballroom crowd: "Why do you want to be Miss Gay America?"

Rachel Wells had nothing to lose as she walked forward to answer this last question.

"As Miss Gay America I will *not* try to represent the gay community as a spokesperson for such a diverse group," Rachel said. "As Miss Gay America, my goal will be to take drag off the streets and put it onstage to help promote the art of female impersonation as a legitimate form of entertainment."

She had competed well in all the segments, and felt confident— but Rachel fought against the feeling of overconfidence as she walked back onstage with the other contestants. She told herself that Hot Chocolate had only missed a win the year prior by a hair, and was the overwhelming favorite, not herself. But Hot Chocolate had caught Rachel before they went onstage and said that Rachel had won. No, Rachel thought—but hadn't Hot Chocolate said the same thing last year when Rachel had won Miss Gay Georgia? The judges cast their votes, and called Donna Drag and Jennifer Fox to the stage. Next the judges called Lady Shawn. Then they announced the first runner-up—and for Hot Chocolate, it was a repeat of the year before.

The Miss Gay America 1979 crown belonged to Rachel. The spectacle was hers. Onstage in a floor-length white gown, ruffled and gathered at the lace sleeves and by the neck, she knelt down under John Austin's Miss Gay America tiara, six feet wide, big enough to span the whole royal court, and bowed as Lady Shawn took the crown off her head and passed it down. Three former Miss Gay Americas placed the tiara on Rachel's head. The crown wasn't new each year, and it was missing a few pieces, but it fit just the same as Rachel walked the runway while cameras snapped and clicked and flashed, that twenty-first night of September, a night that would be forever cast in disco history in joyous peals of pop by the band Earth, Wind & Fire, in their song "September."

The rest of the evening turned blurry. John had been working for five days straight on his costumes and in rehearsals; all he wanted now was a break from Rachel Wells. He left the Fox with friends, and walked back across the street to his room at the Georgian Terrace to take off his character. He worked quickly, wiping off the layers of makeup, straightening out his hair, sliding into his tight jeans and a T-shirt, then rushed downstairs to be John again, and to meet a guy visiting from Michigan that he'd connected with earlier.

When he woke, a faint smile crossed his face as morning steeped the room in soft golden light, as the guy from Michigan took in deep breaths of blissful sleep. God, he thought to himself, sometimes he could be such a whore.

Bill Smith

Atlanta

November 1978

A few dozen people gathered in front of a golden altar at the Metropolitan Community Church, bathed in the glow of a few dozen candles. They sang hymns to commemorate Harvey Milk's death. In New York the flickers would number in the thousands; in San Francisco, in the hundreds of thousands.

Two days before, on November 27, 1978, Dan White had snaked into San Francisco City Hall through a basement window. White had been a city commissioner like Milk, and had resigned, then changed his mind and asked for his job back, but had been turned down. Mayor George Moscone had called a press conference to name a new commissioner that Monday morning. A half hour before his replacement could be named, White had slipped into city hall with a gun and shot Moscone twice in the head. He turned to leave the Mayor's Office, ran into Milk, and shot him in the head as well.

Milk had served less than a year as a city commissioner, but had led astounding progress, even for a city where an estimated one-third of the population identified as gay or lesbian. He got a gay-rights ordinance passed with only one vote against it in March 1978. He took on Anita Bryant's support for an anti-gay measure on the California ballot in 1978, with a ringing speech that capped a Gay Pride celebration in San Francisco that shattered records, a quarter-million marching in its streets. His message for Bryant was not one of hate like hers, but of hope:

Somewhere in Des Moines or San Antonio there is a young gay person who all of a sudden realizes that he or she is gay; knows that if their parents find out they will be tossed out of the house, their classmates will taunt the child, and the Anita Bryants and John Briggses are doing their part on TV. And that child has several options: staying in the closet, and suicide. And then one day that child might open the paper that says "Homosexual elected in San Francisco" and there are two new options: the option is to go to California, or stay in San Antonio and fight . . . there is hope for a better tomorrow. Without hope, not only gays, but those who are blacks, the Asians, the disabled, the seniors, the us's; without hope the us's give up.[11]

His campaign against Proposition 6 led to its resounding defeat at the polls early in November. Milk knew his advocacy had marked him for physical violence. He thought he might be killed. He left a message to the gay community to be released if he died: "Don't be angry or go crazy in the streets. Do something positive in my memory."

Milk was assassinated as gay-rights leaders in Atlanta mulled over an ordinance of the city's own. On the day Milk and Moscone's murders were covered in the newspapers, Atlanta's gay-rights leaders said the measure needed more work, since it might exceed the legal authority of city government and might be in conflict with the state constitution. Mayor Jackson had not dismissed the efforts, but had not rushed in with support either. And by the end of 1978, he no longer had a member of the gay and lesbian community to urge him on to lead the charge.

Bill became an Atlanta city commissioner before Milk, who was one of the first openly gay elected officials in America, but Bill no longer had the power to effect any change. His resignation failed to draw a single news story or television camera. The local gay newspaper didn't even cover it. What would be the final edition of the *Gay News* in Atlanta would only carry a large advertisement for a gala New Year's party at the Sweet Gum Head, with special guest stars Rachel Wells and Hot Chocolate and a $7 cover charge.

Bill might have taken solace in the collapse of Anita Bryant's public life—she was in danger of losing her job as the Florida orange juice spokesperson—or the growth of Pride, or how fundraisers at clubs including the Sweet Gum Head had awoken a new cadre of colleagues. He might have begun to do what Milk had implored him to do: something positive. Instead, he spoke with activist friends more rarely, still sounding like his old sardonic self when he did, even as he gradually withdrew from that life. He found the only relief from the pain he had inflicted on himself—and that others had inflicted on him—in alcohol and cocaine and marijuana, the drugs he prescribed himself, and in the ones his doctors gave him, like Placidyl.

Abbott Laboratories advertised the hypnotic as an aid for chronic insomniacs to fall into deep sleep, billing it as "gentle as a lullaby." Abbott made it known that Placidyl could be psychologically or physically addictive if patients took it for longer than the week it recommended, though longer prescriptions could be written. Doctors observed that Placidyl users might experience mental disturbances when they stopped taking it.[12] Overdoses were notoriously difficult to treat, even with dialysis. Sometimes the only options were life support and prayer.

1979

///

I WILL SURVIVE

Rachel Wells

The Sweet Gum Head

February 1979

Rachel had stepped close to the edge of the stage. A local performer wanted to tip her, and it would be easier to reach for the dollar. As she got closer, Rachel saw the performer reach for a string on her dress, one that held it up. The dress began to slide off Rachel's shoulders and down her body before she caught it. Furious, Rachel kicked the queen in the gut, stormed upstairs, locked herself in the dressing room, and refused to come out.

In the year after Rachel Wells became Miss Gay America, John had let down his introverted guard a bit. He enjoyed a year on the road, touring and raking in cash, though he worried Rachel had been put to pasture like an old Kentucky war horse. The drag queens and fans on the road sometimes treated her that way. She watched as performers cloned her looks, lifted her gestures, mimicked her act, and sometimes it made her angry.

When another performer blocked the audience's view of her Jesus and Mary act, waving a dollar in her face, Rachel coiled back a fist, then thought better of it—what would Jesus do? A cocktail server threw the bill-waver out into the parking lot.

Eight years into her drag career Rachel Wells had ceased to be the fierce Amazonian warrior who ripped up outfits and shredded microphones. She had become a figurehead, the "Sweetheart of the South." Club owners paid her $200 a night to perform in places that made John stop to wonder how they could afford him.

Audiences didn't care if she did her best work. She could get onstage in an easy-to-pack outfit, lip-sync to a single song. She kept her most elaborate acts and impersonations for special occasions—when she felt like it—and no one cared.

Cheshire Bridge was always there when John needed to come home. The apartment he shared with Herman and his boyfriend hadn't changed, except for the paint that obliterated the giant stripe they'd thought was so tasteful when they had moved in. The Sweet Gum Head always welcomed her back for guest shows. He still pitched on the Gum Head softball team, still took pleasure in beating the pants off straight teams who had no idea they'd just lost to a bunch of drag queens. Not that he cared anymore if they knew: John had soared since he had left Alabama. Coming out had refashioned his outlook. He had told the people he loved, the people who mattered, and no longer had the need to lie. He began to speak that truth and other truths in public.

"Tell your mother," he counseled the new women and men who flocked to Atlanta and read about Rachel Wells in gay newspapers and bar magazines. "Your mother is going to know whether you are gay or not. I think anyone can speak to their mothers. It's difficult telling fathers, because it's harder for them to accept it. They're taught all their lives to 'hate queers.' Mothers are a lot more understanding, and they usually know."

Gay people were the most diverse minority group, John told local gay magazine *Cruise*, since the common bond of being gay stretched across cultures, religions, and race.[1] For some, being gay meant having sex in dark alleys, and for others it meant marches for equal rights. That fact would be its biggest hurdle to integrating as a political group.

The battle for equality would be fought for years, but it had already made real progress, he thought. John said he recognized that Anita Bryant probably still spoke for most Americans. She puzzled him, and he could not respect her for leading the bigoted and asinine movement that wanted to destroy people like him.

John had never been very politically aware, but as he grew more comfortable in his identity, his beliefs grew more pronounced and he no longer was afraid to voice them. It was hard to fight during the day when work ended at four in the morning, he pointed out, but drag queens were vital fundraisers in the clubs, where they raised money for operations like the upcoming National March on Washington in the fall of 1979. They were now a highlight at Atlanta's annual Pride march, instead of being relegated to the back where they wouldn't shock and offend on the evening news, as they had been in the past.

John looked forward to his year as Miss Gay America. It was his chance to enjoy touring and to make money from all the hard work he'd put into Rachel Wells. He had reached the pinnacle of a drag queen's career, and now wondered about his future outside of drag. He knew he wanted to usher in the next stage of his life. His title had helped him finish what he had started with drag, but he didn't intend to do it much longer.

Bill Smith

Midtown

Spring 1979

When he was thirty, Bill lived in a cozy bungalow that the *Barb* had once called home. By 1979 the house had been consumed by his fear and anxiety.

He shared the home at 374 Fifth Street with Ariel, whose wife had left him, and with Diane, who had been beaten by her last boyfriend until she left him. The house grew cramped and uneasy. It was a lifeboat, all its passengers praying for survival, clinging to it for safety.

While Ariel and Diane healed their wounds, Bill doted on his dying family pet in a back bedroom. Dottie the dachshund was very old and very weak, and could no longer walk. She had to be held outside to do her daily business. Bill's parents had wanted to put Dottie down, but Bill refused to let them. He brought her to live in Midtown, on his bed, where he could tend to her pain and where he wouldn't have to deal with losing her.

Dottie had grown ill-tempered toward anyone but Bill. He would lift her under her stomach and take her for a walk. A friend came to visit, and Bill warned them not to bother the dog because she was blind and frail and would not tolerate visitors. The guest went too close and Dottie bit them. Bill remained furious at them long after Dottie had died.

Dottie was precious to him, more precious than most people. By then, Bill had disappeared from headlines and from activist circles. He kept in occasional touch with old friends by phone, and when they hung up they felt slightly reassured. He sounded like the same old Bill, at least.

Revolutions spread in unexpected ways, and reveal unexpected truths. They also cause unintended consequences. Bill had always been an anxious person, but he had become incredibly paranoid. He became convinced that the police would find drugs on him and arrest him. There were points in his life when he had sold drugs, but it wasn't a major source of income, Diane thought. Bill hated needles, had never been interested in speed or heroin and, by then, had given up even on his beloved marijuana, she thought—and still he worried constantly about being arrested.

He disavowed drugs entirely to Diane, and told her he would not allow marijuana in the house, that he would not allow hallucinogenics in the house. He questioned anyone who came to the house, shook them down at the door, had them turn out their pockets. "Do you have any drugs? Look in your pocketbook and make sure," he would hiss. "The police are watching me."

When he grew frantic Bill would take pictures inside the drawers of his dressers and put a date on them. If the police came and planted something in his home, he would have evidence to prove his innocence. Diane would try to soothe him while he stalked the house.

But he still used his prescriptions. He drank to numb his anxiety. He took many drugs to dampen his fear. He told his few remaining friends that he would be better off dead. He called and begged his friends for help. Someone had to save him.

Anita Bryant

Florida

Summer 1979

Anita Bryant could see the Atlantic Ocean from the music room in her Spanish-style home on Miami Beach as she played her grand piano or listened to antique discs on an Edison Victrola. The home, built in 1925, had enough room for Bryant and her husband and their four children—twenty-five rooms in all. Artisans had made it fabulous with three stone fireplaces, with lintels over the doors fashioned from coral from underwater reefs, with fountains in the home's front garden.[2] It was her refuge from a growing empire: Her Anita Bryant Ministries had outgrown rented office space near her home, and in 1979 it had paid a quarter-million dollars for a 7,000-square-foot building in Hollywood, Florida, where it would continue to counsel homosexuals to abandon their sinful lives—they were neither male nor female; they were hopeless—and to recover identities lost to alcoholism and drugs.[3]

It had been a year since she waved her red-leather New Testament at the Baptists in Atlanta who applauded her anti-gay screed. She had won the ballot-box battle in Dade County and in cities across America, but Anita Bryant was losing the war against homosexuality itself. Her ministry claimed five hundred recoveries, but in rural Minnesota, gay bars were open on weekends and men danced together safely, more than a hundred of them. In rural Georgia, two gay bars competed for attention from guests, not from police. Harvard Law School had banned discrimination against gays. The nation had watched annual Gay Pride parades swell in the decade since the Stonewall riots, and on the tenth anniversary of that rebellion, the marches would count hundreds of thousands of protesters.

The Stonewall activists couldn't have predicted what their rebellion would ignite. The vivid counterpunch to decades of physical and legal oppression had screamed across television screens and in newspaper headlines. New York had always known it was a haven for homosexuals. Now the rest of the country from Seattle to Atlanta knew it too, and discovered something even more potent—that lesbians and gays who lived in other major cities could take to the streets and fight for their own equality.

The gay-rights movement had gained enormous momentum since Stonewall. In 1979, dozens of "Lavender Anniversary Celebrations" convened in honor of the rebellion at the Mafia-owned hole in the wall, where dirty tub water served as the only place to wash a bar glass, where the fire exits were barred shut, where toilets ran over, where drugs came easily and the cops came once a week to collect the graft that kept the unlicensed bar open.

Gay Pride in 1979 could thank Anita Bryant for its largest, most combative crowds to date. San Francisco officials estimated 200,000 people would march there; New York planned for 100,000. In Atlanta, 4,000 people took to Peachtree Street on June 24, 1979, and made the ninth annual pilgrimage from the Atlanta Civic Center to Piedmont Park to demand equality.

Pride marchers plotted a National March on Washington for October 14, 1979, where they would urge passage of gay-rights legislation across the country. Some worried that a march in the nation's capital would give Bryant more fodder to press her anti-gay agenda in state houses across the country. But gays and lesbians had already begun to outflank Bryant, as her celebrity had begun to implode. Her $100,000-a-year endorsement deal for Florida orange juice was up for renewal in August, and renewal seemed tenuous. She lost $500,000 in bookings almost immediately, and had to raise money from donors to film a ninety-minute TV special after Singer of sewing-machine fame dropped out. Her marriage had begun to crumble and she would divorce her husband the following year.

Bryant had quieted down her rhetoric considerably, but she had already electrified the gay civil-rights movement. Its surge wounded her career. From her oceanfront mansion, she still called God her best friend, but Bryant felt she had been crucified for her beliefs. She saw herself as a martyr.

Gloria Gaynor

Comiskey Field, Chicago

July 12, 1979

Security guards had never seen the White Sox's Comiskey Park so jammed. About 50,000 people had marched through the neighborhood and flooded in through the gates, many without tickets. They swarmed into the baseball field's seats. They hung banners from the stadium's upper decks and matched the slogans with a dark chant: *"Disco sucks!"*

Vinyl records flew from the stands and stuck in the field like falling stars. The game started anyway. Liquor bottles and firecrackers sailed through the air, halting play a few times, but the guards could do little to dampen the electricity in the air. Coaches warned their players to wear batting helmets on the field. The stunt that had riled the crowd still was several innings away.

A Chicago radio DJ named Steve Dahl had dreamed up the idea to demolish disco records on the baseball diamond. Fired on Christmas Eve 1978 from one radio station, WDAI-FM 94.7, when it switched formats from album rock to disco hits, Dahl took his playlist to a rival station, WLUP-FM 97.9, and interspersed his rock standards with the sound of records blowing up. He told listeners he was dedicated to the eradication of disco.[4] He recorded a parody song, "Do Ya Think I'm Disco?" and set it to Rod Stewart's "Do Ya Think I'm Sexy?"

Dahl's schtick brought in listeners; a friend whose father owned a piece of the Chicago White Sox thought it would be a great way to bring in fans to the first game of a double-header against the Detroit Tigers on July 12. Fans were told to bring their hated disco records to the stadium, where they'd be blown up in the break between games. Admission would be just 98 cents if the fan brought a disco record. Promoters thought 20,000 people might show up, a few more than usual.

Dahl's juvenile disgust for disco had tapped into a deeper critique with more vile roots. A late 1977 record had already called for a "Death to Disco." In the months before the July 12 doubleheader, editorials nattered on about the pervasiveness of disco, and the need for something new. Disco had displaced conventional rock music on much of the FM radio band, as it swept away popular music. Its new order was more open, more permissive, more indulgent, more sexually ambiguous—and decidedly more brown and Black and queer than the white-boy rock standards of the day.

Dahl grew nervous when he went to the field at 8:45 p.m., dressed in full army gear. By then, police had closed nearby freeways to stem the tide of protest. Dahl drove around in a Jeep first, then walked out to the box of disco records staged in center field. Players warming up stopped in disbelief while security padlocked all but one gate.

"This is now officially the world's largest anti-disco rally!" Dahl shouted into the mic. "Now, listen—we took all the disco records you brought tonight, we got 'em in a giant box, and we're gonna blow 'em up reeeeeeal goooood." A pitifully small charge detonated the box of albums, but it set off the entire stadium crowd. Dahl drove off quickly as fans piled from the seats into the field. They rioted: They climbed poles, set fires, stole things. A fire raged in center field, where the records had been blown to smithereens. Speakers blared "Take Me Out to the Ball Game" while the scoreboard flashed in a panic: PLEASE RETURN TO YOUR SEATS.

Riot police had to clear the stadium of the rock-music fans. When quiet finally settled in, the stadium was a mess, the playing field ruined by the trampling of feet and by the explosion itself. The White Sox forfeited the second game of the double-header, another defeat in a losing season.

Disco Demolition Night had been planned as a lark, a minor blow-off valve for a decade of war, political implosion, and upended civil order. It had instead tapped into deep-seated anger and into the all-American pastime of civil unrest. It became a skirmish in a culture war about to ensue. Gloria Gaynor, whose hit "I Will Survive" had begun to peak on the Billboard Top 100 and whose albums were among those blown up on Comiskey Field, thought promoters had consciously whipped up the mob mentality, all for the love of money. Chic's Nile Rodgers called it a Nazi book-burning.[5]

Bill Smith

Atlanta

July 16, 1979

O n July 16, 1979, police searched Bill Smith's apartment and found marijuana. Detectives L. Arcangeli and J. W. Carlisle arrested him and took him downtown to book him on three charges.

Under the Georgia Controlled Substances Act, Bill Smith was arraigned in court. He was charged on the first count for selling marijuana to Arcangeli; on the second count, of selling to Carlisle; and on the third count, of possession of more than one ounce of marijuana. According to the law each act was "contrary to the laws of said State, the good order, peace and dignity thereof."

A court date was set for later in the summer.[6]

Mayor Maynard Jackson

Atlanta

July 21, 1979

O n July 9, 1979, Atlantans were warned Skylab could fall out of the sky. They needn't have looked up to see what might put them in danger. It spilled out into the streets in front of them.

The city was in the midst of a "summer of death," a spiraling murder rate unimpeded by a city police force, which was under pressure to reorganize in order to put a stop to the violence. Before the middle of the year more than 130 people had been murdered inside city limits, among them an Ohio doctor of nuclear medicine shot during a downtown robbery. In one twenty-four-hour period in July 1979, seven people were slain in Atlanta. The city had already outpaced its increased homicide rate of the year before.

Crime had been tamped down somewhat during Mayor Jackson's first term, which began in 1974. The year before, Atlanta had been the murder capital of the country. Crime flared out of control in his second administration, and Jackson was forced to ask Georgia governor George Busbee to bring in state troopers to help patrol city streets.

"We're at the point now where we're getting calls so fast we can't handle them all," said retiring police lieutenant Jack Perry.

Local businessmen raised money to put up a billboard near the baseball stadium: WARNING. YOU ARE NOW IN THE CITY OF ATLANTA, WHERE POLICE ARE UNDEREQUIPPED, UNDERMANNED, UNDERPAID. PROCEED AT YOUR OWN RISK.

The city's chamber of commerce complained about the billboard, as did the mayor, who took it personally. J. K. Ramey, who owned a tire business, said Mayor Jackson had come to his store and threatened him if he helped put the billboard up: "I'm going to put your ass out of business."

The mayor's spokesman said Jackson had only wanted the tire store to stop using the street to change treads.

"The mayor doesn't use that kind of language," press secretary Angelo Fuster insisted.

Jackson tried to come to grips with a summer of death. Then, on July 21, 1979, Edward Smith disappeared. Four days later, Alfred Evans went missing. Their bodies were found days later in the woods. Each was shot in the back with a .22. Over the next two years, twenty-two more children and six adults would disappear in Atlanta. All but one would be found dead.

Hot Chocolate

Georgia World Congress Center

August 1979

John's mother sat in the Georgia World Congress Center, where Anita Bryant had hypnotized the masses a little more than a year before. Dolly waited to watch her son give up his tiara to the next Miss Gay America.

Larry Edwards's mother sat nearby, hoping her son would win it. The Miss Gay America pageant would be the first place Larry's mother saw him perform. She had confronted him with her trademark blunt questioning: "I heard you do impersonations. Do you wear female attire?" He confessed, and turned it back on the mother he loved. "I'm getting ready to enter this contest," he told her with nerves jangling, "and I'd love for you to fly out to Miss Gay America."

"I'd like to see that," his mother agreed after a pause that ended not a moment too soon. "I want to see what it's all about."

Before his mother could see him, Larry had to compete in preliminaries held at the Sweet Gum Head. Like John, Larry saw the Gum Head as his home away from home. He could count on the crowd to cheer him on—he could even count on John Austin to sponsor him on behalf of the Gum Head.

None of that mattered in his rush to prepare the perfect gown, the perfect talent act, the perfect swimwear ensemble. He had finished first runner-up two years in a row. He wanted to win. Everything had to be flawless.

Larry had built up lots of experience by 1979. He knew what worked for him—high-energy songs, disco, and some ballads like Natalie Cole's "Inseparable." What didn't work? One night, he came out without makeup and tried to mime to Lou Rawls's "You'll Never Find." He dared to do a male song, out of drag, and it bombed. He wouldn't take that kind of chance with the Miss Gay America pageant, not when he had the chance to succeed his best friend with the crown. Not when his mother would be watching.

In three nights of competition, Hot Chocolate vied for top slots with Dana Manchester and Lady Shawn, but she had held back an unforgettable stage act for the final night of the pageant, when it moved to the downtown convention center.

During the question-and-answer session, judges asked Larry what he would contribute to gay society as a title holder.

"I would tell the gay community that they need to have confidence. I couldn't have come this far in female impersonation without it myself. But I have not always had confidence in myself. Only recently was I able to tell my mother what I do for a living. She told me that I should have been confident enough to tell her a long time ago, because she would always love me no matter what, that I would always be her son. She told me that she was really proud of me. So confidence is something I'd like to give to the gay community that I think is very important.

"Secondly, as a female impersonator I would like to stress the importance of being a man as well as a woman. I can be a man offstage and a woman onstage.

"Finally, I would like to get the gay community together and have respect for each other. If gay people are going to get anywhere, they must have unity."

Hot Chocolate was the acid test at the Sweet Gum Head on a normal night. The first time she had done her special medley there, the Gum Head audience screamed with approval, and stomped the floor for more. Performers didn't want to go after her. As with Rachel's act, they might have to start their performance while people still were clapping for someone else.

Hot Chocolate had brought her fans with her to the Convention

Center. She got up on the stage and then ripped it apart, with choreography Larry had plotted for maximum controversy and effect. A gorilla—Larry in costume—sprang onto the stage, then a second one followed. They fought, while a trainer snapped a whip in the air, cracking it inches away from Hot Chocolate and ushering her into a cage. She took a cue from Rachel's Jesus reveal, and in a split second, dropped out of her gorilla costume to display her sequin-studded gown that glimmered while she performed her go-to rendition of Brainstorm's "Lovin' Is Really My Game." The cage spun to show off a sign with her name on it in lights, the music shifted into a faster and hotter key, and Hot Chocolate segued seamlessly into Linda Clifford's disco remake of the Broadway classic, "If My Friends Could See Me Now."

The audience at Miss Gay America rose up in enthusiasm to give her a huge standing ovation. There was little doubt who had won, except for the order of finishing for the runners-up. When the announcers called out the winners, Satyn DeVille took third runner-up, Dana Manchester second runner-up, and Lady Shawn was first runner-up. Hot Chocolate had done her best, wowed the judges, and finally won Miss Gay America. While she cried through her makeup, her mother hugged her and told her how much she had loved her performance.

Charlie Brown

The Sweet Gum Head

September 1979

John Austin couldn't wait for fall. He planned to attend the March on Washington in October, and had choreographed a series of fundraisers to help pay for the buses that would transport protesters from Atlanta to Washington. He knew it would be a good time. "You won't see so many gay people in one place ever again," he said. "And it won't be like in a bar or at a party. It'll be completely different."[7]

"The bars owe a lot to the gay community, a lot more than they put out. They can do much more."

Until the buses pulled out of the depot downtown, John had work to do. He had adapted once more when Rachel Wells left the Sweet Gum Head to tour. With her Miss Gay America title came dozens of well-paying shows away from Atlanta. Austin would always spare a place for her when she came back home, but he had brought in a raft of new talent, including choreographer Marc Jones, to help plan out the Gum Head's now-complex and costly shows. Jones had raven hair and a muscular body from his years in dance and musical theatre at the North Carolina School of the Arts, then the Juilliard School. He modeled, sang in the lounge at the San Francisco Fairmont, led Ann-Margret's Las Vegas troupe, performed in the 1978 Broadway musical *The Act*, and had won the Ruby Award for male jazz dance in 1979.

He came to Atlanta to dance, but grew disillusioned and took other jobs to survive. He staged a number for the Sweet Gum Head's Lisa King when she entered the Miss Florida pageant, and it won him a job as the dance leader as well as show director.

Austin had installed Charlie Brown in Rachel's place in the lineup, but Charlie also replaced Lavita Allen as emcee. After her Miss Gay Atlanta loss to Hot Chocolate, Lavita mostly gave up drag; as Alan, she became a DJ on the club circuit and a frequent face at the Locker Room baths. Charlie had Lavita's knack for hosting and a quick wit, not to mention a burgeoning collection of gowns. She kept some of them in the small dressing room near the Gum Head stage, which she festooned with strings of beads and long feather boas. They moved gently whenever the door opened or closed, and while she changed from her men's blue jeans into drag.

Charlie transformed himself a few times a week into "The

Bitch of the South," with a filthy mouth and raw attitude utterly incongruous with the quiet, generous man the other performers knew. He loved the process of going from a fat, bald man to what he believed was a lovely old woman.

Charlie had left Nashville and moved to Knoxville to direct the show at the town's Carousel Bar, then had come to Atlanta to create a new show at a club called Timbers. On a night off, out with her husband, Fred, Charlie stopped at the Sweet Gum Head and was offered the spot Rachel had left behind when she went on the Miss Gay America tour. Diamond Lil had been performing the role of host, but when she quit abruptly—Lil was known for being dramatic and hasty—John Austin handed Charlie the microphone even though she'd never hosted before in her life. "You're the new emcee," John told him. "You're funny as hell. You can do it." It was meant to be, Charlie thought.

Charlie became a drag superstar on the Gum Head stage, in the same way Rachel had. Performers from other towns would come to the Gum Head, and would leave starstruck by her. More often than not, they would leave with a part of her act; Charlie would catch drag shows in other towns and regularly hear half of her material regurgitated back at her.

Charlie worked hard with both longtime performers and with new starlets like Tina Devore, a smart and honest performer who hosted the Sweet Gum Head's latest show, the *Diamond Girl Revue*. The Diamond Girls gave the club an early-in-the-week channel for new performers who might never make it to the stage on the big weekend nights.

Charlie was a talented emcee, a versatile moneymaker, and the club's most politically active host yet. The fundraisers for causes and benefits became a regular part of the Gum Head's weekly schedule, and Charlie worked many, if not most of them. She worked tirelessly with Marc Jones to ensure the Showplace of the South kept the honorary tagline it had earned even before Rachel Wells had taken its stage for the first time. Marc wanted more choreography, more productions, and fewer stars. The Sweet Gum Head had to fight a swelling tide of competition, it had to be bigger and better than ever; that would be the only way to stay afloat. The troupe began to focus on long, elaborate shows that reenacted entire Broadway plays and Hollywood movies, because drag acts were beginning to appear at straight clubs around town, discos were hosting "Mr. Buns" contests, and even the Gum Head had more straight guests than ever. All kinds of lines had been crossed.

Bill Smith

Fulton County Superior Court

Fall 1979

Signs read, GAY LOVE IS GOOD LOVE. LESBIANS DESERVE RESPECT. WE LOVE OUR GAY CHILDREN.[8] The snap in the air portended an early winter, and the clouds overhead dulled the rainy sky. But the mood felt more like a florid spring day as men in red jackets chanted lyrics to "We Are Family" while one shook a tambourine and urged bystanders to join them. They were an army of lovers who marched amid the necklace of museums that circled the National Mall.

Lesbians and gays were usually invisible among the other tourists reveling in these buildings containing burned-out husks of rocket ships and priceless gemstones walled off behind bulletproof glass. They could be seen among the canvases and sculptures tucked in more discreet corners, if one knew where to look.

Today they were in plain view during the National March on Washington for Lesbian and Gay Rights, where a crowd of thousands took shape on the Mall. Four buses had left Atlanta in the days before. Arriving at the protest, some of the Atlantans who had traveled hundreds of miles to call for equality remembered the big antiwar marches that stopped the nation's capital a decade before. How many had shown up for this march? It was at least 25,000, according to the Parks Service, or 75,000 according to DC police, or 250,000, if the organizers had it right: Three gay marching bands, a gay men's chorus, religious groups, anti-nuke gays, Socialist Workers' Party gays, parents of gays, and lesbian librarians.[9] The Seussian spectacle left the lawn in front of the Capitol and headed west, toward the Washington Monument.

Gay men and women had rallied behind the idea of a march in Washington after the assassination of Harvey Milk the year before. Throughout the summer of 1979, gay bars and businesses across the country put aside cash to send people to DC on October 14. The march had evolved from a remembrance of the ten years of struggle for gay civil rights since Stonewall into a living memorial for Milk, as well as a protest against the morsels of equality tossed to gays by the Carter administration. Gay leaders accused the Carter White House of begging off when it came to equal protection. Stuart Eizenstat, Carter's domestic policy adviser, had come from Atlanta to serve the administration, but all he could offer gay leaders who knew him were vague platitudes. In December, Eizenstat coauthored a memo of support for "the concept of nondiscrimination on the basis of sexual orientation" and emphasized Carter's protection of "the human rights of all people"—but the memo demurred on support of H.R. 2074, a federal gay rights bill.[10]

The struggle for civil liberties had not gone smoothly, but it had made progress, especially on the coasts, and even in places such as Atlanta. The demonstration of diversity was impossible to miss, particularly when it erupted in song: *When the dykes come marching in!* Marchers sang as they made their way west. The gay-rights networks linked up with one another. No-nukes gays met gay dentists and Mountain State gays and OK gays from

Oklahoma. A community acquired self-awareness, and realized it numbered in the millions.

Some in opposition to gay rights came to heckle marchers or held signs with biblical verses. "The Lord is my shepherd," countered one marcher, "and he knows I'm gay." Happenstance tourists simply were respectful of the marchers, or somewhat amused, even when speakers angrily demanded protections in the law, in the workplace, and in the military—protections that might be granted with a bill in the Congress that year, but one opposed by a Georgia Democrat, Rep. Larry McDonald, who opposed so-called "special rights."

Jerry Falwell Sr. prayed for the protesters to repent and spat out hellfire from the nearby House of Representatives Rayburn Office Building, at a meeting of about seventy-five Protestant ministers gathered ironically in the Science and Technology hearing room. Anita Bryant prayed for "those misguided individuals marching in Washington who seek to flaunt their immoral lifestyle."[11]

Falwell's harangues barely registered with marchers. After Washington, the crowds saw strength in their numbers and went home and organized. They rolled on toward what they assured themselves would be a complete and total victory.[12]

///

While the march gained glory, Bill sat at home and waited for his next court date. He had been arrested and taken to jail. He had been humiliated and shamed. He was angry, but more than that, he was afraid.

On September 25, 1979, the Fulton County Superior Court had returned a true bill in the case of *The State v. William Edward Smith, Jr.,* Violation Georgia Controlled Substances Act (Three Counts). Judge Osgood O. Williams signed a bench warrant, which authorized police to arrest Bill and bring him to jail, where he could be held without bond. With the help of his lawyer, Bill was freed to receive medical treatment while he awaited trial.

He had moved away from Ariel, into a new apartment at 425 Tenth Street, near the corner of Charles Allen, opposite the great green lawn of Piedmont Park where he had fought for the right to move through the dark and find another man with whom to share his body. His vigilance about drugs had morphed into a purer paranoia; when he took on a roommate who brought marijuana into the house, he threw him out onto the street the same day and threw out all the roommate's belongings. The police had planted the pot that brought about his arrest, he nervously explained to friends, and if they had any reason to come back into his house they would plant drugs again.

He believed he was being persecuted because of the position that he had held, because he was a pot smoker, an agnostic, a rabble-rouser, a homosexual. Any friends he had at city hall had abandoned him; it was a tangled place to navigate under normal circumstances.

After his arrest, his family turned their backs on him as well. In the fall of 1979 his parents informed him he would not be welcome at their house for the holidays.

Bill had always been the person who told others to get their affairs straight and to get their act in order. Now his own life was in pieces.

He remained positive. "Diane," he wrote, "a very warm hug, a very very tender kiss, and a most deeply sincere thank-you for helping me take care of me during the past two weeks. I feel rather positive about Bill Smith and I have a good measure of confidence in my ability to feel better about me and take care of me much better than I ever have done."[13]

He told *Gaybriel* magazine that he planned to attend the March on Washington, and still put up the facade of leading the movement he'd helped to found. He said he'd been in touch with former colleagues in local groups and in the National Gay Task Force, and cautioned that there might not be enough housing for those who chose to go. "I would love to go up for the weekend," he said. "If I have a place to stay, I am certainly going to be there."[14]

Instead, he waited for the courts to determine his fate. He had already seen the inside of a city jail, but not for the protest drag he'd worn for the past decade. And he did not want to return.

On December 7, 1979, a judge signed a new bench warrant for his arrest.[15]

RuPaul Charles

Buford Highway, Atlanta

Fall 1979

Irving and Ernestine Charles's home in San Diego wore dazzling yellow paint and had a patio and a two-car garage and a palm tree. They had transplanted themselves out west, and for a young Black couple raised in poverty, the move had proven many people wrong.

In San Diego wife Ernestine wore exquisite pop-art clothes, patterned dresses, and elegant caftans. She knew what it took to look happy.

The couple gave their son RuPaul a Barbie doll when he was five years old; he would create pretend makeup commercials when he was eight. He daydreamed in school and got in trouble because he wanted to be somewhere else, anywhere else, because classmates teased him for being effeminate. He didn't understand why it was bad or wrong. His sister told him to read a magazine story on Christine Jorgensen, the first American transgender woman to go public after her surgery, and he wondered why he had to read it.

RuPaul's parents had a volatile marriage and would scream at each other in the front room while he hid with his sisters until they stopped. One fight ended in broken dishes and lamps flung everywhere, like a storm had passed through. Another time, Ernestine poured gasoline on Irving's car and screamed *I will light this motherfucker* while her husband begged her to stop. The house felt empty when his father left for good. His mother withdrew to her bedroom, and RuPaul's sisters took over his care.

When he was thirteen, RuPaul Charles told himself that the world was trying to shape him, trying to put him in a box that it could understand. *Hold your breath,* he told himself. *Cross your fingers. Do whatever it takes to not get body-snatched into that box.*[16]

RuPaul blossomed in high school like his Afro, which grew to almost a foot and a half deep. He smoked pot. At his school, the cafeteria became a disco in the hours before class, when kids could do the Bump and drink chocolate milk and eat doughnuts while their parents commuted to work. RuPaul usually sat on the side and watched, but screwed up the courage one day to do the Crip Walk—a new dance comprised of intricate footwork and serpentine hip sways that emerged in Southern California in the 1970s—and it made him a school star. He had been judged a freak in elementary school; he became a superfreak in school. He wore his hair in rollers and wore his mother's makeup. His class voted him best Afro and best dancer.

RuPaul's sister Renetta had a boyfriend, Laurence, who wanted to be a businessman. Laurence decided Atlanta would be a better place for a young Black man to make a name for himself. It had a Black mayor, after all. RuPaul only knew it had Hank Aaron. When Laurence and Renetta moved east on July 23, 1976, RuPaul went with them.

///

RuPaul had never seen so many Black people before Atlanta, and never had seen so many freaks. He knew he'd found a home. Within a few months he had asserted his independence and roamed late-night parties at warehouses and underground clubs with his friends in the early hours of the morning.

He loved school, especially drama class. But because the performing-arts school was far from home, getting there was a hassle, and he didn't have time to sort it out. He quit and started driving cars from California back to Atlanta for Laurence, who would flip them for a profit. He would fly to San Diego and drive the cars back, listening to the radio nonstop as he drove.

When he moved out on his own, RuPaul shared apartments with friends in scruffy Midtown. With his friends, he would stumble in and out of clubs there. Sometimes they would make it out to the Great White Way, the Cheshire Bridge strip, where he saw his first drag show: Crystal LaBeija performed Donna Summer wearing a black bustier and fishnet stockings at Numbers. He couldn't believe she lip-synced instead of singing it herself.

He met Todd, a boyfriend who became a friend. They hurtled through the alt-world that sprang out of dingy back rooms and abandoned warehouses while the rest of Atlanta slept. Todd was first to go to the Sweet Gum Head, where someone had given him a pearl of wisdom: *You're born naked and the rest is drag.* He shared it with his friend.

Acting had already transformed RuPaul before he put on his first look. Everyone was wearing some kind of mask, he realized. They controlled who they told the world they were. Drag was at least honest about it.

Born naked and the rest is drag? RuPaul asked himself. *Oh, I love that and I'm going to use that.*[17]

He began to command a new universe around himself, to make it spin and whirl at his behest. He pulled ideas and makeup and outfits into his orbit and pinned them to his jacket, glued them to his T-shirt, absorbed them into his skin. He had begun transforming before Diane saw him in the gas-station parking lot where he danced for no one but himself.

Hi, he would say to Diane sweetly, and she would answer sweetly back.

Diamond Lil

Sweet Gum Head

Winter 1979

To gay men in the pre-Stonewall South, a few names came up often in conversation. A mention of Atlanta always brought up Diamond Lil.

Sister, mother, queen. Diamond Lil told you to call her one of those things, depending on where you were and who you were.

As a sister she traded barbs with other girls. *Oh, Mary! Too much for color television!*

As a mother she cooed to the young gay men who flocked to her for the life prescriptions she wrote in the newspaper: "Remember, it's not good to save what you have for the worms. It's later than you think!"[18]

She told the rest of Atlanta to call her the Queen of the Dunk 'N Dine, an homage to the neon-lit, subway-tiled refuge that offered disco fries soaked in gravy and smothered in cheese to those who stumbled in after shows at the Sweet Gum Head.

In 1979 other girls pushed the boundaries, performed nearly naked, tongue-kissed patrons. Lil still came from Planet Fifties, albeit projected through some jarring, eclectic filters. She danced at the midpoint of a twisted strand of DNA that related the old world of female impersonation to the new frontier of performance art.

"We'll be together for eternity," she sang as she shimmied.[19] Lil's shimmy looked more like a shiver, offbeat and tense. She would stare wide-eyed, arms splayed extravagantly, a Norma Desmond always looking for a Cecil B. DeMille in the crowd.

While the rest of the girls lip-synced to popular songs, Lil had formed a band with some fellow writers from the *Great Speckled Bird*. Together they wrote real music, including an ode to the diner across the street. She barely sang on-key. The crowd rooted for her anyway. Her reedy and rounded falsetto instrument quavered with enthusiasm onstage, fierce and nervous all at once like a Chihuahua. Off the worn oak and out from under the hot lights of the Gum Head, it softened to a lilting drawl, a Minnie Pearl warmth put through finishing school.

"Well, I'm just a wild Tina Turner style," she told friends, admirers, reporters, waiters, herself. "So if you've seen Tina, which I'm sure you have, it's very much like her, very, very much like her."[20] Frail-looking and pale, Lil connected on a deep level with Turner's tumultuous personal life; as an artist Lil pointed out Turner sang more, while Lil rapped with the audience.

Lil changed looks all the time, from blond to redhead to brunette. She morphed in and out of eras with cosmetic perfection. Lil wore ice-cream-blond curls like Thelma Todd. She drew eyebrows like parentheses across her forehead, put on golden straight hair and lightly tinted her cheeks like Sharon Tate, or went beatnik in a dark blouse and natural makeup. She posed like Loretta Lynn on a rustic cabin porch, skirt hiked over a knee, well-endowed with red bouffant hair.

During her on-again, off-again career at the Sweet Gum Head she drifted into the role of emcee, and drifted from her rock-'n'-roll originals to brazen pantomime. She donned a nun's habit for the Gum Head's "Nutty Hot Fudge Sunday" show. She turned the Gum Head into a temporary tabernacle, and injected loopy lunacy to Donna Summer's disco cover of the strange pop smash "MacArthur Park." She kicked props and chairs off the stage, lurching from end to end in a state of delirium.

Lil could pass as a woman, but usually she dressed as a boy, one on the precipitous edge of femininity. She wore a flower-printed tunic and jeans when it was warm in spring, cut her hair in a boyish bob and let her high nose and slanted eyebrows and elfin ears telegraph her bemusement to the world around her.

///

Lil had been born Phillip Forrester, on December 28, 1935. As a boy he dressed in his mother's satin pumps and slip at age five and sang "Don't Fence Me In" for the children who lived in the townhouse across the street. It was a practice his mother looked at quizzically, then put to an immediate stop.

A child during the war years, Lil had sung on Savannah radio on *WTOC's Amateur Hour*. What likely started as a novelty act— a little boy singing grown-up torch songs—evolved into a dangerous flare of sexual ambiguity.

"You can't be a prophet in your own hometown," Diamond Lil wrote. "The town won't let you."[21]

Teenage Lil sang on the riverfront, reveling in the attention of tourists and sailors on leave. In the era of boogie-woogie and blues, pinup-girls were her idols. Her classmates nominated Lil as Miss Commercial High. She was disqualified, but continued to dress in drag with an overweight friend who called himself Sophie. Together on Halloween, Lil and Sophie dressed in evening wear and headed for an American Legion ball on Tybee Island, without an invite. Drinking it up with Air Force cadets, Lil and Sophie passed for women, until Sophie blurted out the truth.

They left in a rush, but two male cadets chased after their car and shot out a tire. The men in uniform held Lil and Sophie at gunpoint, then one raped Lil by forcing her to perform oral sex on him.

"It was so scary," Lil later said. "There's no words for it. But I made a decision that night that I was out. A real weird way to come out, though."[22]

Lil began to take more risks with drag. She performed as a woman in public for the first time at eighteen, singing Ruth Brown's "Three Letters." She sang at cocktail parties and danced for soldiers and sailors headed to Korea. She joined the Air National Guard, served for two years, and ranked as high as corporal—but on one occasion, the good-time girl leapt from table to table in the mess hall singing "The Heat Is On," dressed in women's shorts and a peasant blouse.

Drag cost Lil her Air National Guard post and a job as a private secretary at the Seaboard Railroad. A clerk had seen Lil dancing "The Barefoot Contessa" at an open house on a naval vessel. The sailors cheered Lil in their starched white uniforms, but the clerk had spread the word about Lil's act. She couldn't find another job. She faced arrest after arrest for her performances.

By 1965, Lil knew she could stay and endure the harassment, get arrested, maybe go to jail—or she could leave.

///

Lil settled on the Strip, where she set up her first antique store among the head shops and flophouses. The Strip crowd didn't buy many antiques and repelled customers who might. Lil closed up shop there and headed for genteel Buckhead to sell her wares, but still called the Strip home.

She danced and sang wherever she could once she set foot in Atlanta in 1965 and discovered the underground world of drag just beginning to emerge from private house parties and from a few discreet nightclubs and bars. Drag became her armor, and Lil steeled herself and cultivated her budding celebrity with unadvertised shows in unlikely clubs. Under the weight of seven wigs and six pairs of eyelashes, rhinestones on her eyelids, bright-orange lipstick, and simple crepe de chine gowns, "so as not to take away from facial beauty," she paired painted-on glamour with gritty counterculture dinge.

Lil bestowed an honorary title on herself, the "Queen of All Glamour and Grease," thrilled by the clash of the vain and the vulgar. She layered on superlatives, dubbed queens "voluptuous vamps" and overemoted at every junction. She called one of her bohemian homes "The Temple of the Lonesome Oaks" and her hometown of Savannah "The Land of Famine." She spoke in her own dialect made up suffixes and prefixes, mutated "yes" into "yarr!" and no into "narr!," added French-sounding articles at a whim: *Oh yarr, darling, we're going to ze gay bar tonight, I'm wearing la evening dress*, she might say to another queen, sitting on her porch on Fourteenth Street with freshly shaven legs poking out from women's shorts, an outrageous toupee glued to her head. She was a flaming creature in a day when transsexuals and gay men and drag queens were all lumped together, joined in their supposed shame.

Lil pioneered drag in Atlanta in the waning days of the 1960s at clubs like Mrs. P's, the restaurant in the Ponce de Leon Hotel, which sold filet mignon for $1.25 as a dinner special, then turned more obviously gay at night. The owner had struck a deal with cops: they wouldn't raid the place if the shows took place only during the week, and if they were not advertised. Lil lip-synced to Aretha Franklin and shimmied through rhythm-and-blues hits at Mrs. P's until it was sold and the shows ended. Then she took her act to the even seedier Club Centaur.

The Centaur was no refuge. Outside the police tear-gassed rowdy bikers who mobbed the club and broke out in fistfights. Inside, the bikers threw their chains on the stage and threw beer on it too. Lil dismissed it: They were camping, not harassing. She stepped down from the stage, stepped on their table, swung her skirt high in the air and drank out of the bikers' pitcher of beer— to their delight.

When the Centaur closed, Lil leaned on the other straight and mixed clubs to bring home money. She played Peaches Back Door before it changed its name to the Backstreet, even played the Great Southeastern Music Hall. Their straight crowds worshiped her drag, and gays partied along with her. Both followed her from club to club, since Lil always had a new quip or material; "After all," she said, "others have to have SOMETHING to copy."[23] For her performances of "Big Lollipop" she brought backup dancers wearing jock straps filled with big lollipops. She pulled out the candy during the show and threw it to patrons.

Until the 1970s, Lil got arrested repeatedly for drag. In her last run-in, the police wrote her up for "female impersonation."

"There's no such charge as that!" she complained. "And besides, that particular night I was only in what folks would call cosmic drag. That means a little bit of drag and a lot of men's attire, you know, like no falsies, none of that."[24]

Despite protests in court that she had only tried to fit in with the long-haired hippies, a judge gave Lil a $35 fine for female impersonation. She spent $150 to appeal the fine—and won.

"They just took it off the record, supposedly," she said, "but you know how they are down at the Police Department. Probably still on it."[25]

But the arrests stopped.

///

At the Sweet Gum Head, Lil appeared in a New Year's Eve special in 1979 as Rachel Wells's special guest. They had met years before, when Lil worked at the Sweet Gum Head and raved over Rachel's auburn hair and how much she thought Rachel resembled Rita Hayworth. Rachel had the utmost respect for her and envied her talent; no other drag queen was quite like Lil, and very few sang their own songs. Lil was a singular talent, and she frequently reminded her fans and rivals of that fact.

When Lil came back to the Sweet Gum Head, her fans followed and took over the club with rhythmic chants of *"Lil! Lil!*

Lil!" Lil set the club on fire with a preacher's monologue that converted the Sweet Gum Head guests into her congregation. She swooned through songs in a state somewhere between delirium and ecstasy, the living incarnation of camp.

Other performers tried to upstage Lil, and failed. "The king of spades will never outshine the queen of diamonds!" she crowed.

Lil had quit as the Sweet Gum Head emcee, but she returned in triumph. She vamped for hours, tucked tips in a low-cut sequined halter that framed the pearly skin of her forty-four-year-old breasts. She had already become the stuff of legend, and so had Atlanta's nightlife. Lil had been there when the drag scene was born. She would be there when it started to die.

1980

///

TRAGEDY

Bill Smith

Atlanta

January 21, 1980

On January 21, 1980, police arrested William E. Smith Jr. for possession of more than an ounce of marijuana, and for possession of amphetamines.[1] The charges threatened up to a year in jail. If convicted on his second arrest in a year, Bill might be sentenced to serve at least six months in prison.

Bill Smith

Atlanta

March 7, 1980

In February of 1980, Bill purchased a ticket to the movie theater in downtown Atlanta, near the new arena built for the Flames hockey team. He had been downtown for a court hearing, and due to a computer glitch, had ended up in jail for a few hours while it was sorted out.

He watched *And Justice for All*. In the film, Al Pacino plays a lawyer who rails against the legal system and judicial corruption after a client commits suicide in jail. Bill grew anxious and emotional in the dark theater. When the movie was over, he stumbled around, unable to find a way out.

He had lost nearly everything. He'd lost his place in the community, which stung. He'd lost friends, which drove him into seclusion. He'd lost control over his addictions, which submerged him in a haze of mood relaxers and sleeping pills. He had not yet lost his freedom, but that danger lurked nearby.

By March, Bill had removed all his belongings from his apartment on Tenth Street and had come to stay with Diane and her roommate as he prepared for another court date, a grand jury hearing on his second arrest. Diane had been a practicing psychotherapist for a while, and talked to him for hours to try to calm him down. "You're not going to jail," she tried in vain to reassure him. "You're not going to go to jail. We're going to make sure that doesn't happen to you."

///

The Shriners held their annual circus in downtown Atlanta, and when they came to town in 1969, Bill had invited Diane to attend. Bill's father, a Shriner potentate at the Yaarab Temple, had free tickets for the event at the Atlanta Municipal Auditorium. For a few hours, they could disconnect from the real world and indulge in a made-up one: They could see the gypsy caravan of the Clyde Brothers' three-ring circus, cheer on the Tiska High Wire Troupe as they balanced a motorcycle on a high wire, and would gasp as Princess Tajana spun her magic from there as a part of the spellbinding action.[2]

Bill would bring Diane to events whenever he wanted to convince his family that he wasn't gay anymore. He liked her too, her fierce intellect, her acceptance of herself. They were both deviants of a similar kind.

When the phone rang that afternoon in 1969, it was Bill, just as she'd hoped. Diane could have watched *Mission: Impossible* on TV that night instead. She could have ignored the phone; Bill had been distant and cold to her at a recent party. But she was his go-to when he got lonely or bored, and he was hers.

Bill picked her up that night wearing a gold cotton Nehru shirt and white velvet bell-bottomed slacks. His brown hair almost touched his shoulders, since he had straightened it, removing the kinks from it by sheer chemical force. While she finished getting ready, they bickered like brother and sister about her junior-senior dance, about the money she'd spent on a stereo and records and books instead of clothes she could have worn to the dance. "And the rest is in the bank for college," she responded smartly.

Before the circus, Bill took her to Cheshire Bridge Road and showed off the apartment he shared with his new roommates. It was beautiful, with gold shag carpeting at the entry, a copy of Michelangelo's David, a sparkling new kitchen, and a hallway that led to a living and dining area where a big brown velour chair faced the couch. She sank in and accepted a drink from him. How could he afford it all? she asked.

"I sell drugs to small children," he joked with her. She choked on the drink—not because of his sardonic answer but at the strength of the strawberry daiquiri he served. It was the first alcohol she'd ever tasted, and she grew drunk quickly.

He lit a long Benson & Hedges with a dark filter, and turned half away from her.

"You're pretty and intelligent and I like you a lot. I'm starting to feel a little scared. I've seen you a lot this year and I know by this time you're probably wondering why I don't ever ask you out for days," he said as the flare of a lit match outlined his head for an instant, then died.

"Do you know what homosexual is?" he asked.

"I'm not just telling you this to explain why I haven't asked you out, it's just that you remind me so much of myself," he explained to her. "You're different and nobody likes you except a few close friends who understand. You keep pushing how different you are on everyone around you. And you keep getting hurt.

"You don't have to go around shocking people. You don't have to convince the people at school that the Bible is a pack of lies or tell everyone about your liberal views on sex. You don't have to tell your teachers that people have the right to take drugs if they want to or that you'd like to try marijuana yourself. You outrage and upset everyone around you, and then you hate it when nobody likes you. Do you understand what I'm saying?"

She did, but all she could really hear was that she never would have him. She nodded.

"Which means you don't understand a word. Jesus Christ, you have to pretend to be normal; it's illegal to be a queer. I could be arrested, I could lose my job. Half the people I know would stop seeing me if they found out. It's hell and I have no choice. You, you make your own hell and you don't even have to." His high school girlfriend Linda had been camouflage, pure camouflage, he explained.

"Do you not want to be a homosexual?" she asked him.

"Is that all you've heard? No, I don't want to be a homosexual, but I'm stuck with it. I've known that since I was five."

"Does that mean I can't see you anymore?"

"I don't know," he said.

They were late for the circus. The mausoleum-like auditorium had already filled to its 5,000-seat capacity. Diane sat on the top step of a dirty flight of stairs, and Bill leaned on a wall, standing behind her. She was afraid he would flinch, but she leaned back anyway. His hand fell to her head and he touched her hair gently.

The circus went on, but the thrill had fallen apart. She tried to push pleasure into her mind and push out what she had been told, but could not. Children shouted and carnies hawked *peanuts!* And *popcorn!* And *Coca-Cola!* The smell of freshly shaved sawdust gave way to other senses. She watched as the elephants moved listlessly through the ring while clowns went ape through contrived antics. Princess Tajana and the other acrobats seemed fat and old, with flesh bulging from their tights in Fellini-esque folds. They couldn't defy death. It had all been an illusion.[3]

///

Diane saw no signs of imminent danger in Bill's behavior that night in March. He controlled himself carefully, though she knew his sadness had turned into despair. When he had a lot to drink, he would suggest that maybe he would be better off dead, but for the moment he focused only on his fear of prison, the potential for abuse, the potential for boredom.

When Bill got ready to leave Diane's house, he told her he would seek treatment. He had resisted drug treatment and therapy for many years. He didn't trust psychiatrists after his conversion therapy, but knew Diane believed in psychiatry's power. She told him to stay until after the court had decided his fate.

"I'm not going to be a burden to you," he said, though she told him he wasn't, that her roommate didn't mind. "Well, you know, I don't think Ilene wants me here." He had lost weight, and he looked too thin, too weak.

///

Who we are is never permanent. At best it is a recognizable face to show the world who we are now, who we want to be. At worst, it is a conceit, a deceit, a lie we tell ourselves.

Bill Smith had told himself he wasn't the wayward son of a Baptist soldier, was attracted to women, didn't have a drug problem, could be both a pimp and an elected official, and wasn't beholden to darker impulses and motives. He could never admit that he had run out of solutions and had no way to deal with the irreparable consequences that shame had brought him. He could never admit to himself that he was not the young man in the idealized oil-painting portrait that hung in his parents' home, in his frizzy hair and wide-collared ochre shirt.

He saw no way forward, and no way back. His lover Jimmy would not leave his family to be with him. He felt like a burden to his remaining friends. His family no longer welcomed him. His father would not tolerate anything that upset his mother. He had tried to run away from his past, but could not outrun it as it collapsed around him.

A grand jury was empaneled under an assistant foreman, A. B. Padgett. A true bill writ on March 7, 1980, determined Bill Smith would have to face the charges in court. The court issued a new bench warrant and offered him no bond.

Rachel Wells

Atlanta

March 7, 1980

I n the musical *Chicago*, the "Cell Block Tango" reveals how the women locked up in their prison cages were put there in the first place. One convict warns her husband to stop popping his chewing gum. She fires two warning shots. *Into his head.*

At the Sweet Gum Head, when dark antiheroine Velma Kelly took to the stage, she explained how she'd caught her sister and husband reenacting an acrobatic act from their stage routine. The spread-eagle. She blacked out. *They had it coming.*

Back in the days of the *Red, White & Blue Revue*, Gum Head girls had tap-danced with Phyllis Killer while they beat her with ukuleles. They executed *A Chorus Line* with precision, and *Jesus Christ Superstar*, too, down to the flayings and beatings and mystical transformations.

Chicago burnished the Gum Head's reputation for high-quality theatre, something beyond mere drag. Satyn's Velma gave her free rein to cast her evil eye around the room, and to show off her perfectly coiffed dark hair, but it also gave her a role in which her sly humor found a home. Charlie Brown inhabited the role of the prison matron, a foulmouthed natural at it.

Rachel Wells's Roxie Hart rang particularly true as she mouthed the words to "Nowadays." The ingenue that came to the big city had starred in nearly every major Gum Head production for the last eight years. Roxie's bumpkin-to-beauty transformation mirrored John Greenwell's own metamorphosis into a leggy, beautiful redheaded woman.

By 1980, the Sweet Gum Head looked over its shoulder and saw the ground that Atlanta's discos had conquered. Drag had long been a gay cultural mainstay in the South, but disco became titanic. It was the first genre of music that crossed every line, whether it was race, age, nationality, or gender. It began to deconstruct itself with songs such as "Gett Off" and "Funkytown." It fragmented into dance, house, and new wave. It ridiculed itself with Ethel Merman's disco album. The point of disco was not the song or the dance, it was the change. But it froze in time, and became mundane, in the same circadian cycle that any art movement endured.

What had started as lithe, taut dance music that liberated an underground had become commercial and commonplace. It had already begun to mourn itself, with Gloria Gaynor's 1978 disco triumph "I Will Survive." An insistent plea that no matter what, the world would not crumble, or lay down and die, the song won the Grammy for Best Disco Record in February of 1980.

By then, drag had become ubiquitous in clubs across Atlanta, and the demarcation between show bars and disco clubs had blurred. There was nothing in the Gum Head that couldn't be found in any other club in the city. All sorts of lines had been crossed. The Sweet Gum Head had become almost normal, and John Greenwell's character Rachel Wells had too.

Like Roxie Hart in *Chicago*, John had found a way to emancipate himself at the Sweet Gum Head. That freedom had come with notoriety, and a peculiar kind of fame, one that came with an endpoint. John would turn thirty soon, and he had started to save money for no particular reason other than to gently withdraw from the world he had built for himself and Rachel Wells.

Bill Smith

Atlanta

March 8, 1980

"The moon is good," Bill had written to Diane, long before that midnight, "but like gentle tides on pleasant beaches, destructive waves of powerful fury come also from our moody moon."

A thick pelt of clouds muted the half-moon over Cheshire Bridge Road that Saturday night in early March. Lightning ripped fresh wounds in the sky.

Nearly fifteen years before, researchers had written of drugs such as Placidyl that the self-administered overdose of them had long been a popular means of expressing situational protest. Not infrequently, they were successful in providing the user with the means to take their own life.

What does seem to have been known was that overdoses had to be treated immediately. An overdose of the drug could leave the victim unconscious and confused, unable to summon help if they had changed their mind. Their limbs would go weak, their breath thready and slow, their speech slurred or unintelligible, and their gait unsteady. Their heart would slow. Then it would stop.

In the days before his final court date, Bill exiled himself at a motel outside of city limits, to avoid yet another trip to jail. He wrote friends and expressed hope that he could serve his time and finally receive the therapy they believed he needed. He planned to plead guilty to drug possession, to enter an inpatient facility for treatment, and then to serve six months.

"I'll turn myself in. I'll be fine."

He told Diane he had been too much of a drain on her already. His parents would support him, he said. It pained her that he had tried so hard to forgive them and to love them. She hated them.

On that last night of his life Bill took his prescription sleeping pills. Then he took more of them. And then, still more. He struggled with consciousness. He drove toward Northside Hospital in his blue VW Squareback, an old '72 beater he'd acquired after he had wrecked a Honda two years before.

He pulled into the parking lot at half past ten, going the wrong way. A security guard stopped him. He slurred his speech. He backed his car into a parking space still warm and slick from the day's rain. Bill's breath went shallow, then hitched. He slumped behind the wheel of his car.

"Dependency kills," he had written to Diane a decade earlier. "Like vines on a tree it kills its host and then dies itself."

On March 9, 1980, the sky was swarming with clouds. Morning had not broken through the gray when Bill was found, dead from an overdose. Just before dawn, the medical examiner picked up the phone and dialed the only number found in his wallet.

///

Diane's roommate banged on her door before six in the morning. It was the medical examiner. When she took the call, she assumed one of the women she aided at the community crisis center had been beaten to death by her husband.

She was told it was Bill. At half past five that morning, security found him in his car, amid some blankets and candles and other odds and ends. They found a photo of a blond young man, and slides of other naked men. They found a note. They took him to the emergency room. His blood was overfull with Placidyl, 12.3 milligrams per deciliter when half that could prove fatal. At a quarter to six in the morning a doctor had pronounced Bill Smith dead.

The medical examiner needed to contact Bill's next of kin. Diane fought her grief and pain to recall a friend of the Smiths from church. She dialed and got the number at the Smith home east of Atlanta.

///

As soon as she was able, she raced to Bill's apartment to retrieve a black trunk. Bill had made her promise to remove it if he died. Diane got there after Bill's father and brother-in-law had started to pack away Bill's belongings. The black trunk already was gone. Empty of the last bit of empathy, she lashed out at them: "Maybe he wouldn't have killed himself if you hadn't been so ashamed of him."

///

The next morning, Diane trembled and tried to stay composed while she spoke to the obituary writer at the *Constitution*. Bill had been a city commissioner. He had helped found Gay Pride and the local MCC gay church. He published the South's biggest gay newspaper, and worked on gay issues for the city and the ACLU. When much was at stake, he gave gay liberation a voice, a platform, a channel to city hall, and a reason to believe. When the newspaper landed on her porch the morning after he was discovered dead, no mention of Bill Smith appeared at all.

"Let me check on this," the writer replied.

A half an hour later Diane got a phone call from Bill Sr.

"Diane, please don't do this to us," he pleaded with her. "Don't ask them to put all that stuff in the paper about Bill. His mother can't hold her head up in church as it is."

///

Diane cried through the service in Covington, as did Bill's father.

Bill's gay and lesbian friends had shown up to remember him, and they were not welcome. Bill's mother kept her hostility below the surface but let her family know she was very upset his gay friends had shown. In his eulogy, her reverend absolved the family for what had become of Bill.

Diane cried all the way to the cemetery, where no one spoke a word to her.

Bill had sent a final letter to Diane. He had begun to write it, with a hint of optimism, on February 15. It came in an envelope from the Sheraton airport hotel, with a postmark of March 6, 1980, the day before his bench warrant had been issued. Diane found the letter in her mailbox when she returned home from his funeral.

Mayor Maynard Jackson

City Hall

Summer 1980

That summer, on a humid June Sunday, some 1,500 "gays, lesbians, transvestites and their sympathizers" marched the usual Peachtree-to-Piedmont route and read the proclamation of City Councilman John Sweet, who declared Gay Lesbian and Transperson Week in Atlanta when the mayor would not.

Atlanta had developed a strong gay-rights movement with real political clout, thanks to the city's magnetic draw for gays and lesbians from smaller places in the South. Some saw the movement as a natural extension of the civil-rights era, replacing racial animus with religious opposition.

Among gays themselves, the human range of beliefs and politics curlicued in the predictable, usual ways. Some were stable and staid, others fickle and flighty. Some were old, some were young. Some believed in the "Morning in America" promised by presidential candidate Ronald Reagan. Others were self-professed flaming liberals.

Gays moved out of the closet and into the voting booth, according to the local Atlanta weekly newspaper *Creative Loafing*. They were as disparate in their makeup as any other random slice of society. And while some expected gay candidates to eventually win an election, they had hope that the platform would be something other than just being gay.

Police harassment still was perceived as an issue; police still bothered with inserting clumsy undercover officers into gay bars. This while Atlanta was swept up into the child murders of the late 1970s, and trying to connect them to the gay community. Activist Frank Scheuren went to the police to help them understand the gay community and to understand why homosexuality wasn't a cause in the murders.

Gay-rights supporters, no matter how visible, still would be castigated. One of Atlanta's first female Black news anchors, Monica Kaufman, appeared at a fundraiser for the Atlanta Gay Center. She knew from her own life in the South that the key would be people joining together and challenging the laws. President Carter had signed an order that banned discrimination against gay people in hiring, but for more progress, gay people would have to mirror the Black political experience. They would have to stand by who they were, what they wanted, and what they contributed to society. Kaufman encouraged gay doctors and teachers to come out; she encouraged gay people to spend money at gay businesses and to boycott those that indulged in gay stereotypes.

The 1980 Pride Committee changed its name to Lesbian, Gay, Transgendered Pride. With no small amount of irony, as the movement splintered again into factions that wanted to continue political protests, and those who wanted only to celebrate. The chosen theme was "Let's Get Together."

Mayor Jackson had stopped mentioning "Pride" three years earlier, when he bowed to the Citizens for a Decent Atlanta and referred to Pride as Civil Liberties Days. In 1980 he chose not to say anything at all.

President James Earl Carter

The White House

November 4, 1980

Bartenders mixed expensive cocktails while waitstaff passed fried chicken and barbecue from silver chafing dishes. The ballroom at the Sheraton Washington Hotel had the trappings of a festive celebration but the mood was funereal in spite of the rousing music that blared out of tune with the moment.

"I can't believe every key state would go to Reagan," a party-goer said with fried chicken poised by her mouth.

The warning signs erupted during the summer, when President Carter faced a primary challenge from Sen. Ted Kennedy. He secured the Democratic nomination for the president but had been politically wounded and would not recover.

Carter's human-rights campaigns had fallen aside due to a poor economy, military failures abroad, and a lingering sense that he was stuck in the Vietnam era. The hostage crisis in Iran provided the ammunition voters needed to register their dissent. His opponent proved a savvy television debater. Carter was known in DC circles as evangelical to a fault, a micromanager obsessed with details but not possessed of the means to see grander visions through. He didn't step to Washington's political rhythm.

Carter had flown on *Air Force One* to south Georgia to cast his ballot at home. On the flight to Plains, pollster Pat Caddell told him quietly that it was all over, and Carter burst into tears.

"Don't say anything yet to Rosalynn," Carter told those who knew the results.[4] "Let me tell her."

At home in Plains on Election Day, Carter told a crowd that he was confident in the outcome, then flew back to gloomy Washington, where he stood under an umbrella held by his wife, growing wet at his shoulders as he stared into the abyss.

By nine p.m., as platters of food circulated through the crowd, it was clear that James Earl Carter Jr. would be headed back to Plains for good in a matter of weeks. Carter picked up the phone and placed a phone call to California.

"Let's go and get it over with," Carter told his aides.[5] He officially conceded at 10 p.m., the quickest concession by any candidate for president since the turn of the century.

Carter had lost to Ronald Reagan, former California governor and the herald of a new conservative age and the promise of a "Morning in America." Carter polled 43 percent of the popular vote, Reagan 51 percent. Carter carried three states and the District of Columbia. Reagan swept everywhere else, taking union-loyal voters away from the Democrats as well as nearly the entire South.

Reagan, who had proposed an anti-gay amendment to his state constitution as governor, learned he would be the next president at his home in Pacific Palisades, on a dry and warm day. His campaign aides milled around with the happy energy of victory. His breezy, optimistic tone had proved a facile weapon to skewer Carter's relentless humorlessness, and the gravity with which he approached the hostages held by Iran and a prolapsed economy that refused to heal itself.

The cameras turned their gaze away from the humiliated commander in chief and pivoted toward California, where his successor struck a familiar avuncular pose. "I consider the trust you have placed in me sacred and I give you my sacred oath that I will do my utmost to justify your faith," Reagan told his believers as he accepted Carter's concession.[6]

Billboards sprang up overnight on the western plain: WELCOME TO THE REAGAN REVOLUTION.[7]

Rachel Wells

The Sweet Gum Head

December 1980

Whenever she was in town, Rachel booked weekend shows at the Gum Head, between Hot Chocolate and Diamond Lil and the other regular girls. The weekend shows still were a huge draw; her star power hadn't diminished, though her character had embarked on another sea change. The carefully groomed pageant hair went wild once more, then the Amazon goddess cropped it and added Pat Benatar and more new-wave music to her repertoire. She padded her body for the first time, to create a plush figure. She pulled out the standard crowd-pleasers when she had to, but added new ones like Loretta Lynn, her outfit cobbled together from some of Satyn's old costumes. She didn't rehearse it, didn't even know the words, but with one of Satyn's dresses and a wig and hardly any makeup on, Rachel performed "Coal Miner's Daughter" to enormous applause and a callback.

Costumes were no longer new identities. They were card tricks to be pulled on an amused and anxious crowd with the ease of a dealer.

She ventured into the ridiculous: one night she put on a white bathing suit and a rhinestone tiara, spun herself into yards of cotton-candy-pink tulle, and held a rhinestone scepter. Rachel performed to Olivia Newton-John's "Magic," almost unable to move. She stuck to the back of the stage, only waving her scepter and moving her head until the curtains closed. The crowd roared; Rachel and Satyn laughed themselves silly backstage afterward.

The Gum Head moved into a contentious time. Marc Jones decided the cast would toil on time-intensive dance productions, while guest performers like Rachel and Lisa King would waltz in for four numbers a night, before and after the main event. Performers bickered over favorite songs, and their order of performance. They split into factions, those in the downstairs dressing room against those upstairs.

Dissent struck the ranks of performers and staff alike, and the Gum Head cast let its private spats spill into public in the city's gay publications. Jones said that drug use among performers led to fines and some high-profile firings, which had to be sanctioned by the front office. He promised that the new Gum Head lineup had done away with the star system, and that he would treat cast members as equals, more like a family. He planned ahead for more productions, more legitimate theatre, even a production of *Cabaret*.

Lisa King took to print to rail against Jones and the managers. Mismanagement was the reason the shows and the cast weren't up to past levels, she said. Bar owners were always looking for excuses to get rid of talent, and to hire cheaper labor, which turned performer against performer. She said she would never work at the Sweet Gum Head again.

Lisa had left the Gum Head with a job in hand and opened a Late Night Revue at Numbers, the new club that had opened in the old Locker Room space. Roski Fernandez and Lily White were on board for three shows a night at eleven, one, and three in the morning. King would be the hostess and would perform twice a night. She asked Rachel to join her and perform three songs a night, for $200 a night, just on Fridays and Saturdays.

Rachel decided to leave the Sweet Gum Head's cast of guest performers to join Lisa at its rival club. She didn't say goodbye. What would be the point? The club would be there if she needed to come back. If she wanted to come back.

She had always come back.

1981

///

MIDNIGHT AT THE OASIS

Rachel Wells

Atlanta

Spring 1981

Dressed like a hooker at a political rally, Rachel Wells wobbled toward the basement in four-inch heels, still tired from the 6:45 a.m. makeup call. Downstairs, under bright lights and through thick smoke, she could pick out some familiar faces: Charles Durning at the back of the room, and Brian Keith, who offered her his big hand to shake.

She saw Burt Reynolds and smiled at him.

Filming had begun for *Sharky's Machine*, starring Rachel Ward and Reynolds, whose signature scene had him plunge hundreds of feet off the Westin Peachtree, then the tallest hotel in the Western Hemisphere. At the top of the Westin, a short-lived disco called Burt's—complete with a backlit stained-glass homage to Reynolds built into the floor—had already come and gone. The scene was actually filmed at the Hyatt nearby. Nothing was as it seemed.

A casting call had brought out all the Gum Head family, each drag queen eager to step over the other to get a bit part in the movie. A few insisted they'd won the role, but when Rachel showed up for her audition and passed around pictures of Burt in her Sweet Gum Head dressing room, she was told when to show up for work, no audition required.

You look beautiful, Burt said.

Reynolds had remembered Rachel from his night at the Sweet Gum Head five years before. When she returned to shoot, Keith befriended her while cameras swung into place, while techs set the mood with smoke and lights. Rachel chatted with the burly *Family Affair* actor about the female impersonator who lived upstairs from him in New York. Then, when it came time to shoot her interrogation scene—with Keith as the detective—she improvised with him when he asked her name.

"Rachel. . . . OK, Ralph. My name is Ralph."

Between takes she gave pause to a Lakewood Fairgrounds custodian present at the shoot.

I didn't know which bathroom to send him or her to.

The movie crew invited her to the premiere that winter in Atlanta, but Rachel Wells wouldn't be there. She wouldn't be coming back for anything, even if Burt Reynolds himself had begged her to return.

Mayor Maynard Jackson

Atlanta, Georgia

June 22, 1981

C OME OUT! A string of balloons formed a triangle in the gay newspaper ad. It asked their readers if they would march that Saturday.

"They think we are less than human. Saturday is our chance to show our faces proudly to the world. Saturday is our chance to demonstrate that we are their mothers, fathers, sisters and brothers; that we are their mechanic, their accountant, their waitress and their dentist."[1]

The ad gave a list of five demands: First, to repeal sodomy laws. Only three states had penalties as severe as those in Georgia. Next, to stop police harassment that enforced the law unequally. Third, to enact a human-rights ordinance that would make it illegal to discriminate because of race, religion, age, sexual orientation, gender identification, or any other ridiculous reason. Fourth, to end racial discrimination. And finally, to pass the Equal Rights Amendment.

About 4,000 people saw a street fair, an art show, and a dance that spanned across Seventh Street between Piedmont and Juniper. Some wore faces with painted-on stars while they read gay poetry or cruised other Pride-goers. They sold handmade arts and crafts, they gave speeches, sketched chalk murals, performed impromptu street dances, sipped fresh-squeezed lemonade to beat the stifling 95-degree heat, visited Georgia State University's gay kissing booth, and slurped down chilled watermelon while music wafted over the park.

In 1971 it had begun on the sidewalks of downtown Atlanta, halted by traffic and spat upon by protesters. By 1981 Atlanta's Gay Pride celebration had become a picnic that refused to break up until midnight, long after the marchers had gone by carrying signs of hope: THIS CITY BELONGS TO US TOO.

Despite the thousands that late spring day, the Monday newspapers would not report on the massive festival at all. On the same day as Pride, Atlanta police had arrested Wayne Williams, the chief suspect in the string of child murders that had begun nearly two years before. Mayor Jackson had been informed of the arrest on an official trip to Savannah, and was told Williams had driven to his house the night before in an attempt to elude the police who tailed him.

Williams was in jail. Jackson, grateful and overjoyed, made his way back home to Atlanta. There was hope after all. The city's spiral of death might be at an end.

John Greenwell

Atlanta

Summer 1981

Some days John Greenwell and Rachel Wells missed the Sweet Gum Head. It had taken drag out of sleazy little bars and put it in costumes, under lights, and bathed it in sound, like a real Vegas show. It had given John Greenwell a new life. It had given him Rachel, a beautiful goddess creature, but John had grown weary of putting on her makeup, spending money on wigs and costumes, the hours spent layering on pantyhose, tights, and padding—and the never-ending quest to find a new way to make the audience smile, weep, or cheer. He had done all he could with his drag career, and it just wasn't fun anymore. More than once, he caught himself during a show thinking about other things, performing on autopilot, without any spark or spirit.

John knew the cardinal rule in drag: Do your number, then get off the stage.

He was a wanderer, made one by his move-all-the-time childhood. He only knew the present as something to be disrupted and destroyed. His father's understanding of love and duty had ripped into his life like mortar rounds. As much as he had tried to repair the wounds with psychedelics and sex and road trips and thrift-store drag finds, he knew they would always be raw, always in need of patience and care.

His life in Atlanta had been a time of innocence, but it had not made him content. He did not understand yet that home was the people he chose to love, and it was those who loved him in return.

A friend who owned a bar in Asheville, North Carolina, had

told him to check in if he ever headed that way. John called him to see if he meant it. Buddy had a section in his bar that could be John's—a quiet section, with windows in the front so he could see the world go by. John could tend it as John. He could leave drag behind forever. John looked at his life and realized the only way to go forward was to leave Atlanta.

He went to the gas station, rented a box truck, and filled it with the few things he owned. By the time he had it packed it was dark, and he wanted to be in Asheville before midnight. He cried, and so did Herman as they said goodbye. Then he rolled onto the highway, toward the mountains, in search of a life beyond drag, a life beyond Rachel Wells.

John Austin

The Sweet Gum Head

August 1981

"Come to my office," John Austin told Marc Jones, and his voice hitched. When Marc got into the office, John began to cry.

"I don't know if you've heard some rumors that the place might be for sale," John Austin said. "But it's not for sale."

The Sweet Gum Head had enjoyed a ten-year run. Other clubs burned, closed, or watched their managers run off with the bar receipts. It didn't have a fancy light-up disco floor or million-dollar lighting. It had done the best with what it had.

The Sweet Gum Head had adapted to the world around it. The Atlanta Lesbian Feminist Alliance had its own evening of music and mime, "Some of Our Friends," just before Memorial Day, and drag queens had performed to the songs from *The Wizard of Oz*. Charlie Brown performed an entire evening as Bette Midler, two and a half hours with stunning lip-syncs, special effects, and lighting.

But a rot had set in. Competition among drag clubs meant each of them had polished shows with professional choreography, and even innovative shows bore a time stamp. Austin scheduled a run for *P.S. Your Cat Is Dead,* a play about a depressed New York actor, abandoned by his girlfriend, unaware his cat has died in a pet clinic. The actor puts a would-be burglar into bondage in his apartment, then bonds with him. He discovers the burglar is gay, and they run away together. The Gum Head production framed the play and punctuated it with loud disco music between acts. The upstart gay press glowed, but mainstream reviews were unkind. The trip from New York theaters had patently been rough, according to one take, and the actors at the Gum Head moved through their roles with the emotion of "cud-chewing cattle."

Over the Independence Day weekend, the Sweet Gum Head celebrated with a special show starring Satyn, Tina Devore, Dina Jacobs, and a new queen from Savannah, the Lady Chablis. In August, it mounted a well-attended production of *The Rocky Horror Picture Show,* with Lily White in the starring role pioneered by the sweetest of transvestites, Tim Curry.

Rumors ran rampant that the Sweet Gum Head would close. Attendance was down at clubs across town, thanks to the recession. Some of the discos that had drained away energy from the drag clubs had shut down as that wave ended; the discos rebranded themselves "dance clubs." The Sweet Gum Head didn't have the twenty-four-hour licenses of the Limelight or Backstreet, and the drinking age had gone back up to twenty-one earlier in the year. It didn't have the budget for celebrity appearances and couldn't compete with the likes of Grace Jones, Divine, Donny Most, or three-name celebrities like Vickie Sue Robinson and Evelyn "Champagne" King.

The economics were simple. The Sweet Gum Head had cost pennies to start up back when Frank Powell took over the room.

In 1981 it consumed more money on a nightly basis than a plain old bar that just needed a few drunks and cheap rent to survive. Discos needed bartenders and a DJ—but no talent. The Sweet Gum Head paid choreographers, costumers, eight performers, and male co-stars on top of its DJ, its door staff, bartenders, bar backs, and managers. It had too many mouths to feed.

The owners had decided to go in a different direction. The Sweet Gum Head would close, then reopen as a female strip club.

Marc couldn't believe it. Why?

"I do not have an answer for you," he said. "I'd like you to stay in here when I tell the cast."[2]

On August 17, John Austin called the *Gazette* gay newspaper and delivered the news. At the end of the month, the Sweet Gum Head would close.

The Sweet Gum Head

2284 Cheshire Bridge Road, Atlanta

August 30, 1981

The obituaries ran in the gay newspapers before the Sweet Gum Head had even drawn its last breath. The club had spoiled its guests with a parade of pageant winners, from Rachel Wells to Hot Chocolate to Charlie Brown, and celebrity guests from Freda Payne to Melissa Manchester, Liberace, and Burt Reynolds. The Sweet Gum Head had helped launch the career of Wayland Flowers and Madame, had given space to hypnotists and snake-handlers and Jesus Christ alike. In between, it hosted Miss Gay America, male beauty contests, and theatrical productions from *The Wizard of Oz* to *Chicago*.

Diamond Lil said, "There would never be another den of iniquity to replace it. Booze, Quaaludes, pot, speed, drag, dykes, truck, total debauchery—everybody worshipped at the home of the sinners."

As one man wrote:

Once upon a time, many years ago I actually thought I was straight. Well maybe I really didn't think I was straight, but I sure as hell knew I wasn't queer. I dated women, went to redneck bars and even went so far as to get married, buy a house and have a baby (actually, my ex-wife had the baby . . . I had nothing to do with it). And then, just when I thought everything was going fine, my wife left me and moved to Atlanta. The nerve! What was I going to do? How was I going to cope with being single again?

So what did I do? (I'm sure the suspense is killing you) I packed my bags, put on my little waitress cap and moved to Atlanta. Three days later, my ex-wife introduced me to my first male lover and the rest is history. I came out in the very, very gay city of Atlanta, Georgia. And, I saw my very, very first female impersonation show at The Sweet Gum Head on Cheshire Bridge Road. I went with some very liberal straights and sat there for several hours with my mouth hanging wide open. "Is that really a man?," "That just can't be a man!" and "Now, that one has got to be a woman!," I said over and over. The girl next to me was black and blue from my elbow punching her in the side. I saw Charlie, Lisa and Satyn for the first time. Was I impressed? You bet! Never had I seen or even heard of anything so wonderful. Good crowd entertainment, fabulous gowns and a crowd that just wouldn't say die.

And now, in only three more days, that wonderful club with the funny sounding name will be no more. No more shows, no more contests, no more entertainers. No more Sweet Gum Head.[3]

///

A young blond DJ's voice bounced off the building's dingy paneled walls when she shouted above the din: "This is the last Saturday night any of us will spend in this bar!"

A needle dropped, the record popped, and the last rites began.

On an ordinary night at the Sweet Gum Head, dancers would spin and sweep through unabashedly erotic poses, hungry for a last chance at rapture. That late summer night, on the DJ's cue, they took their seats among the rows of tables lining one side of the club, peered over heads in the back by the bar, or crammed into the nearest available nook. Their laughter kept time with the patter of shoes as the oak dance floor emptied, but a few sobs broke through as the last show of the last evening began.

Since 1971, the Sweet Gum Head had hosted drag shows that made it a modern Southern legend. From the night it opened with a three-way rendition of *Hello, Dolly!,* the Gum Head had seen countless Marilyn Monroes purr for diamonds on its stage, had seen more than one Jesus Christ drag a cross over its worn oak boards. It might have been known as the House of a Thousand Streisands, but everyone knew there was only one Barbra among its talented cast. For a while that Barbra went country, teetering precariously behind an anatomically perfect Dolly Parton ensemble. There were Frank N. Furters and Velma Kellys and Phyllis Dillers, pageant queens and proto-horror queens in bloodstained wedding dresses. There were more conventional celebrities that glinted faintly in the dusky room late at night, sitcom and movie actors and musicians who knew their stardom could hardly outshine the rapier wits and impossibly feminine looks of the performers who had stolen away from their homes and from their pasts, and braved a disapproving world, all for the chance to make someone laugh at them, or lust over them, or just love them.

A new club would rise in a few days from the Sweet Gum Head's ashes. Inside, brass poles would glint and flicker between the legs of beautiful biological women spinning around in an erotic carousel. They would dance in private for men in the old dressing rooms upstairs. But for one more night, the Sweet Gum Head still was "The Showplace of the South." That night, its stars would dazzle as they delivered the club's final drag show, one with free-flowing tears and fabulous gowns and a crowd that just wouldn't say die.

It was August 29, 1981, and closing time would come too soon.

///

John Austin circled the room with his usual military vigilance, even though it was the Gum Head's final night. The ruddy and muscular blond man, a former ballet dancer and ex-Vietnam veteran, had kept a close watch over the club since 1974. He had a knack for catering to all crowds and for making people happy. But he didn't know anything about running a strip club. He couldn't stop what would happen next. He couldn't even fix the broken air conditioner that let the room grow thick and hot with the smell of sweat from the scores of people crammed in the club for the final night, happy to pay the $5 cover. The musk perfumed the crowd as they laughed and clinked their glasses together in celebration.

The aura of cheerfulness was almost enough to mask the base scent of sadness. Drag veteran Satyn DeVille had been in a state of constant tears since John Austin had called the cast into his office and phoned the community newspaper two weeks before to confirm the closing rumors. Satyn had struggled to make it through her performances ever since. Tears threatened to ruin the flawless makeup that drew attention to her patented "evil eyes" and to water down the Wild Turkey never far from her reach.

In the long dressing room upstairs, Lavita Allen carefully drew on her face for her final act. Outside the drag world, Lavita was a successful DJ. She'd long given up her dream of being a respected actor and left behind her teaching job as Mr. Alan Orton. That night, she dazzled in a long gown and a blond bob instead of the Streisand look that had made her famous, the look she eventually grew to despise.

The next weekend, she'd be in a booth spinning records, and a part of her life since her teenage years would be erased.

Near her, Diamond Lil lifted her thin eyebrows into their usual elfin expression, bemused by it all but intent on perfection as she flitted around and soothed jangled nerves, rehearsed her patter and sang little song snippets backstage. Lil had flaunted her gender ambiguity from childhood, when she was Phillip Forrester and when she sang grown-up torch songs on a local radio program. Now she wrote her own music and sang it in her own eerie, shivering soprano. Her performances were less incredible than indelible. Lil carried herself like a star, and when you saw her perform, you were expected to take part in the charade. It was drag, and almost nothing was as it seemed.

///

The DJ hushed the room with the usual signal: an undanceable song that told the crowd the service was about to begin. The lights dimmed, then burst brightly as Billy Jones erupted from offstage, in full Phyllis Killer drag. Reliably adorned in marabou and a huge grin, Phyllis paraded onstage in a black sequined gown trimmed with feathers, and a blond Medusa wig, and she launched into her tried-and-true anthem, with lyrics suitably perverted: *There's NO business. . . . like DRAG business!* The crowd erupted, thrusting bills at her and throwing them on the stage. A family celebrated what was being lost, and what had been won.

The remaining queens painted on their last looks and adjusted their wardrobes in back, while waiters and bartenders offered drinks and thank-yous to the throng. The night people had turned out in force to say farewell to the place they called home, but two were nowhere to be found.

Bill Smith, who had given his voice to the gay-rights movement while he gave himself over to every carnal pleasure, had been gone more than a year—and Rachel Wells, the queen of the Sweet Gum Head stage, had given up drag and become John Greenwell again. Once upon a time the two men had run away from home in a whirlwind, from a place that would not have them to one that would, a city that shrouded itself in an emerald forest, one that glinted with promise. They had thrown themselves into the unknown, on the mercy of hope.

///

On Friday night, its regular cast had performed, but on Saturday night, the Sweet Gum Head opened its welcoming doors to any performer who had ever been on its stage. It ran one continuous show, with no disco breaks, when Phyllis kicked off the show. Frank Powell sat at a table near the front.

Lisa King broke her promise never to appear at the Gum Head again and stepped on the stage for a final bow. Diamond Lil sang "You Made Me Love You" and turned a camp moment into something even more sublime and strange, and touching.

Marc Jones, Charlie Brown, and Satyn DeVille delivered "Don't Cry for Me, Argentina." Satyn hadn't stopped crying most of the week. He would be out of work and would have to look for guest appearances at other clubs. He had a daughter, but his wife, Teddy Bear Julie, had distanced herself from Satyn once they had separated.

Marc hustled the lineup constantly, all night long, as performers showed up early and showed up late. He ran up to the dressing room, down to the other dressing room, turning an eye to DJ Kathy White when he needed help with the music.

"This Is My Life" had moved from drag anthem to drag cliché after years of overuse. Dina Jacobs performed it anyway, as well as "My Way." She introduced Marc for his solo performance; he sang "Bridge over Troubled Water" and got two callbacks.

Charlie Brown did a solo with Dolly Parton's "I Will Always Love You." She could hardly get off the stage before fans and other performers asked to take pictures. They wanted keepsakes, not knowing if they'd ever see the same people again.

Near the end of the evening, a box circulated in the crowd, earmarked for donations for the Atlanta Gay Center. It filled quickly.

To close, the entire cast gathered onstage and sang "United We Stand." A hit in the United States when it was released in 1970 by the British group the Brotherhood of Man, it had been sung as the closing theme of the "Brady Bunch Hour" on TV. Now it closed the Sweet Gum Head, in a final message of unity.

With so many performers and callbacks, it was well into the next morning when the lights went up. People laughed and hugged and cried. They had already emptied out their dressing rooms. It felt too strange to say goodbye.

What was once Frank Powell's idea of a beautiful future now lived in the past. Cigarettes were stubbed out. Car keys swung and clicked and jangled to the door. When the house lights came up that final time, the denizens of the Sweet Gum Head were no longer drag queens or disco children or bar managers or underage kids in search of their future lives. They had grown up.

John Austin, his face wet with tears, pulled Marc aside and hugged him for what seemed like forever.

"Well done," he sobbed. "Well done."

Atlanta

September 1, 1981

Kaposi's sarcoma surfaces on the skin in patches of violet that pass for bruises until they turn dull brown. It swells the lymph glands and spawns lumps as it spreads throughout the body. In patients with compromised immune systems it can rapidly turn fatal.

The disease had no cure, but in the outbreak that began in the summer of 1981 it had a companion. Pneumocystis pneumonia began to appear in tandem with the sarcoma. This form of pneumonia led to weight loss and fever, along with the usual breathing and congestion complications. It amplified the weakness of the patient's immune system. Or it revealed it.

In the months prior to August 30, 1981, 108 Americans received this diagnosis. Nearly all of them were young gay men. Only one female case was reported. Nearly half the patients died during that time.[4]

In its usual patients—elderly Mediterranean men—the sarcoma typically had an incubation period of eight to thirteen years. The 1981 outbreak killed its victims in a year or less.

By the time the Sweet Gum Head closed, doctors and scientists at the CDC had tracked the two diseases to gay men in ten states. Most of the cases had been reported in New York and California, but a few had been reported in Georgia.[5]

The gay newspapers had planned to cover the Sweet Gum Head closing with pages of commemoration, but that story would wait for a week. Instead, the *Gazette* devoted pages to the puzzling illnesses that had broken out in the nation's gay community, in stories that read with alarm.

Scientists scrambled to find a root cause, but it would be too long before a cause was found in a tiny fragment of life that looked like a sweetgum tree seed pod. The National Centers for Disease Control in Atlanta formed a twenty-person task force and told gay men not to panic. They gave the syndrome a name, GRID. Others called it a plague.

Doctors prescribed antibiotics and chemotherapy, but had no real answers. At hospital bed after hospital bed, they stepped aside and let nurses and priests take their place. The world tilted in a frightening new direction.

A generation stumbled into the hard work of dying.

Aftershow

By the time the Sweet Gum Head closed, **Lavita Allen** had already become a DJ and worked at various nightclubs. One night, Lavita—born Alan Orton—came to see Marc Jones backstage at another club. "Why are you getting so thin?" Jones asked. "They don't really know," Lavita said. "But I have a feeling that it's this new gay cancer, maybe." On June 12, 1984, Alan Orton died of AIDS in Washington state. Before he died, he burned his drag and erased all memories of Lavita Allen. On June 15, 1986, the owners of Atlanta's Backstreet nightclub opened a new show bar dubbed Lavita's at 2329 Cheshire Bridge Road, the site of the former Locker Room. Lavita's closed a few years later, after lightning struck the building and caused fire damage.

Onstage, a plush-bodied dancer came out from behind the Sweet Gum Head stage dressed in a tap-dance leotard and sequined jacket. Marc Jones had come to the club and looked for burly gym regular **John Austin**—and found him onstage as Dorothy, a beautiful man transformed into a beautiful woman. "I wanted to see what your reaction would be," Austin told Jones, his date for the evening. "Oh my God," Marc said, laughing, "I don't know if I can look at you the same again now." After the Sweet Gum Head closed, Austin managed several other bars, then opened the Atlanta Hair Salon with a partner. After his HIV diagnosis, he spent a decade raising money and helping others through

AID Atlanta. Austin died on December 17, 1995, at the Veterans Affairs Medical Center in Atlanta.

Berl Boykin spent his final days in a nursing home, where patients left unattended trembled on gurneys, where I helped Berl pull himself up in his wheelchair to relieve his pain. He said that in 1979, a friend had told him about a "gay cancer" that no one wanted to talk about outside the gay community. "That denial caused a holocaust," he said. He died in 2018.

Charlie Dillard doesn't remember a lot about closing night at the Gum Head: "Do you know how many clubs I've closed during my career?" he muses. When the AIDS crisis swept through Atlanta, Charlie raised money tirelessly, and spent her own money to help people who couldn't pay bills when they got sick. Dillard's drag cabaret was chronicled on HBO's 1997 special *Drag Time*. As **Charlie Brown**, he appears weekly at Lips Atlanta.

Anita Bryant's spokeswoman duties had ended when the Florida Citrus Commission declined to renew her contract. Her marriage to Bob Green ended in 1980. In June of 1982, paparazzi photographed her dancing at Atlanta's Limelight disco with the Rev. Russ McCraw, an evangelist who preached to homosexuals. Bryant was furious when the photos surfaced in the *Atlanta Journal*—and some two hundred other publications. In 1990 she said of her anti-gay-rights work, "I don't regret it because I did the right thing." Bryant remarried in 1990 to Charlie Dry. She filed for bankruptcy in 1997. As of July 2020, Bryant preaches to her ministry online from her home and offices in Oklahoma City. She believes her latter days will be greater than those in the beginning.

As of this writing, **James Earl Carter Jr.** is the longest-surviving former president of the United States of America. In

2017 he was treated for brain cancer. He continues to build houses for Habitat for Humanity and to preach and teach Sunday school at his Baptist church at home in Plains, Georgia.

RuPaul Charles says that drag reveals the person you want to be, but don't yet see in yourself. He has won several Emmys as the host of *RuPaul's Drag Race*.

Elizabeth "Mama Dee" DeBoard died in 1980. In November 1982, **Robert Llewellyn** received permission to travel under police supervision to Atlanta to settle his mother's estate. While in Atlanta, Llewellyn was seen at his former club, the Locker Room, and at the Steak and Ale on Piedmont Road. Llewellyn completed his sentence and was given parole in 2013.

When the Sweet Gum Head closed, **Satyn DeVille** struggled to find a place to perform. His former wife had left him because of his playboy existence—one she never had expected when they met when he was in medical school. Clay Hester died from an embolism in 1996.

I never met **Diamond Lil**, but like John Greenwell, I had heard about her performances long before I came to Atlanta. Lil had become a living Atlanta legend by the time she entered hospice care in the summer of 2016. She died that August, days before I began this book.

I sit in a casino, on a midnight date with Larry Edwards after his drag show ends on the Las Vegas Strip. "My first time on a stage, I was a nervous wreck," he says as he tells me about his first appearance as **Hot Chocolate** over the incessant *bling! bling! bling!* of slot machines. Larry has appeared in *Miss Congeniality 2* and *Sharknado 4*, and performs at nightclubs on the Strip regularly, delivering his hallmark impersonations: Diana

Ross, Patti LaBelle, and Tina Turner. "I still get butterflies," he says. "When you start losing that nervous feeling, that's when you need to stop doing it."

In 1977 **Heather Fontaine** left the Sweet Gum Head cast to tour with a group dubbed French Dressing. The troupe required her to live as a man, she says over the gentle rush of a Florida thunderstorm. "They cut off my hair and dyed it brown and all this other stuff. They wanted people to think that we were straight actors."

When Heather moved to California, near Zuma Beach, she walked to the point of a promontory that hung out over the ocean and begged God to remove the hate she had for her stepfather. She filled her heart with love for her life instead, and forgave him. She reconciled with her mother years later, and when he got sober her stepfather apologized to her for all the abuse he had rained down on her.

Heather teaches a "Beautiful Transformations" class near Tampa to share her wisdom and talents with other transgender women. She often closes her messages on Facebook with a simple homily: "Have a great day and be kind to one another."

I descend the escalators into Hartsfield-Jackson International's Plane Train tunnel and look up to see a larger-than-life photo of **Maynard Holbrook Jackson Jr.**, who silently judges me and my progress on this book.

Jackson has been described as the Jackie Robinson of Atlanta, the man who broke the color barrier of political power in the Deep South. At the same time, he also was dubbed a man who did great things badly, or as a friend described him, a man who "pulled teeth without Novocain."

Jackson presided over change that came too swiftly and traumatically for some, not quickly enough for others. He watched over the construction of a new mass-transit system, a new international airport, new parks, jails, fire stations, and schools as

Atlanta boomed. He offered a $100,000 reward for clues on who was killing Black Atlanta children, and in the last year of his second term, saw a man apprehended and convicted for these heinous crimes. He ran for a third nonconsecutive term as mayor and won—and later called it a mistake.

Jackson suffered a heart attack at Reagan National Airport in 2003 and died at a nearby hospital. He is the subject of a documentary, *Maynard*, produced with the guidance and storytelling talent of his family.

With her flawless looks and stunning wardrobe, **Dina Jacobs** still draws crowds wherever she takes the stage. She performs at Hamburger Mary's in Houston and can usually be found on tour across the nation. "It's hard," Dina recalls as we sit in an Atlanta dive bar just hours before the Sweet Gum Head reunion show, "but I love it so much that I'll just keep on doing it until I'm Edith Piaf and I fall out on stage."

A note on a single lined sheet of paper outlines the never-written autobiography of Phyllis Killer, a fragment left for someone else to complete. **Billy Jones** kept printed snippets of his career— programs, photos, newspaper clippings, and letters. Before he died in 2003, he donated them to the Atlanta History Center, where I read his notes and wished he'd been around to read mine.

Marc Jones still dances while he runs an interior decoration business. He emceed a Sweet Gum Head reunion in Atlanta in October 2018 attended by many of the surviving cast. His immense smile never dimmed during the two-hour show, even when his leather harness pinched the hair on his mostly bare chest.

Apple Love tries to explain to me the hesitation she felt when she performed at the Sweet Gum Head. "My whole career, I never felt like I really fit in," she says from her Florida home. "I've always felt sort of like an outsider in drag, even though now, in hindsight . . . I realize that of course I fit right in." She completed gender-confirmation surgery in 1996 and performs in the Tampa area.

Reba would be the name given to five or six snakes Rachel enlisted for her act. We know what happened to four of them. Two escaped. One died in a fire. One died in an air conditioner when Rachel performed on the road. She froze it and hoped to give it a proper funeral before a show in Dallas, but the odor got to be too much.

"Yes, I have been bashed," remembers **Gil Robison** as we sip espresso on the very street where it happened decades before. Late one night, as he walked home down Atlanta's Ponce de Leon Boulevard, a group of men jumped out of a car, knocked him down, and kicked him. Robison flagged down a cop car, and the men were arrested.

Robison ran for the State House in 1988 and advocated for HIV/AIDS awareness in the 1980s. He laments the change in the queer community as he sips. "You poor thing, you've never had a Quaalude, have you?" he asks while he orders another coffee on a hot August day, despite the heavy wine-colored robes that comprise his Buddhist garb. "There was no L, no G, no T, no B, no Q. People were just outside the norm. . . . Anything could happen, anything did happen." He recalls a Pride march where he first noticed how profoundly things had changed. "I saw a couple of guys wearing Mardi Gras beads. I thought, 'OK . . . so that's what we're about.' Consumerism took over," he says, and pauses for a moment. "And things just got rather boring after that, not terribly interesting." Robison recently moved back to Atlanta from India.

She built a character that could resist the ravages of time, one she said she could play at seventy-five as well as at twenty-five, the same "wrinkled old whore" she introduced to Atlanta in the

1960s. **Lily White** retired from performing in 2016, lived in suburban Atlanta and designed costumes and jewelry for drag artists. When we talked by phone, she offered a blunt blanket apology: *I did so much acid back then I don't remember much at all.*

///

After he sold the Sweet Gum Head, **Frank Powell** opened and sold and closed more than a dozen gay bars in Atlanta. Ms. Garbo's, his lesbian bar, opened in October 1973 on Cheshire Bridge Road. Peyton Place opened in May 1975 and closed shortly after.

He christened the country-themed County Seat on Cheshire Bridge Road in August of 1976. At the County Seat, in fictional Gay County, Powell wore the biggest belt buckle, had the biggest drink, and dubbed himself the justice of the peace.

Frank Powell's, his namesake club, opened at Thirteenth and West Peachtree streets on January 1, 1978. Powell held court in the former home where he took confession, bailed out friends, and acted as therapist for his guests and his friends. From his perch by the bar, Frank told stories from late at night until early into the next morning. In one, he recalled how he had performed Atlanta's first gay marriage when he coupled Alan Allison and his boyfriend Travis, surrounded by flowers and fancy guests and a catered reception. He finally had a place where he could minister to his flock.

Powell died on March 8, 1996, from a massive heart attack, dead before the ambulance reached Piedmont Hospital. His sister Pate took him home and buried him in their plot at the Church of Christ Cemetery, at a bend in the road in the middle of nowhere in the Florida Panhandle, in a place called Sweet Gum Head.

///

When she reads I make sure that my recorder captures every word, that my mind stays clear to capture the spirit that leaps from a page not read in years, or maybe in decades.

I am the ghost.
I command the legions of phantom stares which gaze upon me.
Imagining a real body with thighs and a navel.
I am the ghost.

Her broken leg propped on a stack of pillows, patience low but spirits high, **Diane Hughes** mends herself also with the warm memories left behind by the death of her friend Bill Smith nearly forty years ago. She has already shared as much of his life with me as she can remember. On this visit, while the immense magnolia tree outside her front porch sways with the updrafts of a brewing thunderstorm, she opens letters I have yet to read, passes photos I see for the first time.

In the years after Bill died, Diane marched at Pride with his photo and bore the brunt of other activists' self-righteous anger. *Don't you know what he did?* they would sneer.

Yes, she would reply. *I know.*

As long as she is here to revive him, her friend is not a ghost.

Diane earned a doctorate in psychotherapy and practices in Atlanta, where she lives with her husband and son.

///

On one side of the narrow path called Gun Club Road, neatly trimmed emerald grass emits an intoxicating fresh-cut smell, and oaks and pines stand reverent watch over the tombstones that dot the low-rising hills. On the other side of the path, plastic cups and aluminum cans litter the ground and nest in the thicket that knits itself to nearby trees.

I have found friends of Bill Smith by chance and located his family members through near-random text messages. I have read his official memos in remote archives, heard recordings of his voice at the New York Public Library, and discovered fragments of his life in musty city directories that collect dust on shelves at the Atlanta History Center.

I have yet to locate records of his resignations, his notes, or personal journals. His family's home burned in 1986 and nothing of his survived, save for a melted collection of coins. Court records sketch a painful truth, but the Fulton County district attorney long ago shredded his case files. The Atlanta police incinerated his arrest records before that.

I look for a flat marker that rises slightly out of the weeds, according to the photo online, the one that commemorates "our beloved son, Bill Jr." Vines cover the ground, the trees, and the graves. I narrow his location down to a wooded hill, but I cannot find him.

Bill Smith died on March 9, 1980, one of an estimated 300 fatalities from Placidyl overdose in that year. His family buried him at the semi-abandoned Hollywood Cemetery in northwest Atlanta, where he lies in the landing pattern of the airport, near the city landfill, in an obscured grave. But the sky is blue and the sun filters through the trees in patches, brightening the hill where Bill Smith lies among the war veterans and Atlanta history makers, in the shadow of a towering sweetgum tree a hundred feet tall.

///

Asheville proved to be a cold, cliquish place for **John Greenwell.** He enjoyed a break from being **Rachel Wells,** but was convinced to bring her back and to bring himself back to Atlanta, at a new club called the Answer.

It would take the next twenty-five years to leave Rachel Wells behind. Rachel appeared with Tina Devore on local Atlanta cable TV and reported gay news. She toured the country with other Miss Gay America winners. She appeared in a nationally televised female-impersonator pageant hosted by Ruth Buzzi and Lyle Waggoner, and performed as Katharine Hepburn. She returned for a Sweet Gum Head reunion held in the mid-1980s, inside the strip club that had replaced it. The house was packed from eight p.m.

until closing. Friends died, but drugs and sex were easier than ever to score—so John left Atlanta once more and went home to Kentucky for good in 1986.

In 2006 he decided to put away drag, once and for all. He packed a bag with all that remained of Rachel Wells: her wig, costume, makeup, jewelry, some tip money, and a CD. He tucked a short note inside, a message in a bottle for whomever might find it. On his return from a trip to see Larry Edwards, John abandoned all that was left of Rachel Wells at a rest stop on I-65.

When we met for the first time, in 2016, John told me there would be parts of his story that would remain his to tell, when he decided he could, when he settled on the way in which he wanted to tell them. Like you, I await those stories with the kind of anticipation both John and I usually reserve for the baked goods at his favorite café in Louisville.

John earned a master's in education and retired from the field in 2017. He lives in Kentucky, where he writes and produces plays and short stories. He attended the 2018 Sweet Gum Head reunion held in Atlanta with his fellow performers, who came dressed in their finest drag. He received surprised smiles and hugs the entire night until he stood onstage with his friends at the end of the show—in the back row, where the tall girls always stood.

Thanks

I hope you've shared with me the vicarious thrill of reliving someone else's past. I've had it for at least four years, from the day I
first read about a world long gone before I knew it existed.

A host of performers brought it to life again for me. John Greenwell published his memoir online, where I could fall deeply into it.
This book would not have happened without his recollections and
his patience and his honesty.

Diane Hughes sat for hours to discuss the sometimes painful
circumstances of Bill Smith's life. Gil Robison answered my questions with perfectly bemused amity.

Berl Boykin, Charlie Brown (Charles Dillard), Maria Hel-
ena Dolan, Hot Chocolate (Larry Edwards), Heather Fontaine,
Dave Hayward, Dina Jacobs (Cliff Montalbo), Marc Jones, Leslie
Jordan, Apple Love (Angela Morales), Melissa Manchester, Tina
Devore (Cliff Taylor), Pate Waller, Gary Poe, and Lily White helped
me piece together complex relationships and narrative arcs.

Though some stories still elude me, I remain stunned at how
much I could reconstruct from archives, including those at the
Atlanta History Center and Georgia State University.

I wrote much of this story in the MFA program at the University of Georgia's Grady College of Journalism and Mass Commu-
nication. Valerie Boyd has created a community of writers, and
has been a tireless advocate and friend. She inspires us all to
become better writers, and to be better people.

John T. Edge urged me toward this resonant story and to take the time to do it justice. Moni Basu helped me tightly weave the key narrative threads, and to pluck the stray ones. Along with Lolis Elie, Pat Thomas, and Jan Winburn, they have all nurtured our community of writers and helped it thrive.

I owe a special thanks to friends who lent their time to this book—Rosalind Bentley, Max Blau, Samantha Bresnahan, Katoya Ellis Fleming, André Gallant, Emanuella Grinberg, Lourdes Follins, and my Lambda Literary colleagues, Jeffery Johnson, Richard Read, and Mary Ann Scott. I thank Beth Marshea, who took a chance on a fifty-year-old debutant, and to Amy Cherry and Zarina Patwa, who loved this story like their own.

I owe an enormous debt to my work colleagues, especially ACT UP veteran and inveterate grammarian John Voelcker, and to my Maryland and Georgia families, who let me be a writing hermit without question.

I thank my husband, Jack, most of all. With him, no idea is too big to go along with, no plans for the evening too small. With him, there truly is no place like home.

Notes

Introduction

1. Sam Lucchese, "These Theaters Fit into Stores," *Boxoffice* 93, no. 24, September 30, 1968.
2. "Case Against Warhol Film Is Continued by Court Here," *Atlanta Constitution*, August 7, 1969, 13B.
3. Michael Waters, "The Stonewall of the South That History Forgot," *Smithsonian*, June 25, 2019, https://www.smithsonianmag.com/history/stonewall-south-history-forgot-180972484/.
4. "Atlanta Moviegoers Harassed by Police Shutterbug," *Independent Film Journal*, August 19, 1969, 3.
5. Margaret Hurst, "More Raids on Movies Coming," *Atlanta Constitution*, August 9, 1969, 9A.
6. Bob Hurt, "More Movie Raids Promised," *Atlanta Constitution*, August 15, 1969, 5A.
7. Dick Hebert, "They Meet Without Fear," *Atlanta Constitution*, January 3, 1966, 1, ProQuest ID 1612064601.
8. Dick Hebert, "Clear Out Piedmont Park Perverts, Grady PTA Urges," *Atlanta Constitution*, May 11, 1966, 1, ProQuest ID 1556887087.
9. Dick Hebert, "Detectives Watch Hangouts and Curb Some of Activity," *Atlanta Constitution*, January 4, 1966, 1, ProQuest ID 1611927581.
10. Alex Coffin, "Loner Massell Sets Own Style," *Atlanta Constitution*, January 17, 1971, 1A.
11. Bill Shipp, "Carter Pledges Fight on Hip Area Crime," *Atlanta Constitution*, January 1, 1971, 1A.
12. "Massell and the Hippies," *Atlanta Constitution*, June 6, 1970, 4A.
13. "More Hip Raids Seen Despite First Failure," *Atlanta Constitution*, October 17, 1970, 1A.
14. "Atlanta Police Use Tear Gas to Quell Riot in Hippie Area," *New York Times*, October 12, 1970. 23.
15. Alex Coffin, "Nightclub Is Shut Here," *Atlanta Constitution*, November 21, 1970, 1A.
16. Sam Hopkins, "10th Street Change Benefits Some, Too," *Atlanta Constitution*, June 3, 1970, 1A.

1971: Bring the Boys Home

1. Celestine Sibley, *Dear Store* (New York: Doubleday, 1967), 133.
2. Cyclops, "Celebration . . . Very Gay," *Great Speckled Bird*, July 5, 1971, 2.
3. Bill Smith, interview by WSB-TV: "Gay Rights Protestors March in Atlanta," June 27, 1971. Clip no. wsbn58227.
4. UPI, "50 in Atlanta Mark Gay Liberation Day," *Atlanta Journal*. June 28, 1971. 9A.
5. Cyclops, "Celebration," 2.
6. Dave Hayward interview, November 11, 2017.
7. Reg Murphy, "Carter's Inaugural Speech: Like 1966," *Atlanta Constitution*, January 13, 1971, 4A.
8. Berl Boykin interview, November 30, 2017, Atlanta.
9. Ron Taylor and Tom Crawford, "Commandos Storm Park," *Atlanta Constitution*, August 8, 1971, 2A, ProQuest ID 1563283535.
10. WSB-TV. Students demonstrating against the Vietnam War and an appearance by Fannie Lou Hamer at the demonstration, Hurt Park, August 7, 1971, Atlanta, Georgia, Clip no. wsbn63671
11. Wendy Eley Jackson and Samuel D. Pollard, *Maynard*, dir. Samuel D. Pollard (2017; Atlanta, GA: Auburn Avenue Films), streaming. Interview with Dr. June Dobbs Butts.
12. Boyd Lewis, Facebook update, June 13, 2016. "Atlanta, in a sense, set out in the 1970s to fulfill King's dream of a 'Beloved Community," https://www.facebook.com/boyd.lewis.16
13. Bill Seddon, "Atlanta Needs Blacks' Aid, Says Massell," *Atlanta Constitution*, October 7, 1971, 1A, ProQuest ID 1616054271.
14. Alderman Henry Dodson, interview by WSB-TV. Newsfilm clip of African Americans reacting negatively to mayor Sam Massell's speech on politics and government, October 10, 1971, Clip no. wsbn64296.
15. Advertisement, *Atlanta Constitution*, June 5, 1968, 13.
16. Tony Romano, Facebook comment, https://www.facebook.com/groups/4110539 73126140/.
17. *David* magazine, December 1971, Billy Jones Papers.
18. Farnum Gray, "Female Impersonation Is Big Business," *Atlanta Constitution*, October 4, 1974, 15C, ProQuest ID 1616114370.
19. "Who Is Danny Windsor?" Unidentified publication (believed to be *David* magazine), Billy Jones Papers.

1972: What Makes a Man a Man?

1. Judith Lambert and Bill Cutler, "Gay Pride Week," *Great Speckled Bird*, June 19, 1972, 4–5.
2. Sam Kindrick, "Red, White, and Blue Revue Reviewed," *San Antonio Express*, May 25, 1972, 82.
3. John R. Greenwell, *Teased Hair and the Quest for Tiaras*, http://www.jrgreenwell mga79.com/Teased%20Hair%20webpage.html.
4. Greenwell, *Teased Hair*.
5. Jim Auchmutey, "The Shaping of Atlanta: Part 5: Three Communities," *Atlanta*

Journal and Atlanta Constitution, August 13, 1987, Local News, A1. Accessed April 21, 2017.

6. Maria Helena Dolan interview, August 1, 2019, Atlanta.
7. Ron Taylor, "Gay Can Be a Sad or Dangerous World," *Atlanta Journal,* May 12, 1975, 1A.
8. Dave Hayward interview, November 11, 2017, Atlanta.
9. Maria Helena Dolan, "You Can't Be a People Unless You Have a History," *The Body*, June 25, 2004, http://www.thebody.com/content/art32194.html.
10. Steve Abbott, "British & Klaus," *Great Speckled Bird*, October 30, 1972, 18.
11. Greenwell, *Teased Hair.*
12. Tom Linthicum and Jeff Nesmith, "Massell Brother Is Called 'Atlanta Crime,'" *Atlanta Constitution,* September 22, 1972, 1A, ProQuest ID 1612254289.
13. Linthicum and Nesmith, "Massell Brother."
14. Jeff Nesmith and Tom Linthicum, "Atlanta Is in a Showdown with Crime, Massell Says," *Atlanta Constitution*, September 26, 1972, 1A, ProQuest ID 1557115226.
15. Nesmith, Jeff. "Reported Mobster Loan to Massell Pal Probed," *Atlanta Constitution*, September 20, 1972, ProQuest ID 1556630670.
16. Sam Hopkins, "Governor Calls Wolcoffs Threat to City and State," *Atlanta Constitution,* October 20, 1972, 1A, ProQuest ID 1616508504.
17. Sam Hopkins and Tom Linthicum, "Massell Lashes Inman, Threatens to Fire Him," *Atlanta Constitution,* October 25, 1972, 1A, ProQuest ID 1556639934.
18. Alex Coffin, "Jackson Lashes Massell Concepts," *Atlanta Constitution*, April 6, 1972, 6A, ProQuest ID 1616497798.
19. After the grand-jury investigation, Burton Wolcoff moved to Florida and he and his company sued Mayor Massell, Police Chief Inman, and others for allegedly violating his civil right to earn a living.

1973: Who's That Lady?

1. Taylor, "Gay Can Be a Sad or Dangerous World."
2. Taylor, "Gay Can Be a Sad or Dangerous World."
3. "Entertainer of the Month," *Barb* 1, no. 7, 7.
4. "Miss Gay America Crowned," *Advocate*, June 6, 1973, 24.
5. "Carters Abroad for 16 Days," *Atlanta Constitution,* May 14, 1973, 11A.
6. "Gay Donation Is Turned Down," *Atlanta Constitution,* May 6, 1973, 11C.
7. "Thousands Join Gay Parade," *Atlanta Constitution,* June 25, 1973, 8B, ProQuest ID 1557038438.
8. Nancy Lewis, "Ballet Benefit: 'Rachel Wells' Is Out of Show," *Atlanta Journal,* September 1, 1973.
9. Lewis, "Ballet Benefit."
10. Kevin Stevens, "Frank Powell: A Man of Vision," *Guide*, November 1988, 5, Atlanta History Center, Kenan Research Center, Atlanta Lesbian and Gay History Thing papers and publications, ahc.MSS773.
11. Jackson and Pollard, *Maynard.*
12. WSB-TV. Victory statements by Mayor Jackson and City Council President Fowler; Election Night Party, October 16, 1973. Clip no. wsbn37941.

1974: Rock the Boat

1. William Safire, "The Right to Be Gay," *Atlanta Constitution*, April 22, 1974, 5A, ProQuest ID 1617339292.
2. Atlanta Gay Information Service Interview, March 7, 1974, Manuscripts and Archives Division New York Public Library, International Gay Information Center collection, #206123.
3. WSB-TV. Female Impersonators Compete for Miss Gay America, May 5, 1974. Clip no. wsbn16926
4. "Miss 'Gay America' Pageant Attracts Thousands to Atlanta," *Atlanta Barb* 1 no. 2, 1974, 1, folder 1.
5. "Inman Orders Investigation on Harassment of Gays," *Atlanta Barb* 1, no. 6, 1974, 1.
6. Bill Smith, "Editor's Notebook," *Barb* 2, no. 4, 1975, 2, folder 3.
7. Bill Smith, "Editor's Notebook," *Barb* 2, no. 9, 1975, 2, folder 4.

1975: The Hustle

1. "Night Life's Not Dull in Atlanta," *Atlanta Constitution,* November 16, 1975, 1A, ProQuest ID 1619818966.
2. "Night Life's Not Dull in Atlanta."
3. "Night Life's Not Dull in Atlanta."
4. "Night Life's Not Dull in Atlanta."
5. Bill Smith, "Editor's Notebook," *Barb* 2, no. 3, 1975, 2, folder 3.
6. Smith, "Editor's Notebook," *Barb* 2, no. 3, 1975, 2, folder 3.
7. Bill Prime, "Yum Yum Tree Action Upheld," *Pensacola News,* May 24, 1976, 1.
8. *State v. Michael S. Day et al.*, Case No. A34160 (1977).
9. Cliff Green, "Trio Still Missing, No Leads," *Atlanta Constitution,* March 28, 1976, 17C, ProQuest ID 1614054199.
10. "A Mafia Takeover in Atlanta?" *Great Speckled Bird*, July 1, 1974, 5.
11. Ron Taylor, "The Gay Life: 'Bashers' on Prowl Break Up 'Cruising,'" *Atlanta Constitution*, May 11, 1975, 10A, ProQuest ID 1557944946.
12. Taylor, "'Bashers' on Prowl."
13. Gore Vidal, "The State of the Union," *Esquire,* May 1, 1975. https://classic .esquire.com/article/1975/5/1/the-state-of-the-union.
14. Bill Smith, "Editor's Notebook," *Barb* 2, no. 8, 1975, 2, folder 4.
15. Bill Smith, "Editor's Notebook," *Barb* 2, no. 5, 2, folder 3.
16. Taylor, "'Bashers' on Prowl."
17. Incorporation papers filed with Fulton County, Georgia. Lee says he never lived or worked at this address.
18. Dave Hayward interview, November 11, 2017.
19. Taylor, "'Bashers' on Prowl."
20. "Homosexuality: Gays on the March," *Time*, September 8, 1975, http://content .time.com/time/subscriber/article/0,33009,917784,00.html.
21. Charles Morel, "Atlanta, Atlanta, Atlanta," *Advocate*, September 10, 1975, 34. Duke University Rubinstein Library, Newspaper #9, no. 170–180 (1975) c.1.
22. Maynard Jackson, "Opinions," *Advocate*, October 8, 1975, 22. Duke University Rubinstein Library, Newspaper #9, no. 170–180 (1975) c.1.
23. "Fowler Rejects Petition," *Barb* 2 no. 12, 1.

24. The newspaper published a note that it had asked Fowler for comment; Fowler called the article unfair and said it mischaracterized his views.
25. "NGTF Comes South," *Barb* 2 no. 10, 14.
26. Bruce Voeller, letter to Bill Smith, November 13, 1975. Bruce Voeller Papers, 1956–1990, Collection Number: 7307, Division of Rare and Manuscript Collections, Cornell University Library, box 37, folder 45.
27. Bill Smith, letter to Bruce Voeller, December 2, 1975. Bruce Voeller Papers, 1956–1990. Collection Number: 7307, Division of Rare and Manuscript Collections, Cornell University Library, box 37, folder 45.

1976: Disco Inferno

1. Rex Granum, "Hectic Opening for Peachtree Plaza," *Atlanta Constitution,* January 13, 1976, 2A, ProQuest ID 1621638900.
2. John M. Lee, "The Southeast Sobers Up," *New York Times,* March 14, 1976, F13, ProQuest ID 123021769.
3. DeWitt Rogers, "'Top' Officially Put on 70-Story Hotel," *Atlanta Constitution,* October 3, 1975, 12D, ProQuest ID 1617406827.
4. Paul Goldberger, "Complex Use of Spaces Marks Portman's Design," *New York Times,* March 17, 1976, 82, ProQuest ID 122773865.
5. Green, "Trio Still Missing."
6. Green, "Trio Still Missing."
7. Allecia Freels, "Presenting: The Evil Eyes of Satyn DeVille," *Gazette,* December 18–24, 1980, Atlanta History Center, Kenan Research Center, Atlanta Lesbian and Gay History Thing papers and publications, Box MSS OS box 2.270, folder 1.
8. Ken Willis and Robert Lamb, "Police Say 3 Men were Executed," *Atlanta Constitution,* April 27, 1976, 6B, ProQuest ID 1617588927.
9. "Gay Honor Awarded to Jackson," *Atlanta Journal,* May 6, 1976, 2E.
10. "Atlanta Mayor Wins Phyllis Killer Oscar," *Barb* 3, no. 4, 1976, 1, folder 5.
11. Bill Smith, "Editor's Notebook," *Barb* 3, no. 1, 1976, 2, folder 5.
12. Gil Robison interview, May 11, 2018, Atlanta.
13. Dave Hayward interview, August 19, 2018, Atlanta.
14. Bill Smith, "Editor's Notebook," *Barb* 3, no. 4, 1976, 2, folder 5.
15. Interview with Richard Evans Lee, by email, March 21, 2019.
16. Heather Fontaine, Facebook post, July 22, 2018, https://www.facebook.com/heather.fontaine.9/posts/10204409715839621.
17. Heather Fontaine, Facebook post, September 11, 2018, https://www.facebook.com/heather.fontaine.9/posts/10204569125784770
18. Heather Fontaine, Facebook post, June 4, 2018, https://www.facebook.com/heather.fontaine.9/posts/10204261320409828
19. Bill Smith, "Editor's Notebook," *Barb* 3, no. 1, 1976, 2, folder 5.
20. "Councilman Pierce Calls For End of 'Sexual Orientation' Protection in Atlanta," *Barb* 3, no. 2, 1976, 1, folder 5.
21. "Mayor Stands Firm," *Barb* 3, no. 6, 1976, 1, folder 6.
22. John York and Ann Woolner, "Gay Day Stays, Jackson Says," *Atlanta Journal,* June 26, 1976, 11A.
23. "Gay Pride Week 1976," *Barb* 3, no. 5, 1976, 16, folder 6.
24. Neil Swan, "Gay Pride Rally Without Incident," *Atlanta Constitution,* June 27, 1976, 7B, ProQuest ID 1557748406

25. "Gay Pride," *Atlanta Constitution,* July 26, 1976, 4A, ProQuest ID 1617547178.

26. "Gay Pride."

27. "Atlanta Stages Gay Pride Day," *Arizona Daily Star,* June 27, 1976, 60.

28. Swan. "Gay Pride Rally Without Incident."

29. WSBN-TV. Supreme Court Upholds State Laws Forbidding Homosexual Acts Between Consenting Adults in Private, March 30, 1976. Clip no.: wsbn07532, Walter J. Brown Media Archives & Peabody Awards Collection, University of Georgia Special Collections Libraries.

30. Bill Smith, "Editor's Notebook," *Barb* 3, no. 3, 1976, 2, folder 5.

31. Bill Smith, "Community Activities," *Barb* 1, no. 7, 1974, 8, folder 2.

32. Joe Brown, "The Gay Life," *Atlanta Constitution,* April 24, 1976, 8B.

33. "Sex for Sale—And City's Paying Price," *Atlanta Constitution,* June 27, 1976, 1A, ProQuest ID 1557750939.

34. "Sex for Sale."

35. Scheer, "The Playboy Interview with Jimmy Carter."

36. Jimmy Carter interview, 1976; audio clip from the "Have a Nice Decade '70s" CD box set.

1977: Star Wars

1. "Mayor Appoints *Barb* Editor to CRC," *Barb* 4, no. 1, 1977, 11.

2. Marion Gaines, "Car Restrictions Hit Perverts in Piedmont," *Atlanta Constitution,* May 17, 1966, 10.

3. Bill Smith, "Editor's Notebook," *Barb* 4, no. 1, 1977, 11.

4. The club would become the Locker Room Disco in October 1976, to align it with the Locker Room bathhouse next door, also owned by DeBoard and Llewellyn.

5. "Interview: Lavita Allen," *Cruise,* July 1980, 17.

6. Rob Jewett, "Does She or Doesn't He? Some Men Play Vixens for a Price," *GSU Signal,* February 14, 1977, 25.

7. "Dade in Uproar at Anita's Outcry," *Atlanta Constitution,* Mar 27, 1977, 4B.

8. The ordinance had been proposed by Commissioner Ruth Shack, who was married to Anita Bryant's agent.

9. *Time,* "Homosexuality: Gays on the March."

10. "'America's Greatest American' Award Protested," *Barb* 41, folder 8.

11. Larry Laughlin, "Gay Pride March Is Very Moving Experience," *Barb* 4, no. 6, 1, folder 7.

12. Phone interview with Gary Poe, March 23, 2020.

13. Steve Warren, "Gay-ing to the Movies," *Barb* 4 no. 6, 6, folder 7.

14. Bill Smith, letter to Diane Hughes, June 27, 1977, Bill Smith Papers.

15. Grace Lichtenstein, "Poll Finds Public Split on Legalizing Homosexual Acts," *New York Times,* July 19, 1977, 17, ProQuest ID 123073106.

16. "The Anti-Gay Vote: Is Backlash Ahead?" *Atlanta Constitution,* June 13, 1977, 1A, ProQuest ID 1617613160.

17. Joyce Leviton, "Loser and Still Champion, Atlanta Mayor Jackson Is a Sliver of His Former Self," *People,* December 5, 1977, https://people.com/archive/loser-and-still-champion-atlanta-mayor-jackson-is-a-sliver-of-his-former-self-vol-8-no-23/

18. "Mayor Jackson Hedges on Gay Rights," *Barb* 43, 1, folder 8.

19. "Mayor Jackson Hedges."

20. Jay Lawrence, "Mayor Vows to Rock the Boat," *Atlanta Constitution,* October 6, 1977, 1A, ProQuest ID 1619699177.

21. Bill Smith, letter to Diane Hughes, November 9, 1971, Bill Smith Papers.

1978: Fuck Anita Bryant

1. Grace Lichtenstein, "Laws Aiding Homosexuals Face Rising Opposition Around Nation," *New York Times,* April 27, 1978, accessed September 30, 2018, https://www.nytimes.com/1978/04/27/archives/new-jersey-pages-laws-aiding -homosexuals-face-rising-opposition.html.

2. W. E. Bill Smith, Jr. "No: Gay People Can Not 'Teach' Sexuality," *Atlanta Constitution,* April 23, 1977, 1B, ProQuest ID 1619682625.

3. Thom Schafer, "Gay Theatre Off-Broadway and in Other Cities—Some Triumphs, Some Tragedies," *Gay News,* September 1978, 20, Box 43.

4. "Interview: Lavita Allen," *Cruise* 3, no. 8, July 1978, Lesbian, Gay, Bi-Sexual, and Transgender Serial Collection, Atlanta History Center, Kenan Research Center, box 4, folder 5.

5. Alice L. Murray and T. L. Wells, "1,800 Demonstrate Against Singer Here," *Atlanta Constitution,* June 12, 1978, 1A, ProQuest ID 161460440.

6. Bill Montgomery, "Baptists, Gays Exchange Sneers over Barriers," *Atlanta Journal,* June 12, 1978, 7A.

7. Anita Bryant, Speech to Southern Baptist Pastors' Conference, June 12, 1978, Atlanta, Georgia. Audio recording from the Southern Baptist Historical Library and Archives.

8. Spelling is per Coe.

9. Repeated requests for City of Atlanta records have not been productive. They either never existed, were later destroyed, or will not be produced.

10. Mark Segal says he remembers nothing of the end of his business relationship with Bill Smith.

11. Harvey Milk, "The 'Hope' Speech," delivered throughout 1977 and 1978; https:// www.youtube.com/watch?v=X9vol-8HYEc.

12. Lawrence K. Altman, "Drug Rehnquist Used Carries Strict Warning," *New York Times,* January 7, 1982, https://www.nytimes.com/1982/01/07/us/drug -rehnquist-used-carries-strict-warning.html.

1979: I Will Survive

1. "Interview: Rachel Wells," *Cruise,* 1979, 15.

2. "Rooms," *Miami Herald,* August 12, 1979, 354.

3. Margo Harakas, "Homosexual Counseling, Anita's Way," *Palm Beach Post,* June 28, 1979, 20; "Anita Bryant Would Do It All Over Again," *Mattoon Journal-Gazette,* April 18, 1980, 11.

4. Dahl's remarks were widely reported; a great resource for all things disco is Alice Echols's *Hot Stuff: Disco and the Remaking of American Culture* (New York: W. W. Norton, 2011).

5. Daryl Eslea, "Disco Inferno," *Independent,* December 11, 2004, https://www .independent.co.uk/news/world/americas/disco-inferno-680390.html

6. *State v. William Edward Smith, Jr.,* (GA case A46378), September 25, 1979.

7. "News Update," *Gaybriel,* August 31, 1979, 31.

8. Carol Anne Douglas, "The National March on Washington for Lesbian & Gay Rights," *Off Our Backs* 9, no. 10, November 30, 1979, ProQuest ID 197141695.

9. Douglas, "National March on Washington."

10. Anne Wexler and Stuart Eizenstat, "Re: National Gay Task Force Questionnaire," memo, December 20, 1979, Office of Staff Secretary, Presidential Files, Folder [12/20/79-Not Submitted-DF]; Container 143; Jimmy Carter Library.

11. Courtland Milloy and Loretta Tofani, "25,000 Attend Gay Rights Rally at the Monument: 25,000 March in Gay Rights Parade," *Washington Post,* October 15, 1979, A1, ProQuest ID 147107340.

12. Dolan, "You Can't Be a People."

13. November 20, 1979, letter to Diane Hughes.

14. *Gaybriel,* "News Update," 31.

15. The judge's signature is nearly illegible, but compared with directories for the court, it appears to be Judge Osgood O. Williams.

16. RuPaul, on @worldofwonder Instagram. Accessed November 15, 2019, https://www.instagram.com/p/BnZkL88guWS/?igshid=p5o7vypa4qts.

17. RuPaul, *What's the Tee?* Podcast episode 165, "Lady Bunny," August 14, 2018.

18. "Dear Diamond Lil," *Gaybriel,* 1979, 6, Atlanta History Center, Kenan Research Center, Atlanta Lesbian and Gay History Thing papers and publications collection, ahc.MSS773, box 33, folder 2.

19. Diamond Lil, "The Queen of the Dunk 'N Dine Grill," YouTube, https://www.youtube.com/watch?v=WJyClwJTe8Q.

20. J. D. Doyle, "Those Singing Drag Queens," *Queer Music Heritage.* March 2006, Part 1, http://www.queermusicheritage.com/mar2006s.html.

21. Tray Butler, "God Save the Queen," *Creative Loafing,* October 9, 2003, http://www.thestripproject.com/wp-content/uploads/2016/08/God-save-the-Queen-Creative-Loafing-Atlanta.pdf.

22. Butler, "God Save the Queen."

23. Robin Roberts, "Diamond Lil: Queen of All Glamour and Grease," *Cruise,* November 1978, 9.

24. Roberts, "Diamond Lil."

25. Roberts, "Diamond Lil."

1980: Tragedy

1. *State v. William Smith, Jr.,* Fulton Superior Court, case A48789.

2. Terry Kay, "Shrine Circus Sets Play Dates," *Atlanta Constitution,* March 30, 1969, 9F, ProQuest ID 1554859628.

3. Diane Hughes read this story to me from her personal archives in July 2019.

4. Douglas Brinkley, *The Unfinished Presidency: Jimmy Carter's Journey Beyond the White House* (New York: Viking, 1998), excerpted by *The New York Times,* http://movies2.nytimes.com/books/first/b/brinkley-unfinished.html.

5. Brinkley, *Unfinished Presidency.*

6. Jeff Nesmith, "Reagan Landslide: Carter Loses His Grip on 'Solid South,'" *Atlanta Constitution,* November 5, 1980, 1A, ProQuest ID 1621295351.

7. Brinkley, *Unfinished Presidency.*

1981: Midnight at the Oasis

1. "Come Out!" *Gazette* 2, no. 25 (1981).
2. Marc Jones interview by phone, October 14, 2018, Atlanta.
3. James Heverly, "First Word," *Cruise Weekly,* August 28–September 3, 1981, from the private collection of John Greenwell.
4. Philip J. Hilts, "2 Mysterious Diseases Killing Homosexuals," *Washington Post,* August 30, 1981, A15.
5. Charles Seabrook, "Outbreak of Rare Form of Cancer Among Gay Men Baffles CDC," *Atlanta Journal,* August 28, 1981.

Bibliography

Where not otherwise noted, biographical information and anecdotes were related by those interviewed in person, by phone, and by email from 2016 to 2020. Unless otherwise noted, all online sources were accessed and verified once more in November of 2019.

The following abbreviations are used in citations:

ALFA archive: All items have been acquired as the Atlanta Lesbian Feminist Alliance (ALFA) Periodicals collection, David M. Rubenstein Rare Book & Manuscript Library, Duke University Library.

Atlanta Barb/Barb: All editions courtesy of Atlanta History Center, Kenan Research Center. Unless otherwise noted, these are filed with the Atlanta Lesbian and Gay History Thing papers and publications collection, ahc.MSS773, Box MSS OS Box 2.273.

Cruise **magazine:** All editions have been acquired by the Atlanta History Center, Kenan Research Center. They are located in the Atlanta Lesbian and Gay History Thing papers and publications collection unless otherwise noted.

Gazette: Unless otherwise noted, issues have been acquired by the Atlanta History Center, Kenan Research Center, MSS OS box 2.270, folder 3.

Great Speckled Bird **and** ***Georgia State (GSU) Signal:*** All issues are located online in the Digital Collections of Georgia State University Library.

Billy Jones Papers: All items have been acquired as the Billy Jones Papers, Atlanta History Center, Kenan Research Library, ahc.MSS1106, box 5, folder 1.

Bill Smith Papers: All items have been acquired as the Bill Smith Papers, 1970–1980, Atlanta History Center, Kenan Research Library, ahc.MSS735f.

WSB-TV: All video clips come from B-roll acquired by the Walter J. Brown Media Archives & Peabody Awards Collection, University of Georgia Special Collections Libraries.

Atlanta, Maynard Jackson, and Jimmy Carter
Atlanta Constitution. "Massell Doesn't Regret 'Think-White' Statement." November 19, 1971, 19B. ProQuest ID 1613107831.

———. "'Organized Crime Not New to Area.'" October 16, 1972, 6A. ProQuest ID 1557118120.

Bell, Chuck. "Crime Always Here—Jackson." *Atlanta Constitution*, October 20, 1972, 3B. ProQuest ID 1616507855.

Berkeley, Bill, and Morse Diggs. "The Man Who Did 'Great Things Badly.'" *Atlanta Constitution*, December 13, 1981, 1A. ProQuest ID 1622447555.

Coffin, Alex. "Nightclub Is Shut Here." *Atlanta Constitution*, November 21, 1970, 1A. ProQuest ID 1616485273.

Dodson, Henry. Interview by WSB-TV. Newsfilm clip of African Americans reacting negatively to Mayor Sam Massell's speech on politics and government, October 10, 1971. Clip no. wsbn64296.

Dolman, Joe. "Few Traces Left of Eaves' Secret Squad." *Atlanta Constitution*, December 30, 1979, 1A. ProQuest ID 1639191357.

Drue, Abby. Interview, June 26, 2019, Atlanta, Georgia.

Flowers, Johnny. Letter to the Editor. *Atlanta Journal-Constitution*, December 29, 2009. https://www.ajc.com/news/local/back-the-early-70s-the-drinking-age-had -dropped-when-did-that-happen-and-how-long-did-stay-until-went-back-age -johnny-flowers-lilburn/JLsbYTsSTAFFulw83qn5xN/

Jackson, Harold, and Alex Brummer. "Aides Tell Tearful Jimmy Carter That 'It's All Over.'" *Guardian*. November 5, 1980. https://www.theguardian.com/ world/1980/nov/05/usa.alexbrummer1

Jackson, Wendy Eley, and Samuel D. Pollard. *Maynard*. Directed by Samuel D. Pollard (2017, Atlanta, GA: Auburn Avenue Films), streaming. Interview with Dr. June Dobbs Butts.

Jet. "Maynard Jackson, Wife, Announce Separation." April 29, 1976.

———. "Atlanta Mayor Jackson and Wife to Divorce." August 5, 1976.

Ledlie, Joe. "Summer Murder Wave Has Atlantans on Edge." *Washington Post*, August 5, 1979. https://www.washingtonpost.com/archive/politics/1979/08/05/ summer-murder-wave-has-atlantans-on-edge/2a915ebe-ec4e-44a5-b228 -cec96acb8128/?utm_term=.20975c5f32ff

Leviton, Joyce. "Loser and Still Champion, Atlanta Mayor Jackson Is a Sliver of His Former Self." *People*, December 5, 1977. https://people.com/archive/loser-and -still-champion-atlanta-mayor-jackson-is-a-sliver-of-his-former-self-vol-8-no-23/

Lewis, Boyd. Facebook update, June 13, 2016. "Atlanta, in a sense, set out in the 1970s to fulfill King's dream of a 'Beloved Community.'" https://www.facebook .com/boyd.lewis.16.

Linthicum, Tom. "Aldermen to Conduct Liquor License Study." *Atlanta Constitution*, October 3, 1972, 1A. ProQuest ID 1557649162.

———. "Inman, Slaton End Rift." *Atlanta Constitution*, October 10, 1972, 1A. ProQuest ID 1557117828.

———. "Massell Won't Drop 'Racist' Blasts." *Atlanta Constitution*, October 11, 1973, 2A. ProQuest ID 1899771251.

Nesmith, Jeff, and Tom Linthicum. "Spurned Nightclub Deal—Inman." *Atlanta Constitution*, October 26, 1972, 1A. ProQuest ID 1563226916.

Scheer, Robert. "The Playboy Interview with Jimmy Carter." November 1, 1976. *Playboy*. https://www.playboy.com/read/playboy-interview-jimmy-carter.

Street, Barbara Gervais. "The Gaying of Atlanta." *Atlanta Constitution*, December 12, 1982, 10. ProQuest ID 1623144489.

Bill Smith and the LGBTQ Civil-Rights Movement

American Civil Liberties Union of Georgia. "American Civil Liberties Union of Georgia Records 1938–2014." Richard B. Russell Library for Political

Research and Studies, University of Georgia Library, RBRL/025/ACLU, Box R.I.1, folder 24–25.

Associated Press. "Right to Ban Homosexual Acts Upheld." *Atlanta Constitution,* March 30, 1976, 1A. ProQuest ID 1619735676.

Atlanta Constitution. "Gay Pride." July 9, 1976, 4A. ProQuest ID 1617595592.

———. "Gay Pride." July 26, 1976, 4A. ProQuest ID 1617547178.

———. "Dade in Uproar at Anita's Outcry." March 27, 1977, 4B. ProQuest ID 1617491391.

———. "Study Raps Stereotypes About Gays." August 9, 1978, 1B. ProQuest ID 1614076002.

Barb. "Atlanta Mayor Wins Phyllis Killer Oscar." Vol. 3, No. 4, 1976, 1, folder 5.

———. "Councilman Pierce Calls for End of 'Sexual Orientation' Protection in Atlanta." Vol. 3, No. 2, 1976, 1, folder 5.

———. "Gay Week 1976." Vol. 3, No. 5, 1976, 16, folder 6.

———. "Georgia Sodomy Law Repeal Dies in Committee." Vol. 2, No. 2, 1975, 1, folder 3.

———. "Mayor Stands Firm." Vol. 3, No. 6, 1976, 1, folder 6.

———. "Season's Greetings from the Barb People." Vol. 3, No. 10, 1976, 16, folder 6.

Battenfield, John. "15 to 20,000 Join Homosexual March." *Atlanta Constitution,* June 29, 1970. Accessed November 11, 2019, ProQuest ID 1616099238.

Boykin, Berl. "Atlanta Gays Harassed." *Great Speckled Bird,* July 22, 1974, 15.

———. An Interview with Atlanta Gay Rights Pioneer Berl Boykin, AIB Network. YouTube, https://www.youtube.com/watch?v=bYIpq_KP9js.

Bryant, Anita. "The Downfall of Anita Bryant," SuchIsLifeVideos, published December 30, 2009. YouTube, https://www.youtube.com/watch?v=UX6i5Y6t1nI.

Cutler, Bill. "Gay Atlanta Out Front." *Great Speckled Bird,* July 2, 1973, 8.

Cyclops, "Celebration . . . Very Gay." *Great Speckled Bird,* July 5, 1971.

Epstein, Gail. "Activist Briefing Police on Homosexual Lifestyles." *Atlanta Constitution,* May 1, 1981, 15A. ProQuest ID 1614202751.

Fiedler, Arthur. Arthur Fiedler and the Boston Pops/Abbott Laboratories, liner notes, *Music to Nudge You to Sleep,* 1963. Personal archive.

Fleischmann, Arnold, and Jason Hardman. "Hitting Below the Bible Belt: The Development of the Gay Rights Movement in Atlanta." *Journal of Urban Affairs* 26, no. 4, 407–26. ProQuest document 60670482.

GSU Signal. "Gay Students Meet for Recognition," April 20, 1972, 5.

———. "If Editor for a Week, What Would You Alter?" October 30, 1969, 5.

Globe and Mail. "BRIEFLY Anita Will Promote Juice Another Year." July 27, 1979, 13. ProQuest ID 387051369.

Great Speckled Bird. "Gay Life in Atlanta." June 12, 1975, 6. Digital Collections, Georgia State University Library.

———. "Vixen, Si! Viva, No!" August 11, 1969.

Hayward, Dave. "I Was There and I'm Still Here!" *Georgia Voice,* August 6, 2018, https://thegavoice.com/community/features/i-was-there-and-im-still-here/.

———. Interviews: November 11, 2017 and August 19, 2018, Atlanta.

Hyer, Marjorie. "Bryant's Campaign Against Homosexuals Marches to Atlanta." *Washington Post,* June 12, 1978, https://www.washingtonpost.com/archive/politics/1978/06/12/bryants-campaign-against-homosexuals-marches-to-atlanta/69556a23-dee8-4972-9553-e10e22b1716e/?utm_term=.897c5a90d1bb.

Jackson, Maynard. Memo from Maynard Jackson to Tony Riddle, June 22, 1976, Gay Pride Week, 1976. Maynard Jackson mayoral administrative records. Robert W. Woodruff Library of the Atlanta University Center. Box 56, Folder 10.

———. Memo from Mayor's Office, June 17, 1977. Maynard Jackson mayoral administrative records. Robert W. Woodruff Library of the Atlanta University Center.

———. Proclamation for Gay Pride Day, *Great Speckled Bird,* August 1976, 8.

Johnson, Jennifer. Interviews via text and phone, April 2018.

Kay, Terry. "Shrine Circus Sets Play Dates." *Atlanta Constitution,* March 30, 1969, 9F. ProQuest ID 1554859628.

Lambert, Judith. "Gay Pride Week." *Great Speckled Bird,* June 19, 1972, 4

Lee, Richard Evans. Interview by email, March and May 2019.

———. "Peddling Flesh." LiveJournal blog, https://richardevanslee.livejournal.com/245605.html.

———. "Young Richard Works for a Gay Newspaper." LiveJournal blog, https://richardevanslee.livejournal.com/254927.html.

Lorraine. "Are Gay Rights an issue in the '72 Election?" *Great Speckled Bird,* October 23, 1972, 7.

Martin, Lyn. "Group Praises Mayor on 'Liberties Days.'" *Atlanta Constitution,* June 25, 1977, 6A. ProQuest ID 1617617632.

Martin, Lyn, and Ken Willis. "There'll Be No 'Gay Pride Day.'" *Atlanta Constitution,* June 24, 1977, 1A. ProQuest ID 1617616933.

Merzer, Martin. "Anita Battles On." *Atlanta Constitution,* November 5, 1978, 20C. ProQuest ID 1620435738.

Robison, Gil. Interviews, May 11 and November 23, 2018, Atlanta, Georgia.

Saunders, Patrick. "Georgia Gay Liberation Front and Atlanta's First Pride March." *Georgia Voice,* June 10, 2016, https://thegavoice.com/georgia-gay-liberation-front-atlantas-first-pride-march/.

Smith, Bill. "Gay Is Gone." *Great Speckled Bird,* July 23, 1973, 7.

Smith, Bill. Audio interview, Bill Smith and a female voice, "Atlanta Gay Information Service," March 7, 1974. International Gay Information Center collection 1951–1994, New York Public Library ID A00526.

Smith, Bill. "Community Activities." *Barb,* Vol. 1, No. 4, 1974, 2, folder 1.

———. "Community Activities." *Barb,* Vol. 1 No. 5, 10. 1974, folder 1.

———. "Community Activities." *Barb,* Vol. 1, No. 7, 1974, 8, folder 2.

———. "Editor's Notebook." *Barb,* Vol. 3, No. 1, 1976, 2, folder 5.

———. "Editor's Notebook." *Barb,* Vol. 3, No. 3, 1976, 2, folder 5.

———. "Editor's Notebook." *Barb,* Vol. 3, No. 4, 1976, 2, folder 5.

———. "Editor's Notebook." *Barb,* Vol. 4 No. 2, pg. 6, folder 7.

———. Letter to Diane Hughes, February 15, 1980. Bill Smith Papers.

———. "Publisher's Perspective." *Barb,* No. 41, pg. 6, folder 8.

———. "Traveling South." *Barb,* Vol. 4 No. 6, pg. 7, folder 7.

Smith, Bill, and Gary W. Poe. "Barb Endorsements." *Barb,* October 1, 1977, No. 43, 4, folder 8.

Swan, Neil. "Gay Pride Rally Without Incident." *Atlanta Constitution,* June 27, 1976, 7B. ProQuest ID 1557748406.

Taylor, Ron, and Tom Crawford. "Commandos Storm Park." *Atlanta Constitution,* August 8, 1971, 2A, Accessed November 11, 2019, ProQuest ID 1563283535.

Time. "Sexes: How Gay Is Gay?" April 23, 1979, http://content.time.com/time/magazine/article/0,9171,920281,00.html.

U.S. House of Representatives. H.R.14752—Equality Act. 93rd Congress (1973–1974). https://www.congress.gov/bill/93rd-congress/house-bill/14752.

Westervelt Jr., Frederic B., MD. "Ethchlorvynol (Placidyl®) Intoxication: Experience with Five Patients, Including Treatment with Hemodialysis." *Annals of Internal Medicine,* June 1, 1966. https://annals.org/aim/article-abstract/680813/ethchlorvynol-placidyl-intoxication-experience-five-patients-including-treatment-hemodialysis.

Witherspoon, Roger. "CDC Seeks a Gay Link to Diseases." *Atlanta Constitution,* August 29, 1981, 2A. ProQuest ID 161978703.

Wooten, James T. "The Life and Death of Atlanta's Hip Strip." *New York Times,* March 14, 1971, SM34. ProQuest ID 119324009.

WSB-TV. Newsfilm clips of Gay Pride march and rally at Piedmont Park, Atlanta, Georgia, June 25, 1972. Clip no. wsbn66752.

———. Supreme Court Upholds State Laws Forbidding Homosexual Acts Between Consenting Adults in Private, March 30, 1976. Clip no.: wsbn07532

Disco

Cohn, Nik. "Tribal Rites of the New Saturday Night." *New York Magazine,* June 7, 1976. http://nymag.com/nightlife/features/45933/.

Dodson, Jim. "Disco Dollars." *Atlanta Constitution,* October 8, 1978, SM19. ProQuest ID 1612109396.

Emmrich, Stuart. "Disco Fever." *Atlanta Constitution,* March 25, 1978, 1T. ProQuest ID 1621468911.

Greene, Andy. "Flashback: Watch 'Disco Demolition Night' Devolve into Fiery Riot." *Rolling Stone,* July 12, 2019. https://www.rollingstone.com/music/music-news/flashback-watch-disco-demolition-night-devolve-into-fiery-riot-206237/.

Terry, Josh. "'Disco Demolition Night' Was a Disgrace, and Celebrating It Is Worse." *Vice,* June 12, 2019, https://www.vice.com/en_us/article/8xzke5/disco-demolition-night-was-a-disgrace-and-celebrating-it-is-worse.

Drag Performers and Clubs

Advocate. "Disco Update." April 7, 1976. Duke University Rubinstein Library, Newspaper #9, no. 181–193 (1976) c.1.

Andres, Sean. "Applause: Rachael [*sic*] Wells," *David,* March/April 1973, 25. From the personal archive of John Greenwell.

Barb. "Miss 'Gay America' Pageant Attracts Thousands to Atlanta." Vol. 1 No. 2, 1974, 1.

Cruise. Advertisement, August 1977 issue. Box 19, folder 2.

———. February 1976 issue. Box 19, folder 1.

———. "A History of the Conference Room." Billy Jones Papers.

———. "Interview: Frank Powell." Billy Jones Papers.

David [?]. "Who Is Danny Windsor?" Unidentified publication (believed to be *David* magazine), Billy Jones Papers.

Devoreaux, Cara. "A Conversation with Marc Jones." *Gazette,* 1981. Atlanta History Center, Kenan Research Center, MSS OS box 2.270, folder 1.

Fontaine, Heather. Facebook post, May 24, 2018, https://www.facebook.com/heather.fontaine.9/posts/10204227000431850, accessed November 14, 2019.

———. Facebook post, June 4, 2018, https://www.facebook.com/heather.fontaine
.9/posts/10204261320409828, accessed November 14, 2019.

———. July 22, 2018, https://www.facebook.com/heather.fontaine.9/posts/1020
4409715839621, accessed November 14, 2019.

———. September 11, 2018, https://www.facebook.com/heather.fontaine.9/posts
/10204569125784770, accessed November 14, 2019.

Gallagher, Kathleen. "Field of 27 Starts 'Miss Gay' Event." May 11, 1973, *Tennessean.*

Gazette. "Sweet Gum Closes as Gay Bar." August 20, 1981, 1. Atlanta History Center, Kenan Research Center, MSS OS box 2.270, folder 3.

Geneva County Reaper. "Bob Jones College." March 5, 1926, 3.

Gray, Farnum. "Female Impersonation Is Big Business." *Atlanta Constitution*, October 4, 1974, 15 C. ProQuest ID 1616114370.

Greenwell, John. Interviews in Louisville, Atlanta, and by phone, November 2016, June 2017, August 2018, October 2018, and June 2019; and by email.

Harris, Art. "The Night People." *Atlanta Constitution*, March 7, 1975, 7B. ProQuest ID 1644155722.

Henry, Scott. "Atlanta punk! A Reunion for 688 and Metroplex." *Creative Loafing,* October 1, 2008, https://creativeloafing.com/content-165784-atlanta-punk-a
-reunion-for-688-and.

Hess, Vi. "Billy Jones Finds Show Biz 'No Drag.'" *David* Magazine, December 1970, 7. Billy Jones Papers.

Hesser, Fran. "Raising Drinking Age Is Gaining Support." *Atlanta Constitution*, January 1, 1980, 1C. ProQuest ID 1620851172.

Hollis. "Miss Gay America Founder Jerry Peek on a Life in the Business of Drag." *Out and About Nashville,* January 1, 2013, https://outandaboutnashville.com/
miss-gay-america-founder-jerry-peek-on-a-life-in-the-business-of-drag/.

Hudspeth, Ron. "Some Yes, Some No; and a Few Are Both." *Atlanta Constitution*, April 8, 1978, 2A. ProQuest ID 1619722971.

Jacobs, Dina. Interview by phone, October 13, 2018.

Martin, Cliff, and John Greenwell. Interview October 20, 2018, Atlanta.

Jones, Billy. "Phyllis Killer's Nite Notes." *Barb*, Vol. 2, No. 2, 1975, 9, folder 3.

Jones, Marc. Interview, October 14, 2018, Atlanta.

Kavanaugh, Richard. "Miss Gay Georgia Pageant 1977!" *Cruise*, August 5, 1977, 5. Lesbian, Gay, Bi-Sexual, and Transgender Serial Collection, Atlanta History Center, Kenan Research Center, Box 4, folder 1.

———. "The Sad Saga of British Sterling." *Cruise*, 1977. Atlanta History Center, Kenan Research Center, Atlanta Lesbian and Gay History Thing papers and publications, ahc.MSS773, Box 19, Folder 2.

King, Barry, and Robert Lamb. "The Night People: Glimpses of Atlantans Whose Day Starts at Sundown." *Atlanta Constitution,* November 12, 1977, 1A. ProQuest ID 1617622822.

Love, Apple. Interview by phone, April 23, 2018.

Oosterhoudt, Tom. "Drags' Queen Hits Hot-lanta." *Barb,* No. 44, 7, folder 8.

———. "Miss Gay America Wants to Keep Reign Simple." *Gay News,* November 1978, 28. Atlanta Lesbian Feminist Alliance (ALFA) Periodicals collection, David M. Rubenstein Rare Book & Manuscript Library, Duke University Library, Box 43.

———. "Tom's Cup O' Tea." *Gay News,* July 1978, 25. Atlanta Lesbian Feminist

Alliance (ALFA) Periodicals collection, David M. Rubenstein Rare Book & Manuscript Library, Duke University Library, Box 43.

Perry, Charles. "Unconsciousness Expansion: The Sopor Story." *Rolling Stone*, March 29, 1973, https://www.rollingstone.com/culture/features/unconsciousness-expansion -the-sopor-story-19730329.

Raines, Howell. "'Deliverance' Excels Technically." *Atlanta Constitution*, September 21, 1972, 20D. ProQuest ID 1616505448.

Reston, Tom. "The Hound's Tooth Is Doggone Profitable." *Atlanta Constitution*, August 16, 1965, 18A. ProQuest ID 1637041643.

RuPaul. *Lettin' It All Hang Out*. New York: Hyperion, 1995.

Saunders, Patrick. "Catching Up . . . with Deana Collins." *Georgia Voice*, December 23, 2014, http://thegavoice.com/catching-deana-collins-former-hoedowns-3 -legged-cowboy-owner/.

Sears, James Thomas. *Rebels, Rubyfruit, and Rhinestones: Queering Space in the Stonewall South*. New Brunswick, NJ: Rutgers University Press, 154.

Smith, Helen C. "Hosanna Is Emotional Play." *Atlanta Constitution*, December 22, 1977, 4B. ProQuest ID 1619913867.

Stevens, Kevin. "Frank Powell: A Man of Vision." *Guide*, November 1988, 5, Billy Jones Papers.

Waterhouse, Jon. "Ghosts of Hotspots Past." *Creative Loafing*, April 23, 2003, https://creativeloafing.com/content-165126-Ghosts-of-hotspots-past.

WGST News. "Atlanta's Gays: A Life of Their Own." August 17–20, 1981. Peabody Awards Collection, 81003 NWR 1 of 1. Walter J. Brown Media Archives & Peabody Awards Collection, University of Georgia, Athens.

Wikane, Christian John. "The Spirit in Her Soul Is Free: An Interview with Linda Clifford." *PopMatters*, February 16, 2017, http://www.popmatters.com/feature/ the-spirit-in-her-soul-is-free-an-interview-with-linda-clifford/P0/.

Wortham, Jenna. "Is 'RuPaul's Drag Race' the Most Radical Show on TV?" *New York Times*, January 24, 2018, https://www.nytimes.com/2018/01/24/magazine/is -rupauls-drag-race-the-most-radical-show-on-tv.html

Gay-Bar Wars

Atlanta Constitution. "3 Bodies Found in South Fulton." *Atlanta Constitution*, April 25, 1976, 1A. ProQuest ID 1614055073.

Barb. "Arson Stops the Show at Magic Garden." No. 42, 1. Atlanta History Center, Kenan Research Center, pending digital archive.

———. "Fire Destroys Cabaret After Dark." Vol. 2, No. 4, 1975, 1, folder 3.

Gaybriel. "A Conversation with Mama Dee." Issue 3. Atlanta History Center, Kenan Research Center, Atlanta Lesbian and Gay History Thing papers and publications, Box 33, folder 2.

Gazette. "Sensations Disco Escapes Fire Damage." August 27–September 2, 1981, Vol. 2 No. 35, 1. Atlanta History Center, Kenan Research Center, MSS OS box 2.270, folder 3.

Henderson, Barry. "Triple Slaying Charge Dropped." *Atlanta Constitution*, June 12, 1976, 8A. ProQuest ID 1617503367.

Hendricks, Gary. "Had Offer to Change Story—Witness." *Atlanta Constitution*, March 26, 1977, 1A. ProQuest ID 1617596076.

———. "Jury Refuses to Indict Five Fulton Deputy Sheriffs." *Atlanta Constitution*, August 25, 1978, 1C. ProQuest ID 1613301024.

————. "Three Get Life Terms in Slayings." *Atlanta Constitution,* May 3, 1977, 9A. ProQuest ID 1614117962.

Hendricks, Gary, and Jim Stewart. "DA Investigating Loans, Jail Favoritism." *Atlanta Constitution*, June 24, 1978, 1A. ProQuest ID 1613297821.

Stewart, Jim, and Paul Lieberman. "Charred Ruins Mark Feud of Gay Clubs." October 12, 1977, 1A. ProQuest ID 1619867610.

Willis, Ken. "Club Owner Charged in Killings." *Atlanta Constitution,* January 12, 1977, 1A. ProQuest ID 162036098.

Willis, Ken, and Robert Lamb. "Police Say 3 Men Were Executed." *Atlanta Constitution,* April 27, 1976, 6B. ProQuest ID 1617588927.

Index

Drag names are not inverted.